W. R. (William Robinson) Pirie

Natural Theology

An inquiry into the fundamental principles of religious, moral, and political science

W. R. (William Robinson) Pirie

Natural Theology
An inquiry into the fundamental principles of religious, moral, and political science

ISBN/EAN: 9783743394759

Manufactured in Europe, USA, Canada, Australia, Japa

Cover: Foto ©Lupo / pixelio.de

Manufactured and distributed by brebook publishing software (www.brebook.com)

W. R. (William Robinson) Pirie

Natural Theology

NATURAL THEOLOGY

AN INQUIRY INTO THE FUNDAMENTAL PRINCIPLES OF RELIGIOUS, MORAL, AND POLITICAL SCIENCE

BY THE

REV. W. R. PIRIE, D.D.

PROFESSOR OF DIVINITY AND CHURCH HISTORY IN THE
UNIVERSITY OF ABERDEEN, AND DEAN OF
THE FACULTY OF THEOLOGY

WILLIAM BLACKWOOD AND SONS
EDINBURGH AND LONDON
MDCCCLXVII

PREFACE.

THE true theory of religion, morals, and politics constitutes the grand question of the day. We have arrived at a period of human progress, in which mere authoritative or traditional belief is held comparatively as of little value. Education is so widely spread that the majority of men think more or less for themselves, and demand evidence for that which they are called on to believe. As in all cases of a great movement of the human mind, they consequently are led to appeal to first principles, and of course the most plausible, though it may be the most superficial theories, are in the first instance generally adopted.

This, accordingly, is the case with respect to the sciences of religion, morals, and politics. The vast mass of mankind, while occasionally speculating with regard to them, have yet a sort of unconscious impression that we neither know, nor can know, anything *definite* about them whatever. Even the most intelligent thinkers are content with theories which either rest on assumptions of innate ideas, or which only imperfectly explain the phenomena.

Under those circumstances, Revelation has been left without any firm foundation on which to rest. So much is this the case, indeed, that many excellent persons assume its authority to depend exclusively on some sort of mysterious belief communicated directly by superhuman influence. Others take it for granted that the miracles recorded in Revelation must be true, and sufficient to sanction its authority, apart from natural religion; though it is perfectly evident that this cannot be the case, as the very value of the testimony for those miracles must depend upon the moral character of the witnesses, and the object on account of which the miracles themselves were performed. *No amount of testimony could be probative of miracles that were intended to sanction a scheme inconsistent with natural religion.* Nay, the very words expressive of spiritual states used in a revelation must be interpreted by natural religion. The words " goodness," " justice," " mercy," and " truth," as well as the words " right," " wrong," " ought," " duty," and many others, must be interpreted by natural religion, or we could attach no definite meaning to them at all.

Not only, therefore, would the evidences of Revelation be uncertain, or rather baseless, apart from natural religion, but there could be no such sciences as those of morality and politics. It is unnecessary to dwell upon this, because that it is so will be fully proved afterwards.

From these remarks it will be manifest that I publish this work under the conviction that the principles of natural religion have never been thoroughly vindicated. Hitherto, indeed, this has not been felt to be absolutely necessary. Until a very recent period the evidence of authority, combined with the half-conscious assurance involved in our feelings, seems in so far to have served the purpose. If anything be clear, however, it is clear that this state of things cannot last in the present age. Not merely infidelity, but gross materialism and pantheism are widely spread, and are rapidly spreading farther. Moral and political duties are beginning to be regarded, consequently, as without any obligation, and merely invented by influential parties to serve their own self-interested ends. Nor are these views merely put forward as speculative theories. They are unconsciously adopted by persons who know nothing about philosophical theories, and are practically affecting the character and conduct of immense masses of the people.

It was under these impressions, which have been specially forced on me by circumstances, that I entered on the consideration of this subject, and it is under the same impressions that I now offer the result of my investigations to the public. It has been my object to reason out every step of the argument demonstratively, and with the utmost plainness. With the exception of one chapter, therefore (Preliminary Inquiries, chap. i.), I have avoided all approach to metaphysical speculation; and even that chapter is not essential, having been introduced for the sake of those who may desire to examine more profoundly the primary principles on which my argument rests. I have endeavoured to state every particular, moreover, in such a way as may be universally intelligible. In this view I have carefully separated the argument for the moral attributes of God from those which prove His omnipotence and omniscience, these latter being necessarily proved in the evidence for the existence of an intelligent First Cause. A mixing up of the proofs for these two classes of attributes has greatly tended to confuse the argument and weaken the power of the evidence for both.

I consider myself bound to add, that I believe

the main argument to be perfect demonstration. Objections may no doubt be taken to the illustrations, or to the incidental and practical inferences, but the argument for the being and attributes of God, and the moral and political *principles* flowing therefrom, seems to be as certain as any proposition of geometry, assuming that the laws of nature are to be trusted. If these are not to be trusted, of course there could be neither physical nor spiritual philosophy, nor truth of any kind. We have too many crude and half-true theories already on religion, morals, and politics. Had I not believed the argument, therefore, from beginning to end, both plain and logically irresistible, I should not have presumed to intrude it on public notice. I have published it under the conviction that it will conduce to the interests of truth, specially with reference to the most important subject that can engage the attention of rational beings, by resting the faith of the religious world on foundations which cannot be shaken.

CONTENTS.

	PAGE
GENERAL INTRODUCTION, ...	1

PRELIMINARY INQUIRIES.

CHAPTER I.

SOURCES AND LIMITS OF HUMAN KNOWLEDGE.

No such thing as innate or intuitive ideas—Knowledge is primarily derived from feelings—Process—How knowledge may be derived from others—How knowledge may be derived from a comparison of effects produced by causes external to ourselves with effects produced by the operation of our own faculties—How knowledge is further implied in the desire of co-relatives capable of gratifying such desire—Universality of the conclusions of reason, ... 21

CHAPTER II.

NATURE AND DIVISIONS OF SPIRITUAL SCIENCE.

Nature of spirit—Theory of materialism—Mode of studying spiritual science and its parts—Process under which we discover the existence of spirits external to ourselves—Process under which we discover the relations in which these spirits stand to ourselves—Division of the spiritual sciences, . . 41

PART I.
SCIENCE OF RELIGION.

INTRODUCTION.

Universality of belief in higher spiritual existences—Outlines of the causes of this—Origin of polytheism—Relation of morality and politics to the belief in higher spiritual existences—Universal expectation of a revelation—How this is to be accounted for, ... 53

CHAPTER I.

ARGUMENT FROM OUR SENSE OF WEAKNESS AND DEPENDENCE; OR, A PRIORI ARGUMENT FOR THE EXISTENCE AND ATTRIBUTES OF A GOD.

Explanation of the nature of the argument *a priori*, as contradistinguished from the argument *a posteriori*—Doubts connected with *a priori* arguments as hitherto adduced—Proof that there must be an *a priori* argument of some kind, sufficient to convince every one of the existence of a Supreme Power, omnipotent, omniscient, true, just, benevolent, and eternal—Relation of this *a priori* with the *a posteriori* proof —Its character and limits indicated, ... 69

CHAPTER II.

ARGUMENT FROM THE ARRANGEMENTS AND ORGANISATION OF THE UNIVERSE; OR, A POSTERIORI ARGUMENT FOR THE BEING AND NATURAL ATTRIBUTES OF A GOD.

Our proof for the exercise of intelligent agency in contriving and constructing the universe, is precisely the same as our proof for the intelligent agency of our fellow-creatures in contriving and constructing artificial arrangements—It consists in our assurance from the knowledge which we have of the nature of our own reason, that intelligence alone, or some equivalent attribute, is competent to contrive and construct adjusted arrangements—The possible eternity of the phenomena of nature does not affect the question at issue— A possible power of development in the products of nature does not affect the question at issue—This still further realised in the necessity of supposing that the elements of things must have been endowed with the precise properties competent to work out the phenomena—According to the development theory, these properties must have been infinitely numerous, if not contradictory, in each molecule—These considerations obviate every form of difficulty which can possibly arise from the assumption of that theory, or of any other theory—Extent and application of the proof to the power, wisdom, and immutability of God—Summary of the argument, ... 79

CHAPTER III.

ARGUMENT FOR THE MORAL ATTRIBUTES OF GOD.

Definition and character of morality—God cannot be an immoral being—Proved from the position and relations of man to his fellow-creatures and his God—Objection arising from the rigour of God's justice obviated—No difficulty exists on the subject, except in so far as arises from the limited nature of the human faculties—Conclusion, . . . 109

CHAPTER IV.

RELATION BETWIXT GOD AND MAN.

God has created us for the purpose of seeking intense and permanent happiness, through victory in the struggle betwixt selfishness and love—This consideration necessarily opens to us the prospect of an immortality—The voice of nature heard in those laws which assure us of an immortality—This immortality will be intensely and permanently happy to those who seek it in the way which nature indicates—Such happiness involved in trust in God—This trust imperfect or wanting in all men under ordinary circumstances—Mode in which nature indicates that it is to be sought, ... 141

PART II.

ETHICS, OR THE SCIENCE OF MORALS.

INTRODUCTION.

The theory of the relation betwixt God and man applied to human circumstances—Subject little understood—Definition of ethics—The various moral theories that have been proposed, and why unsatisfactory, ... 155

xiv CONTENTS.

CHAPTER I.
SPIRITUAL LAWS OF NATURE.

Difference in character betwixt the physical and moral laws of nature—Different kinds of happiness—We have in this a distinct indication of the mode in which our conduct should be regulated—In the struggle betwixt love and selfishness, selfishness conquers in the first instance—Process described—Power of habit and association—Only mode in which love can be generated—It must be stimulated and strengthened by the same means as selfishness is stimulated and strengthened—The object cannot be attained apart from religion—This proves the truth of religion, even if it had no other proof, ... 191

CHAPTER II.
NATURE AND OBLIGATIONS OF MORALITY.

There is in all human beings a certain feeling of love for others—This the source of a high measure of happiness from the beginning, which grows greater and greater—Morality essential to the existence of our race—This proved from our relations to one another, our sense of approbation and disapprobation, and our prospect of a future life—How a sense of religion operates on the human mind—The obligations of and motives to morality definitely stated, as discoverable from the preceding considerations—Mode under which we discover right and wrong in each case—Mode in which we can realise right—Conclusion, ... 208

CHAPTER III.
DETAILS OF MORALITY.

Recapitulation—Details of morality—Morality consists not in acts, but in intention and a state of mind—Illustrated—Categories under which the details of morality are comprehended—Love of ourselves—Love of our fellow-creatures—Love of our God—There can be no sufficient motive or obligation to morality apart from religion—Nature of moral law according to this theory, and mode of its realisation—Effect of this realisation on character, ... 234

PART III.

SCIENCE OF POLITICS.

INTRODUCTION.

Definition of political science—Its origin—Its relation to moral science—It concerns conduct rather than states of mind—Necessity of governors for administering political law—No direct natural law entitling one man to rule over another, except the law of the stronger—No political rights, therefore, under direct natural law—Misconceptions on the subject, ... 273

CHAPTER I.

NATURE AND FOUNDATION OF POLITICAL RIGHTS.

Immediate sources of political power—In so far the words "right," "ought," and "duty" can have no place in political science—Theory of compact, as the foundation of political rights, untenable—Theory of a tacit admission of such compact untenable—Submission to a government does not necessarily imply a recognition of its authority—Utility of government does not necessarily imply a recognition of the rights of those that administer it in any particular case—Paley correct in resting political rights on "the will of God," but wrong in assuming "the will of God" to be collected from "expediency"—"The will of God" declared in the actually existing constitution of things—This theory explained and vindicated, ... 283

CHAPTER II.

LIMITS OF POLITICAL RIGHTS.

Limits of political rights—They are limited by the moral rights of others, as of superior authority—Classification of moral rights as relating to governed and governors: 1. Right of personal liberty—2. Rights of labour and property—3. Right of political power, ... 309

CHAPTER III.

SUMMARY OF THE PRINCIPLES ESTABLISHED IN THE PRECEDING CHAPTERS, AND DEVELOPMENT OF POLITICAL SCIENCE AS FLOWING THEREFROM.

Summary of the principles established in the preceding chapters—Governments arise from circumstances, so as to be more or less suitable to the progress of society—This is a declaration of the will of God—Evils arising from a sudden change on the essential character of any government—Common result of such changes, and the causes thereof—Further changes following on such result—Probable mode of restoring a government under such circumstances to working order—Illustrated in the case of Cromwell, and in the present proceedings of the French Empire—Liberty of the press—Class of persons in whom political power may be safely vested—Dangerous classes—Point of view in which political power ought to be regarded—Cause of misconceptions on this subject, ... 320

APPENDIX.

A. Positive philosophy, ... 339
B. Theories of development, ... 349
C. Examples of extreme theories of political right, and argument involved in them, ... 351

NATURAL THEOLOGY.

GENERAL INTRODUCTION.

No one who has anything like a just appreciation of the nature of religion, can regret the objections which have been taken to it during recent years. Those who mourn over the propagation of infidel and rationalistic theories, cannot sufficiently know that religion *must be everything, or it is worth nothing*. Our belief, so far as it goes, must be clear, precise, and full, or it is a mere delusion. We do not indeed deny that at certain stages of human history, the evidence of authority and tradition may be sufficient to a greater or less extent. Such evidence, combined with more strictly logical proof, may not only at such times satisfy the human mind, but may in reality constitute a much more trustworthy ground of belief than many people in their pride of supposed intellectual superiority are apt to imagine.

As, however, the energy of human thought develops in the progress of scientific discovery, it is impossible that difficulties should fail to suggest themselves with regard to a subject implying such profound and complicated considerations. It was clearly intended that it should be so. The evidences and truths of religion are so interwoven with other sciences, that they can only be appreciated in their fulness, as the philosophy of these sciences becomes more and more accurately known. Wherever a sudden impulse is given to general knowledge, difficulties will naturally arise with respect to views of religious science transmitted from former generations. Yet these will gradually become fewer and fewer. Sceptics, indeed, seem already to have reached their last possible objection to Christianity *on principle*, and as the last, so also the most important, for everything else, as we shall presently see, is dependent upon it. It is the conclusive battle-field, on which, if religion be victorious, there may be skirmishes on isolated and unimportant points; but as to principles, the contest will be at an end, for no enemy can ever find another position of the same character which can be occupied against her.*

* It is manifest that there can substantively be only two theories as to the constitution of the universe. It must either exist as it now is, by the very essential nature of material existence, or

The fact is, that the progress of science has done more to remove difficulties with respect to religion on the one hand, than to suggest them on the other; and hence it is that sceptics have been driven back, till, as has been said, they have reached the only position which on principle it seems possible for them to occupy. That position is substantively Atheism. It is the doctrine that, in so far as we, at all events, have an opportunity of knowing, there is no personal Deity; that nature is God, and God is nature. It might be supposed that multitudes would have eagerly pressed forward to oppose theories involving such a doctrine, which takes away from men all security for peace on earth, and all hopes of happiness in a world to come. But this was not the result. On the contrary, religious men turned away with disgust from even thinking on a philosophy from

it must be the work of an intelligent Agent. No third supposition appears possible. The one is the assumption of the Atheist, the other of the Theist. The question is therefore reduced to a very narrow compass. If the one be true, the other must be false. It will be our object to show that the one is not only probably true, but is demonstrably certain. If we succeed, all dispute as to the principle is at an end. "There may," as is said in the text, "be skirmishes on isolated and unimportant points," but the only difference thereafter must be as to the mode in which these can be educed from the fundamental fact. No doubt there is a vast number of *apparently* different theories upon the subject, the *apparent* differences arising from the use of metaphysical and frequently unintelligible terms. But in reality they are all reducible to one or other of those stated.

which their intuitive feelings revolted. They regarded theories involving such a philosophy as unworthy of notice. To examine them was considered as equivalent to giving them circulation, and was therefore counted mischievous, if not sinful. This notion was so intense and so widely spread, that even those who doubted its validity were intimidated from making the attempt. They were afraid of being charged with doing evil instead of good, and doubted the soundness of their own convictions when opposed to those of the great mass of the Christian world. The consequence was, that plausible arguments, left entirely unnoticed, began to ferment silently in men's minds, and especially in those of the young and thoughtless. In this way, under the form of insinuations, doubts, and conjectures, they acquired daily a wider circulation and more extended influence. It was only through pressure from without that men ultimately awakened out of this most delusive dream, to find that a new generation had been growing up around them, amongst whom, in many instances, apathetic indifference had taken the place of religious zeal, and not unfrequently the very foundations of religion had been shaken.

The contempt thus exhibited towards such theories had therefore been a grievous error from the beginning. It is quite true, as we shall by-and-by more particularly show, that there is an intuitive feeling compelling us to believe in a

God; and that feeling will, of course, more or less retain its influence in all circumstances. But, as with respect to every other feeling, the conviction originating from it is vague and indefinite. To give it practical power by making it precise, it is absolutely necessary that its character should be logically determined, and its tendency logically ascertained. Consequently, if plausible objections can be taken to the proof proposed without any reply being attempted, the result must of necessity be the generation of religious indifference and practical Atheism.

This is by so much the more to be expected in the present age, because it is a mistake to suppose that those objections to religion which the almost exclusive prosecution of physical science during modern times has infused into the minds of a large mass of society, had been thoroughly anticipated either by heathen or by Christian philosophers. On the contrary, heathen philosophers left even the general question most imperfectly argued; and since the date of Christianity, the subject has been held in a great measure settled, and its details have been taken for granted. Until a recent period, consequently, Atheism has been almost unknown, except either under such gross or such subtilely metaphysical forms as to be incapable of doing any material evil. Latterly, however, this has been entirely changed. The rapid progress of physical science among all classes of society, has fixed men's minds almost exclusively on the operation of physical causes. Hence there has been generated during the present age a tendency to materialistic modes of thinking, such as we believe was never known during any previous period of human history. Thus has arisen a sort of habitual, though often scarcely conscious, belief in the action of a series of causes and effects operating in a circle, under which the phenomena of the universe may be regarded as an eternal succession altogether away from an efficient Creator. We say phenomena, because, according to this theory, phenomena are all that can be known; though what may be the precise meaning attached to the word phenomena in this case, or how much it may embrace, it is certainly not very easy to ascertain. The absurdities of the theory, however, are kept out of view by its disciples; and it is easy to understand how effective, on minds unaccustomed to think on almost anything save material objects, would be a philosophy which taught that doctrines affirming phenomena to be referable to the action of a God, were the products of an ignorant age, and in the enlightened nineteenth century were at once therefore to be repudiated. It followed, of course, that henceforth we are to trust exclusively to the information of our senses, and that those things consequently which we can see, hear, taste, touch, and smell, are to be the alone foundations of our reasoning. With respect to the evidence of these, it is indicated that there can be no mistake.*

Under this theory, not only is profound thought rendered unnecessary, but a mode is pointed out under which the grossest of men's desires and worldly passions may be gratified without ultimate danger or present shame. It is not wonderful that a philosophy so simple, and so well suited to the ordinary character of the human mind, should, when uncontradicted, propagate itself widely, and at the same time take a strong hold on the feelings of those who are induced to adopt it. In these circumstances, it is a blessing to society that Christians have been compelled to conquer their superstitious dislike of even examining opinions which call in question the primary elements of religious truth. Such a line of procedure prevented the possibility of obviating misconceptions arising from the changes which the progress of various sciences wrought out on the character and tendencies of human thought. As

---

* This tendency is farther strengthened by the difficulty of reducing spiritual phenomena to their causes. It is a so much simpler method to assume an apparent though insufficient cause for phenomena than to trace the real cause, that we need not be astonished at men being seduced into adopting it. We shall find, however, that the true cause, when once discovered, is felt in all instances to be plain and unmistakable, and such is specially the case with the conclusions of a sound spiritual philosophy.

has been said, it was a complete mistake, originating in a misunderstanding of the constitution of human nature, and the arrangements under which Providence has provided a means for gradually generating a full appreciation of the ways and wonders of Almighty God. The most minute and sedulous examination of any objection that can be proposed against religion, can never be dangerous to religion, because religion is the highest and purest truth, and her lustre is dimmed by every shadow of doubt which is allowed to rest on the entire and unhesitating faith which she demands. It is clearly, therefore, the duty of all who revere religion and appreciate its infinite importance for the welfare of the human race, to meet every objection which may be taken to it, so far as this can be done effectually.

But there is still an additional call on our efforts for this purpose. On the determination of the principles of religion, however little it may be understood, depends the validity of those obligations which bind men together as members of society and portions of political combinations. Few, indeed, seem to have any notion of the length to which some of our most popular modern theories with respect to religion would lead us, because few seem to know the only solid foundation on which moral and political obligations can by possibility be rested. Apart from religion, it is demonstrable that the selfish theory is the only foundation either of morals or politics, and *it* can imply no obligation.

It may be said that even under this theory men would feel the necessity of allying themselves with each other, and of practically asserting relative duties, for the sake of their personal and selfish interests. But it must be remembered that different people look upon their personal and selfish interests under very different aspects, and that under such a theory it must be left to each individual to determine what in each case he might deem most advisable for the promotion of his own interests. Granting, however, that the mass of intelligent men would feel the necessity of defending and assisting each other under ordinary circumstances, it is clear that the extent of the feeling must in every instance depend on the measure of advantages which the several parties might believe themselves to have realised in comparison with others. The rich and the powerful no doubt would be zealous defenders of conservative principles, but it is absurd to suppose that the poor and the outcast would under any form of the selfish theory sympathise with them. They, on the contrary, would uphold the rights of physical force and the justice of the equalisation of property, and they would naturally combine for the purpose of giving effect to their theory. We must satisfy the poor and the outcast, not merely that there is a higher law than the law of selfishness, but that they have it in their power to realise a far higher position, and a far greater happiness, than the utmost gratification of selfishness will afford, or there can be no real security either for life or property.* The amount of security which we have for either the one or the other depends on the universality and degree of such a conviction, which no doubt prevails more or less among all classes, though its effect be materially impaired by the vague form under which it is too often entertained. The Atheistic philosophers are in fact indebted for their own safety to the silent operation of the very principles which they seem to be zealous in repudiating and denying. For all human beings, even the most degraded, have some respect for life and property while they have

* There has been a most singular verification of this in the recent inquiry into the working of trades-unions, among which robbery, perjury, fire-raising, and murder have been systematically practised. It is a natural and necessary consequence of men without religious principle having an opportunity of secretly combining for the purpose of resisting measures which they believe inconsistent with their own interests. Had these men been influenced by religious principle, nothing could have induced them to do such deeds; but apart from religious principle, they have acted a perfectly intelligible part, and we should like to know on what ground they can be condemned. They are strictly following the utilitarian theory, seeking what they believe the "greatest happiness of the greatest number." This investigation into the working of trades-unions began after this book had been substantively finished, but we felt called upon to refer to an event which not only illustrates, but practically demonstrates, the validity of its whole argument. How thoroughly it does so will appear from the sequel.

the most shadowy idea that they are under the guardianship of an omnipotent Lawgiver. But convince them theoretically that any other man has as much right to property as its actual possessors, that there is just as little harm in taking the life of a man as of an ox or of a sheep, that no one has any authority, save from accident or force, to rule over his fellow-creatures, and as surely as human nature is human nature the theory will sooner or later be practically realised. It was for a few months nearly the theory of the French revolutionists, and the results, as is well known, are recorded in letters of blood. It is the theory of all thieves, murderers, and traitors.

The consequences will be exactly proportional as men are taught to approximate to the belief of such a theory; and it will not be very difficult in so far to teach it, since it is a theory in some respects most pleasing to humanity, and is indeed, apart from religion, the only possible theory, as we shall subsequently endeavour more particularly to prove.

We by no means deny that there are feelings of mutual relationship naturally existing in every human being. But experience demonstrates that these feelings will in a great measure be eradicated by that adoption of the selfish theory which results from doubt, and still more disbelief, of the moral attributes and moral superintendence of a God. Such feelings in that case can only act as motives to the extent that they overbear the impulses of our personal interests and passions; and how trifling this would be, and is, need not be farther illustrated than by referring to the conduct of others, or even to the consciousness of our own minds. In fact, such feelings, apart from religion, merely constitute a form of selfishness, which practically has little or no influence when opposed to the gratification of our personal desires.

This becomes still more entirely the case as men advance in life, because we have no encouragement under the selfish theory to cherish relative feelings. They therefore must gradually though necessarily die away, like every other tendency of the mind which is neglected, or rather crushed, under the operation of more powerful influences. Such, indisputably and obviously, would be the condition of the world, supposing the influence of religion to be destroyed, and such proportionally the condition of the world in so far as its influences are weakened or impaired.

Let it not, however, be supposed that we figure this condition of things as deprecating discussion on subjects involving such tremendous consequences. Far otherwise; on the contrary, from the very importance of the subject, we hold that every objection to religion should be examined, and that every doubt with respect to its evidences should be removed. We simply desire to show that there is no time to lose. Some of the opinions from the adoption of which such consequences would necessarily follow, are already widely prevalent. It therefore becomes all who have anxiously considered the subject, and who believe that they can rest the principles of religious, moral, and political science on a more precise and unassailable foundation, to lend their aid. Men need not delude themselves by supposing that theories of natural law will restrain human passions under any system of selfishness: unless moral and political duties rest on religion, they can have no foundation except such as even the most illiterate will discover the weakness of.

It may, however, still be said that natural religion would to some extent form a foundation on which moral and political obligations might be rested. This is true, although natural religion would never of itself afford motives sufficiently strong for the purpose of at all efficiently subduing our passions, or generating that trust in God which can alone constitute real and permanent happiness. But, in point of fact, this is not the question, as may be easily inferred from the previous part of our argument. The avowed attacks of sceptics have generally been made upon Christianity, from whatever cause; but the attack in modern times is not on the *characteristics*, but on the *foundations*, of Christianity. The theories to which we have adverted do not therefore strike at Christianity as a revelation, but as resting on natural religion. It is natural religion itself which is assailed, as incapable of constituting a satisfactory ground on which any system can be reared.*

For example, the assumption that miracles are impossible, or at all events incapable of proof, sweeps natural religion utterly away. The adjustment and arrangements of the universe constitute the greatest of miracles; but if the adjustment and arrangements of the universe, as the productions of an intelligent Being, be incapable of proof, then it follows that instead of being the creatures of an intelligent God, we may be the product of some natural law operating throughout eternity. Human beings, according to this theory, have had no beginning, and will have no end; but this im-

* I have recently heard it suggested as an objection to miracles, that the occasional interposition of the Supreme Being would interfere with the certainty of the conclusions of physical philosophy, because the interposition of the supreme power would thus render the operation of general laws uncertain. The objection is evidently absurd. It assumes the interventions of the Supreme Being as *without reason, or under reasons which cannot be known or discovered.* The intervention of the Supreme Being, if it take place at all, *is a law of nature*, and the occasions on which it will happen or may happen can be ascertained by means analogous to those used in other cases. It would be just as reasonable to say that the occasional interposition of human beings so as to prevent physical consequences which might otherwise occur, would interfere with the certainty of the conclusions of physical philosophy. It would indeed be more reasonable, for the one interposition must be in conformity with perfect wisdom, while the other will usually imply more or less of caprice.

mortality is not an immortality of individuals, but of race. The race may therefore never cease, but the individuals of whom it is composed, when they die to this world, perish for ever.

Nor is this attack on the principles of natural religion merely incidental to such systems. It is of the very essence of them all, since if the possibility of proving the truth of miracles be conceded, all the other objections which are proposed to Christianity become trifling and untenable. A sound theory of inspiration would supersede them so thoroughly, as to make those infidel and rationalistic works which have acquired the widest circulation during recent years absolute defences of the evidences of Christianity.

It is clear, therefore, that from the progress of science we have now got back to first principles. All attacks on the details of Christianity, or rather on its characteristics, have failed, apparently from their own inherent weakness, and would seem to be given up. Its excellence as a system, the purity of its precepts, the transcendent sublimity and effectiveness of its doctrines, are admitted. No Christian could describe them in more glowing terms than Strauss or Renan. The infidel has been forced back to his last stronghold. Christ is recognised as the most perfect of human characters, and Christianity as the most perfect system of spiritual science. It is now only maintained that Christianity cannot be proved to have come from God, *because we can have no satisfactory proof that there is a God.** All that we know, or can know, according to the rationalistic theory, is the existence of an operating system of unchanging laws, by which all things were and are and will be regulated. It may be that in certain instances this is not avowed. It may even be that some rationalists are not themselves † thoroughly aware of all that is involved in their theory. But it is no less certain that through all rationalistic works such assumptions are implied. The principle of the ultra-materialistic philosophy lies latent in every one of them. Here indeed we have the essential distinction betwixt Socinianism, which has now been almost universally abandoned, and Rationalism, by which it has been absorbed. Socinianism fully recognised natural religion, and attempted to reduce revelation to a form of it. Rationalism, on the contrary, denies the validity of the Christian evidences on the ground of their assuming the truth of natural religion, which it maintains more or less avowedly and explicitly to be itself incapable of proof.

* In the same way, if morality be obligatory on all human beings, and essential for their happiness, then the perfect morality of Scripture may prove its truth. But if morality be a mere incident in human relations, or depends purely on selfishness, then, instead of proving the truth of Christianity, it would prove the very reverse.

† There are still professing clergymen and others, who from their position dare not avow pure Rationalism, that maintain in its place a sort of spurious Socinianism.

It is to first principles, therefore, we repeat, that we must manifestly address ourselves, in order in any measure effectively to answer the rationalistic theories of modern times. Mere attempts at answering the incidental theories of rationalists, by which they undertake to trace the origin of Christianity to natural causes, are useless; because, while the essential assumption of rationalism, flowing from its adoption of the most objectionable form of materialistic philosophy, remains untouched, such attempts, however successful, still leave a painful sense of deficiency on the mind of the reader. He feels that there is something wanting which lies a great deal deeper than the clearest answer to such incidental and superficial theories can supply. He feels that a mistake as to the mode in which Christianity originated can be of no consequence, while a primary objection to the possibility of a revelation, founded on a denial of the possibility of the superhuman altogether, at at least as knowable by us, remains behind.

Supposing, therefore, all the various modes in which it has been proposed to account for the origin of Christianity from natural causes to have been refuted, it would only prove the conjectures of those who proposed them to have been wrong, but would leave the primary assumption, that a proof of any superhuman phenomenon is impossible, perfectly untouched. The doubt originating in such an assumption would still inhere in the mind of those who had no sufficient means of ascertaining its groundlessness. The possibility of some other conjecture proving more satisfactory would still suggest itself, so that to a person harassed by such a form of scepticism no amount of evidence in favour of Christianity would be considered decisive, or constitute a sufficient foundation for any approach to full assurance of faith.

To meet that apathetic indifference to religion, therefore, with which a tendency to rationalistic opinions has imbued multitudes—of whom, however, many know little about the matter, except that they dislike to think on spiritual subjects at all—we must evidently deal with principles; we must show on sufficient grounds, stated in the plainest and most practical manner, what are the real evidences on which natural theology rests. Thus, as will now be manifest, can the system of God's moral government be in any measure clearly understood, and an assurance of his direct action on human affairs logically established. This being done, it will be comparatively easy to determine the fundamental principles of moral and political science, and to demonstrate the only possible manner in which these sciences can in any proper sense be practically realised.

Until all this be done, moreover, we cannot be in a position to appreciate the full value of the Christian evidences. The conclusions derived from natural theology constitute, on the contrary, the very basis on which these evidences rest. When this basis has been thoroughly laid, the evidences of Christianity can be reared upon it in their strength. The nature and necessity of a revelation become manifest, because natural theology, *though essential as a basis*, is yet found to be only a basis, and consequently useless for any other purpose in itself.

PRELIMINARY INQUIRIES.

CHAPTER I.

SOURCES AND LIMITS OF HUMAN KNOWLEDGE.

NO SUCH THING AS INNATE OR INTUITIVE IDEAS—KNOWLEDGE IS PRIMARILY DERIVED FROM FEELINGS—PROCESS—HOW KNOWLEDGE MAY BE DERIVED FROM OTHERS—HOW KNOWLEDGE MAY BE DERIVED FROM A COMPARISON OF EFFECTS PRODUCED BY CAUSES EXTERNAL TO OURSELVES WITH EFFECTS PRODUCED BY THE OPERATION OF OUR OWN FACULTIES—HOW KNOWLEDGE IS FURTHER IMPLIED IN THE DESIRE OF CO-RELATIVES CAPABLE OF GRATIFYING SUCH DESIRE—UNIVERSALITY OF THE CONCLUSIONS OF REASON.

THEOLOGIANS have generally more or less rested our religious beliefs on certain elementary ideas which they assume to be born with us. These were formerly called innate ideas, but as it was found that the existence of such innate ideas could hardly be defended, they have subsequently reappeared under the name of maxims and intuitions. These are manifestly the same thing under another designation; and so, in order to evade the difficulties involved in the assumption, recent German philosophers, and their followers in this country, have assigned to them the character of mysterious suggestions. With these, consequently, religion has become a sort of mysticism, but can rest on no precise evidence, nor exist in any precise form as matter of intelligence. They therefore repudiate the use of logic altogether in religion, which they say depends upon a state of mind which they are pleased to call faith, resulting from those supposed mysterious intuitions which they have discovered or invented for the purpose. The theory is evidently nothing new. It is, indeed, as old as the human race, although never perhaps expressed in precisely the same words. It has been exemplified in the Pythagoreans among the Greeks of old; in the Essenese Therapeutæ of the Jews; in the innumerable sects of visionaries among the Christians. It is the religion of imagination, where it is any religion at all, substituted in place of the religion of reason. Indeed, they sometimes call those mysterious suggestions reason, as if implying something greater and nobler than the mere understanding could discover; and hence this reason becomes a very different thing from understanding, sanctioning conclusions even which are often directly opposed to those derived from the understanding.

But although this theory be evidently untenable,

and would reduce faith to a mere matter of imagination or caprice, differing in different individuals according to the special conditions of each; yet we cannot believe, considering the multitudes practically influenced by it under some form or another, that it is devoid of every element of truth. This, indeed, is very far from being the case. For though there are neither innate ideas, nor intuitive ideas, nor mysterious suggestions, nor any other form of absolute notions existing in the human mind, there are unquestionably innate or intuitive *feelings.* * These *are developed under the operation*

---

* Some philosophers, from an entire misconception on this subject, deny innate feelings as well as innate ideas. The theory is not only inconsistent with every man's experience, but necessarily leads to absurdity. They say that *all* our knowledge is derived from experience of external perceptions. But *our belief in experience must itself have some foundation on which to rest.* Experience of external perceptions, moreover, can only teach us what is past, and can never assure us of what is to come. It would teach us, therefore, that certain sequences of phenomena had occurred, but could not possibly teach us that in future the same sequences would be invariable. There must be some innate feeling made known to us in its exact character by reason which compels us to believe this. That feeling is our personal sense both of physical and specially efficient power as the cause of every phenomenon. The nature of it is explained afterwards. But it signifies little what the nature of the feeling may be. It is sufficient that we are assured, as matter of certainty, that there *must* be such a feeling, be it what it may. This theory, that all our knowledge is derived from experience of external perceptions alone, and which constitutes pure scepticism as implying a disbelief not only in effects having causes, but even in mathematical axioms, has nearly run its course. The mass of mankind consider it rather as a subject for ridicule than for reasoning.

of the faculty, or whatever it may be called, of reason or understanding. It is that faculty, and that faculty alone, which teaches us the proportions and powers both of modes and existences. It is that faculty by which, in other words, we compare feelings, and thus are enabled to discover in how far they and their causes are *identical with* or *different from* each other. It is that faculty, consequently, by which we *know, as contradistinguished from feeling;* and hence, of course, our knowledge of the relations of things depends on its degree, and the degree in each specific case, in which it has been brought into operation.

In the primary stage of its operations, therefore, it gives us notions of the simplest kind. It teaches us the identities and differences of colours, and of the other feelings which are discovered by our senses. In the same way it teaches us the identities and differences of lines and figures, and all the other *modes* of the feelings that originate with our senses. Further, it gives us a knowledge of power as distinguished from the absence of power, so as to teach us the relation of cause and effect. Now, it is these and similar simple notions, resulting from the primary operations of reason on our perceptions, and impressed upon our minds by continuous experience, so as that at length we can hardly tell whence they came, that philosophers have imagined to be innate, intuitive, or mysterious. But they are no such thing.

They are, it will now be manifest, merely the knowledge which reason gives us of the nature of our own feelings and faculties, and of the simplest relations of external qualities and modes, as they affect our feelings and faculties.

The man who knows, for example, what is implied in the feeling of equality, must also know the truth of the axiom, "Things equal to the same thing are equal to one another," because it is a mere expression of one characteristic of equality. For to argue that any one knows what is implied in the feeling of equality, and yet does not know its characteristics, is a contradiction in terms. The man who knows the feeling of power, again, in his own experience, must also know the truth of the axiom, "Every change must have a cause," inasmuch as we know from our feeling of power that it is power, and *power only*, which changes. Thus all knowledge is the result of our reason teaching us what is implied in our feelings, and in how far each feeling is identical with, or different from, every other feeling. That which we call our knowledge of external things is evidently a form of this. It arises from an inference, that the causes of certain feelings are to be found in objects external to ourselves. We are conscious of those causes which are within us, and reason, discriminating these from *the only other causes of which we are cognisant*, teaches us that they are without us. The whole process is so obvious, that it hardly can be misunderstood. At the same time, it is not to be supposed that the mind is a mere *tabula rasa*, on which reason is to rear a purely intellectual superstructure, as if we were creatures of intelligence, and nothing else. This is an idea not uncommon amongst persons devoted to certain classes of studies, after they begin to discern that some of their earlier opinions were prejudices, resting merely on authority, and more or less unfounded. They are thus led to imagine that all their former principles are to be swept away, and the whole constitution of their mental characters to be changed, so that every notion shall be a matter of rational deduction, to which no objection can be taken, and with respect to which no difficulty can be suggested.* They forget that reason must have foundations on which to rest; and that

---

* We have observed that when men thus throw off all belief in authority, they usually go to the opposite extreme, and despise *all* that they had been formerly taught, and *all* that the mass of their fellow-creatures believe. This strength of prejudice is owing to an unconscious fear that, after all, authority may be right and they themselves wrong. Hence such persons generally substitute the author of some plausible system in place of the belief of mankind, and, contriving to differ from him on some incidental or trifling particular, they delude themselves into supposing that they are independent thinkers. Almost all of this class of thinkers, if thinkers they can be called, end *for a time* in the adoption of pure unadulterated scepticism, only modified by a love for disputation, which, of course, is necessarily inconsistent with the very essence of a system which can believe nothing, and therefore cannot consistently argue about anything.

every one of these foundations must consist in a feeling or tendency implying belief, for which *no cause can be assigned*, except that such is the constitution of our natures, and that we cannot help more or less trusting in them. They forget that the very feelings or tendencies which thus exist as very parts of our beings, originate our prejudices, which, while they may be partially erroneous as modified by circumstances, yet in every instance contain a certain admixture of truth, which cannot be swept away without undermining the foundations on which truth ultimately rests, and thus generating universal scepticism. They forget that trust in the authority of others is itself one of these tendencies which more or less regulates the beliefs of every human being, which is not in any case to be repudiated lightly, and which cannot, indeed, be eradicated without almost annihilating the use of reason, which, were it limited in its exercise to facts within our own personal experience, could never carry us beyond the most elementary knowledge. We are not, therefore, when we come to years of discretion and to the capability of self-thought, to sweep away all our former opinions, and endeavour, on the mind as a *tabula rasa*, to rear a totally new superstructure. In such a case we are almost sure to fall into monstrous errors. We are to ascertain, not rashly but very cautiously, how much they involve as arising from natural tendency, which must to us be true, whether the tendency of any individual mind, or the tendency of all minds, as realised by society at large; and how much, on the contrary, is the result of mere circumstances, which must be more or less tinctured with error, and therefore ought in so far to be rejected. We have thus a basis on which reason may rear its superstructure, and it is the only possible basis on which a firm and trustworthy superstructure *can* be reared.

All knowledge, then, must *primarily* be derived from our feelings and tendencies; or, in other words, from our own personal experience. Thence we have our primary facts, and thereafter reason teaches us what they respectively imply; or, in other words, enables us to know them. The more thoroughly we *know* what is implied in our feelings, the more thoroughly, of course, we also farther know their relations—that is to say, the extent to which they are identical with, or different from, other feelings, and the power, consequently, of the one to act upon the other. In the same way, the more thoroughly we know what is implied in external objects, the more thoroughly do we know also *their* relations, or the extent to which they, in like manner, are identical with, or different from, other objects, and the power, consequently, of the one to act upon the other. As we thus know feelings and objects in our own experience, we come to be in a position to receive information with respect to other facts of the same kind from our fellow-creatures. We say facts of the same kind, because we can form no conception of facts of which the kind or the elements are not known from our own feelings. They alone can give us primary knowledge. No description could enable us to appreciate a primary colour, or taste, or smell, or sound, or emotion, or any primary sensation or feeling whatever. But we are quite capable of understanding a description of the combinations or relations of the facts, of which we have known the kinds or elements before, from our personal experience. The facts thus derived from the information of others thereafter become our own, and we can reason upon them just as well as upon those which our own experience may have made known to us. In other words, we can be assured that the thing which happened once, will, under the same circumstances, happen again, and may determine the relative character of the facts with which others have made us acquainted, just as we would determine the relative character of those that we had discovered for ourselves.

If, for example, they told us of a new species of soil, we could determine the species of plants for which such soil is most suitable; or if they told us of a new species of metal, we could determine the uses to which it might be applied.

There is, however, it will now be seen, a mode under which we may reason from the facts of our own experience with perfect certainty, but can in no degree be assisted by the knowledge which other people can afford us. This is where we discover, from the nature of the feelings or faculties of our own minds, that a certain result can only be explained under the operation of such feelings and faculties. If, for example, we find a living creature manifesting in its proceedings the remembrance of a past fact, as where a horse seeks to return to the place where it had been formerly fed, we infer that it has the faculty of memory. In other words, we identify in the horse the faculty which we know to be essential to the production of a similar result in ourselves. There is something in the very nature of the faculty, *as felt in ourselves*, which assures us that either the identical faculty, or at all events some cognate faculty, must exist in the horse likewise. This clearly proceeds from our experimental knowledge of the character of such faculty as discovered by reason, which teaches us what it can do, what it cannot do, and what *it alone* is competent to effect.

This consideration, however, carries us a great deal farther, for it assures us that a knowledge of facts must, in so far as it extends, imply a knowledge of their relations. Whatever fact, in other words, we know, must be known relatively, so that, from the very nature of the case, we must in so far know what it can do, and what it cannot do, and, as our knowledge becomes more perfect, *what* *it alone is capable of effecting.* Except, indeed, in so far as we know our minds and their feelings, we cannot know anything in the strictest sense absolutely.* We can only know external things relatively. We can only know sound, for example, in relation to our sense of hearing, and odours in relation to our sense of smelling, and so in all other cases. Hence, except in so far as we know external objects as relative to ourselves, in their actions on ourselves, we do not know them, and cannot know them at all. All our knowledge of such objects, in the first instance, is a knowledge

* Our own feelings in their essence we know absolutely, though it be from internal experience. When we hear, we know what hearing is, apart from the sound heard, which we intuitively distinguish from it. When we see, we know what seeing is, apart from the object seen, which we intuitively distinguish from it. When we remember, we know what memory is, as apart from the subject remembered, which we intuitively distinguish from it ; and so in all other cases. It is one of the grossest absurdities of modern speculation to say that, because we cannot know without experience, therefore the feeling which enables us to know, and the object or subject of that feeling, cannot be known as distinguished ! How such a theory could be admitted for a moment seems wonderful, since it is directly contrary to never-ceasing experience. The man who maintains that practically it is impossible to distinguish between the light which we see and the perception of sight by which we see it, seems too much confused by metaphysics to be capable of logical argument. It is evidently the theory of a man who attends only to words, and altogether neglects realities. It is in fact a manifestation of that intellectual pedantry which grows out of the vanity of speculative knowledge, unchecked by knowledge of the world. Intellectual paradoxes, *honestly* maintained, are almost all referable to this condition of mind.

of the mode in which they act upon ourselves, and a distinct appreciation of this will be found greatly to simplify our ulterior inquiries. We thus discover that a knowledge of their power—or, in other words, of what they can do, and cannot do, as this is discovered by our feelings and faculties—is all the knowledge of them which we can by possibility realise.

The fact of our being able, however, even in thus far to appreciate the nature of objects external to ourselves, shows that there is a connection between us and them subsisting under the very constitution of our minds. Hence it is that our feelings give us a sort of anticipatory expectation of their existence, enabling us to appreciate the origin of a series of beliefs, the nature of which has never been thoroughly explained, but which have a material bearing on our ordinary conduct in life, as well as on the philosophical development of spiritual truth. For it is evident that there must be a series of beliefs under which we are induced to act with a view to the gratification of our desires. No desire could of itself induce us to act, unless there were involved in it some sort of belief that there were means provided by which it could be gratified. Desire, apart from such belief, would be a mere feeling of pain; each desire must therefore involve a farther feeling, however generated, that it has a co-relative without us, suited for its gratification. Without this, as it has been said, that which we call desire would not be desire, but a mere sense of suffering. This, of itself, would originate no effort of any kind. It might, no doubt, generate a physical action where the cause of the suffering exerted a physical power, but it would originate no voluntary effort. Yet a sense of suffering does, beyond all doubt, originate voluntary effort, from which it clearly follows, that a sense of suffering must in itself imply some belief in the possibility of a remedy.

It is this belief which causes the infant to scream, or, at all events, it is for the purpose of procuring aid, which comes to the same thing, that nature urges it to scream, and to manifest other symptoms of suffering. Nature, in other words, teaches infants the signs by which their wants may be made known to those who have the means and inclination to relieve them.

It is the same species of belief that impels us, at all stages of life, to seek relief when we are afflicted, under the irresistible impression that there are means of relief, if we could only procure them. Under such an influence, we appeal to our fellow-creatures, and if they cannot or will not aid us, *we appeal to a higher power*.

Still, as has been said, in all cases of mere physical suffering, our notions of co-relatives must in the first instance be exceedingly general. The infant, when it first feels hungry, must believe in the possibility of relief from some external remedy, or else it would not be compelled by nature to indicate its want; but it can have no notion of the precise nature of the co-relative by which its suffering is to be removed, or, in other words, its desire is to be gratified. The moment, however, that the precise co-relative is known, its appreciation of the connection betwixt the desire and the gratification is complete; and as, in advancing life, it discovers more and more accurately the nature and purpose of the desire, so does it learn to modify, according to circumstances, the form of the gratification.

The constitution of these beliefs, however, and the mode in which they tend to greater precision in ascertaining their co-relatives, is brought out with special clearness in the relationship of the sexes. It is a relation which only develops itself at a somewhat later period of life. Children of different sexes seem sensible of no other relation than that which unites them as human beings. But boys and girls, at an early age, begin to mark each other's distinguishing characteristics. In some instances, strangely enough, there seems a sort of repulsion betwixt them, from the difference of their tendencies. But no sooner do they begin to discover the nature of sexual difference, and the purpose on account of which it has been constituted, than a feeling of their being co-relatives to one another is appreciated. They recognise each other by their feelings as parts of a whole, and essential therefore to each other morally, mentally, and physically, for the full enjoyment of domestic and of social life.

The same result is perhaps less precisely, but not less certainly, exemplified in respect to other relationships. Our sense of weakness and dependence, which is forced upon us almost every instant by the lessons of continuous experience, necessarily generates the assurance of existences, external to ourselves, who can and will protect us, sustain us, and sympathise with us. We have thus in our personal feelings a sort of anticipation of *external* intelligent existence, and involved therein a bond uniting us to those intelligent beings with whose existence we are made acquainted, which is stronger or weaker according to the measure of the relationship which nature has constituted betwixt us and them.

In fact, in every primary desire there is an expectation involved that a co-relative essential to its gratification is provided; and in every instance, so far as our experience extends, this expectation is realised. How can we doubt that such must be the case? Were it otherwise, our natures would be a delusion and a lie. They would urge us to seek co-relatives which either do not exist, or, at all events, are not attainable. Now this we cannot believe. Were it indeed possible, all belief would be at an end, since the information of nature is all we have to depend upon for any of our beliefs; and did she deceive us in one case, we could have no confidence in her as to any other. What nature teaches, therefore, we *must* accept as true. We cannot help it, since in all attempts at distrusting her we shall ultimately find that we have been mocking and deceiving ourselves. But if nature teach any one thing more certainly than another, it is, that every primary desire has its co-relative, through which alone it can be adequately gratified, and this teaching is found in the assurance involved in the very nature of our desires themselves.*

This conclusion will be ascertained under yet another form in the determination of a particular which still remains to be considered. That particular regards the extent to which rational deduction is valid. Is reason, in other words, a universal principle, giving us valid conclusions with reference to everything to which it applies; or does it only embrace those relations which we could discover by observation, though under a more circuitous process? Thus, reason teaches us to believe in human testimony, and under that belief we repose confidence in those who testify to us as to the phenomena of astronomy. We ourselves, however, by acquiring a knowledge of astro-

---

* This is true not only of strictly primary desires as involved in our primary natures, but of every desire *which necessarily flows from our primary natures*, and must necessarily be common, therefore, to the whole human race.

nomy, might take the observations and make the calculations essential for ascertaining such phenomena, or for confirming their truth. Now, is it because this could be done, or because we think it could be done, that we repose confidence in the testimony of such parties; or would we be justified in such confidence, supposing that they, *as good and sufficient witnesses*, professed that they had received their information, so far as they were capable of judging, by a direct communication from Heaven?

Again, if we hear of certain beautifully organised machinery in a distant land, we immediately conclude that it must have been contrived by minds possessed of the same kind of intelligence as our own. We ourselves, however, might perhaps ascertain the truth of this by visiting such lands. Now, is it because this might be done, or perhaps might be done, that we are justified in such a belief; or would we be justified in the same belief supposing such machinery to have fallen, ready made, in so far as we could discover, from the sky, as being framed of materials of which we never heard before, and of a kind to which our world, so far as we know, contains nothing similar?

There cannot be a doubt upon the subject, as regarded in connection with these and similar illustrations. Our conclusions are determined from the very nature of reason, apart from all incidental considerations. Reason has nothing to do with any such considerations. *If the evidence be liable to no objection,* it is equally valid with respect to all things, and that whether they be natural or superhuman.* It is a universal faculty, and if its legitimate conclusions rest on legitimate premises, they are universally true. We feel that this is the case *in our knowledge of the nature of the faculty as realised in our own experience.* No doubt, in arguing on effects as to which the causes or operating powers are beyond the reach of our observation, we can only conclude as to classes of causes, and not as to individuals. We can only,

* We use the word superhuman rather than supernatural, because the latter word leads and has led to grievous misconceptions. Nature is merely a short name for that which actually occurs in the universe, whether through the operation of animate or inanimate existences. There can therefore be no supernatural existence. All is natural which exists. It is no interruption of the course of *nature,* nor therefore *supernatural,* when a *human* being by his intervention modifies the action of causes, so that different effects are produced from those which inanimate existences would have produced had they been left alone. Neither is it *supernatural,* therefore, if a *superhuman* being in the same way modifies either effects or causes; his being *superhuman* by no means makes him *supernatural.* Superhuman agency, on the contrary, is manifest in all parts of the universe, and at every moment. Reason, therefore, must be perpetually engaged in observing it, and philosophising upon it. Miracles, as probative of a divine revelation, may have ceased. But miracles, in the sense of the action of superhuman power, are continuous everywhere *around* us, and, as Christians believe, *within* us. Whether this superhuman power be intelligent or non-intelligent, is just the question which we propose to determine.

in the case of machinery for instance, conclude that it has been contrived by an intelligence without specially determining the particular intelligence. But the conclusion is no less certain. It is attained, moreover, not merely from our experience that, so far as we have observed, contrivance is the effect of intelligence exclusively, *which is the general impression,* but from our own experimental knowledge of the nature of intelligence, which assures us that the contrivance implied in organised machinery *cannot possibly originate in any other cause.* It is thus not merely a probable, but to this extent a demonstrative, conclusion. Were it false, there would be implied not merely a misconception of evidence, but a misconception of the nature of a faculty of our own minds, which is made known to us in our consciousness. There would be implied, in fact, a denial of the validity of the law of nature as a ground of belief.

Wherever, therefore, we perfectly understand the nature of causes or powers, we can draw certain and universal conclusions as to what must be their effects; and wherever we perfectly understand the nature of effects, we can draw certain and universal conclusions as to what must have been the causes or powers which produced them.

It has indeed been argued that reason sometimes contradicts itself, and consequently that its conclusions cannot in all cases be trusted. But the assumption is utterly false. Reason never does, and never can, contradict itself. In every instance where by different processes of reasoning seemingly opposite conclusions are attained—as in the case, for example, of philosophical necessity and human responsibility *—the phenomenon is owing to our ignorance of the facts on which, either in the one case or the other, the reasoning is founded. We reason, therefore, in such instances from false premises, and must attach the blame to our own ignorance, and not to the uncertainty of the faculty which we employ.

The sources from which our knowledge can alone be acquired, and the limits by which such knowledge is bounded, being thus ascertained in so far as necessary for our purpose, we shall find the process greatly simplified under which are to be determined the fundamental principles of religious, moral, and political science.

* The difficulty connected with the subject of philosophical necessity arises from the unfounded assumption that motives act upon the human mind in the same way that physical force acts upon a physical machine. Yet if we would only endeavour to think with some accuracy, our own consciousness would satisfy us that this is not the case. *Every one* has the conscious power of either yielding to motives, and thus acting under impulse; or resisting them, and thus acting with a view to ulterior and more permanent happiness. The decision of the question is, however, of no importance to our present subject, as even if the doctrine of philosophical necessity were true, it would only constitute the stronger cause of leading us to appreciate the motives that must secure for us, by the assumption itself, the most intense and permanent happiness.

CHAPTER II.

NATURE AND DIVISIONS OF SPIRITUAL SCIENCE.

NATURE OF SPIRIT—THEORY OF MATERIALISM—MODE OF STUDYING SPIRITUAL SCIENCE AND ITS PARTS—PROCESS UNDER WHICH WE DISCOVER THE EXISTENCE OF SPIRITS EXTERNAL TO OURSELVES —PROCESS UNDER WHICH WE DISCOVER THE RELATIONS IN WHICH THESE SPIRITS STAND TO OURSELVES—DIVISION OF THE SPIRITUAL SCIENCES.

SPIRIT is that which feels, thinks, remembers, reasons, or, in other words, which possesses the qualities that we attributed to the mind of man. It is usual to call this form of existence immaterial, but this is only as compared with those qualities of physical matter with which we are made acquainted by means of our senses.* This

---

* Although we cannot form any definite idea of existence except under the character of matter, it by no means follows that there may not be existence of a different character. There may be spiritual existence altogether different, therefore, from any kind of material existence. As it is manifest from the text, however, that we can never positively determine any theory on the subject, *because the nature of essence is beyond us*, it follows that all discussion and disputes upon the subject must be mere metaphysical trifling. We have two classes of phenomena dif-

limitation of the meaning of the word immaterial at once puts an end to the absurd discussions which are so common with respect to what is called the theory of materialism, and which really originate, like many other disputes with respect to spiritual questions, in a mutual misconception of the sense of the term which is employed. For no one would assert that spiritual phenomena are hard, coloured, divisible, or possessed of any of the properties by which physical phenomena are characterised. Nor will it be maintained that physical qualities, under whatever form of machinery they might be combined, could produce spiritual phenomena, so as that a physical mill could grind ideas, or a physical loom weave emotions. Physical machinery can only change the form of matter, but cannot produce results *generically* different from the material subjected to its action. Thus, the brain as a machine might combine the rays which the optic nerve conveys to it, so as to give to them a new form, but could not constitute them thoughts, and still less generate through them desires or feelings with respect to other existences which are not involved in them, and which could only have originated in the brain

---

ferent in kind, and therefore, *so far as we are concerned*, we *must* refer them to different kinds of causes. It is of no consequence whether we regard the essence of mind and matter to be different, or assume that there is only one essence, but endowed with qualities of perfectly different kinds. It is a mere dispute about words.

by an utterly different process, unlike anything which the physical world exhibits to us.* On the other hand, that spirit is not some kind of matter we hardly believe that any thinking man will venture positively to affirm. We do not indeed know what the essence of matter may be, or what qualities it may involve. There may be some kind of matter which thinks, feels, and desires. Indeed, the essence of matter and spirit, for anything we can tell, may be one and the same.†

* I recently met with a materialist of the medical profession, who proposed a theory having the appearance of some plausibility. According to him, the ideas and emotions usually attributed to mind are what he denominated the waste of the brain. This waste of the brain he regarded as analogous to the perspiration which violent bodily exercise causes. As a proof, he averred that after earnest thought particles of cerebral matter were found mixed up with the excretions of the body. But he evidently not only reasoned erroneously, but, admitting his facts, the conclusion should have been precisely the reverse of that which he drew from them, and constitutes indeed a most logical proof that the mind and the body are two different existences. For the cerebral particles are the waste analogous to perspiration produced by bodily exertion. According to the assumption, however, there is in the ideas and emotions *another product* to which there is *nothing analogous produced by bodily exercise.* The phenomena, therefore, would prove that there are two actions in thought; viz., a physical action, consisting in the efforts of the brain, and a mental action, consisting in the efforts of the mind, the cerebral particles found in the excretions being the product of the one, and ideas and emotions the product of the other. Assuming the facts to be true, the argument is consequently destructive of the theory of materialism under a form of reasoning which it does not seem possible to gainsay.

† The absurdities which we sometimes read or hear under the use of such phrases as "educating the brain," or "educating

There seems to be no impossibility involved in such a supposition. Nay, to conceive existence, which in some sense of the word is not material, seems, to say the least, exceedingly difficult. It is like conceiving an existence, which to us, at all events, would be nothing at all. What the essence of spirit may be, is, however, of no practical importance whatever. We know all that we need to know for our purpose when we know its qualities as contradistinguished from the qualities

the spinal marrow and the nerves," arise from the very misapprehension here indicated. To educate the physical brain or physical spinal marrow and nerves, in the sense of educating the physical elements under the form in which *our senses make us acquainted with them*, is simply nonsense, and has no meaning at all. If these phrases have any meaning, it must be that the brain and spinal marrow and nerves have qualities distinct from their physical qualities, *with which our perceptions do not make us acquainted*. But under this assumption there is really no dispute at all, since we do not dispute that such spiritual qualities may be interwoven with the others. We do not profess to know anything about the matter, nor have we the means of ascertaining whether the theory be true or false. We have indeed heard it maintained that sensations are merely motions of the nerves, and that therefore feeling is merely a species of motion; so that any moving body feels, though not so sensitively as nerves, whether a stick, or a stone, or a plant, or anything else. This is the legitimate fruits of materialism. Such notions, however, are not likely to do much harm. If those who profess to believe in them be asked how they know that there is such a thing as matter, they reply that they do not know it except relatively to their minds. If they be asked how they know that they have minds, they reply that their minds are merely the motions of matter. In other words, they do not know that there is either mind or matter. Curiously enough, the logical *materialist* must be a pure *sceptic*.

which we know to exist in ordinary matter, and these we know, because we feel them in ourselves to be different from the ordinary qualities of matter.

The same qualities we infer as existing in others, from observing them as manifested in the various phenomena of human life. We have no means, except from our observation of phenomena, of knowing the existence of spirit out of ourselves; because, be its essence what it may, it is, at all events, something so different from physical matter in its qualities, as to be perfectly inappreciable by the bodily senses, from which our knowledge of physical matter is alone derived. Except in so far as we may be conscious of emotions spiritually relating us to other spirits, we can have no knowledge of their existence at all, unless from perceiving that the acts which they do are identical with those acts which our own spirits induce and enable us to accomplish.

It is only, therefore, through our own consciousness in the first instance, and then through the exercise of our reason, that we can discover the qualities of spirit, or the various forms under which it appears to exist, or the relations in which these various forms of spirit stand to each other. This being premised, it will be obvious that the mode of studying spiritual must be precisely the same as the mode of studying physical science, *mutatis mutandis*. We have first to determine what are the qualities of spirit, and then ascertain the relations under which different forms or kinds of spirits are connected among themselves. To determine the qualities or powers of spirit is the business of intellectual philosophy. To determine the degree in which those qualities or powers exist in different spirits, and the relations under which they are connected among themselves, is the object of the higher sciences of religion, morals, and politics.

That there are spiritual beings external to ourselves, is not denied by any one, in so far as our fellow-creatures are concerned. That there are others, or, at all events, that there must be one other, we shall prove, *from the very same evidence under which we all believe in the spiritual existence of our fellow-creatures.* If we believe that our fellow-creatures have spirits because we are conscious through perception of certain physical phenomena which they have organised, consistency compels us to attribute the far more complex phenomena of the universe, which in so far is exactly of the same kind, to spirits or a spirit of a proportionally higher order. No doubt it might be argued that our belief from first to last on this subject is a mistake; that our fellow-creatures have no intelligent natures, inasmuch as we cannot see them, nor taste them, nor touch them, nor, in a word, perceive them by any of our senses; that our fellow-creatures, as we call them, are therefore merely physical machines, without any intelligence whatever; but no one could possibly believe it. Such an argument *could not be proved to be false.* We could only reply to it, that it is utterly inconsistent with the teaching of reason, which compels us to attribute identical effects to identical causes or powers, more especially when we know what those causes or powers are, and thus know from our own consciousness *that none other could have produced such effects.* It is just the same with regard to the pantheistic argument, as we shall by-and-by show more particularly, which attributes the organisation and arrangements of the universe to the inherent power of matter. The universe no doubt involves a much more vast and complicated system of workmanship than any machine made by human beings; and thus the argument, as applied to it, admits of being more easily perplexed by appeals to irrelevant considerations. But the phenomena in mode are precisely the same, and thus, if reason be a universal faculty, must be referred to causes or powers identical in kind, however much they may differ in degree.

That, again, there are certain relations existing among spiritual beings, appears from the notorious fact, that human beings feel emotions allying them to other spirits. As a result, consequently, they indirectly act and react upon each other's spirits not only by precept and example, but through various forms of innate desires and sensibilities. There may, however, be higher spirits which can do much more than this, by acting immediately on other spirits through some species of direct influence. There is no *a priori* objection against such a supposition. Like everything else, the facts must be determined by evidence. The existence of such beings, and, if they exist, their relations to us, and their modes of operation, can only be ascertained by *our own* feelings and by *their* actings. Their actings, again, can only be known to us through experience, whether our own personal experience, or the experience of others, communicated to us in such a way as to satisfy us that their testimony is worthy of confidence.

It has indeed been maintained that on such a subject we cannot receive testimony, because that which is superhuman is inconsistent with our own personal experience, which must to us constitute an evidence stronger than any testimony. But the absurdity of such an objection is manifest, from the very terms in which it is expressed.*

---

* Besides the argument in the text, which rests the proof on a special ground, it will be obvious that according to the argument recently indicated, and which will subsequently be illustrated at length, intelligent power, of which we have had no direct knowledge, is not only not inconsistent with our personal experience, but is every instant forced upon our personal experience, *unless we be prepared to deny that our fellow-creatures are intelligent agents.* We have exactly the same proof for the existence of superhuman, as we have for the existence of human intelligent agency. If we deny *either,*

For if we have never witnessed the thing personally at all, it is self-evident that we can have no personal experience upon the subject one way or another. There are thousands of phenomena of which we have had no personal experience, but which we believe firmly on the testimony of others. Probably, indeed, the greater proportion of our beliefs rest upon testimony. *There is nothing incredible which is possible.* There is nothing, therefore, which cannot be proved by testimony which can be proved by our own personal experience, provided we be capable of understanding the kind of the fact which is submitted to us. The evidence of testimony, it is true, may generally be less satisfactory than the evidence of our feelings or our senses, but that is in consequence of its being generally more or less imperfect. Let such evidence be full and complete, and it is as satisfactory to our reason as personal observation is to our senses.

From these remarks we can easily understand how, in the first instance, the higher spiritual sciences divide themselves. It is a division which in its general character is perfectly precise, although, as in all other sciences, the facts to a certain extent

we must deny *both*. In one word, the use of the word *supernatural*, we repeat, is a mistake. If powers superior to man, or superhuman powers, act under certain circumstances in human affairs, they must act *under natural laws* just as much as human beings do. Nature is a mere name for the arrangements of Providence.

run into each other, and could not be accurately appreciated apart. How this is the case, and how they serve to illustrate each other, will strikingly appear in their subsequent development. This division embraces three particulars:—

1. The relations in which human beings stand to higher orders of spiritual existences. This constitutes the subject of the science of religion.

2. The relations in which human beings stand to each other. This constitutes the subject of the science of morality.

3. The artificial arrangements and laws under which human beings endeavour to provide for the order and peace of society. This constitutes the subject of the science of politics.

These particulars we shall consider in order.

PART I.

SCIENCE OF RELIGION

SCIENCE OF RELIGION.

INTRODUCTION.

UNIVERSALITY OF BELIEF IN HIGHER SPIRITUAL EXISTENCES—OUTLINES OF THE CAUSES OF THIS—ORIGIN OF POLYTHEISM—RELATION OF MORALITY AND POLITICS TO THE BELIEF IN HIGHER SPIRITUAL EXISTENCES—UNIVERSAL EXPECTATION OF A REVELATION—HOW THIS IS TO BE ACCOUNTED FOR.

To whatever part of the world we direct our attention, or to whatever class of society, we find, without any exception, that every individual has a more or less clear belief in the existence of spiritual beings of an order superior to the human race. In ancient times we find all nations recognising the existence of superhuman agencies. Indeed, neither in ancient nor in modern times, so far as we can discover, was there ever a tribe, however barbarous, that did not manifest some tendency to superstition, which is just religion misapprehended. The tendency may be very slight,—so much so, as to require considerable knowledge of their habits and customs in order to appreciate it; but a minute investigation of these invariably ends in the same result. Some traces of worship are discovered, or at all events some fear of unknown causes as involving mysterious powers. It thus seems indisputable that a belief in superhuman agency is of the very constitution of our natures, as occurring under circumstances which preclude the possibility of its being derived from the conclusions and conjectures of a more cultivated intellect. Accordingly, the same belief is discovered under a similar investigation, even in the case of those who during more enlightened times profess scepticism. They cannot help themselves. Their feelings give the lie to their professions. We have investigated the matter with care, and we have never known a single exception to the general principle. Such persons are themselves invariably liable to the influence of that tendency, which in others they would regard as superstitious weakness.

We remember specially the case of one gentleman, with whom we were intimately acquainted, and whose opinions approached as nearly to pure scepticism as it was well possible to do. He had indeed been trained in scepticism. He was a man of great ability, extensive knowledge of the world, and occupied no humble position in society;

but a gay and busy life had precluded him from cultivating logical thought, or making any serious effort at determining the grounds of that scepticism which he had adopted almost from childhood. His scepticism was therefore absolute and unconditioned. He seemed to consider the superhuman as essentially beyond the sphere of our cognisance, so that our very natures were incapable of realising it. His cosmological theory, in one word, was pantheism of the most broad and unqualified character. Yet on the general principle we were not at all surprised that this same gentleman assured us in a moment of excitement, caused by family distress, that he had seen the ghost of a near and dear relative, who had died under circumstances which to him were of the most exquisitely painful description. His conviction of the reality of this phenomenon, seemingly so destructive of his philosophical theory, was full and strong. He exhibited, indeed, an irritability upon the subject very unusual with one whose manners were generally in the highest degree polished and tranquil. It appeared to us that he felt how inconsistent was his philosophical theory with the belief of his feelings. We mention this case particularly, because it forms a striking example of the fact which we are illustrating, especially considering the uncompromising firmness and sound worldly judgment of the man. We have, however, known many cases of a similar character; and indeed, as has been said, we have never known a single exception to the general principle, when we have had an opportunity of becoming intimately acquainted with the private history and inner feelings of the parties.

The same seems to have been the experience of Sir Walter Scott. This appears from many portions of his writings, but there is one passage which bears so directly on the particular under consideration as to afford a summary of the whole. In his novel of 'Woodstock,' in speaking of the character of a sceptic of the Puritan age, he says, "In short, with the shadowy metaphysical exception aforesaid, Mr Joshua Bletson of Darlington, member for Little Creed, came as near the predicament of an atheist as it is perhaps possible for a man to do. But we say this with the necessary salvo: for *we have known many* like Bletson, whose curtains have been shrewdly shaken by superstition, though their fears were unsanctioned by any religious faith. The devils, we are assured, believe and tremble; but on earth there are many who, in worse plight than the natural children of perdition, tremble without believing, and fear even while they blaspheme."

There is still another writer whose authority we would farther quote upon this subject, as less likely to be biassed by prejudice than even Sir Walter Scott. We allude to Lord Byron, who, in a work where his opinions seem to be put forth precisely as they arose, and with the most entire indifference to public feeling, expresses himself in these terms :—

> " Grim reader ! did you ever see a Ghost ?
> No ! But you have heard—I understand—be dumb !
> And don't regret the time you may have lost,
> For you have got that pleasure still to come ;
> And do not think I mean to sneer at most
> Of these things, or by ridicule benumb
> That source of the sublime and the mysterious ;
> For certain reasons my belief is serious.
>
> " Serious ? You laugh. You may, that will I not ;
> My smiles must be sincere, or not at all.
> I say I do believe a haunted spot
> Exists—and where ? That shall I not recall,
> Because I'd rather it should be forgot ;
> Shadows the soul of Richard may appal.
> In short, upon that subject I've some qualms very
> Like those of the philosopher of Malmesbury."
>
> 'Don Juan,' canto xv. stanzas 95, 96.
>
> " And therefore, mortals, cavil not at all—
> Believe ! If 'tis improbable, you must,
> And if it is impossible, you shall :
> 'Tis always best to take things upon trust.
> I do not speak profanely, to recall
> Those holier mysteries, which the wise and just
> Receive as gospel, and which grow more rooted,
> As all truths must, the more they are disputed.
>
> " I merely mean to say what Johnson said,
> That in the course of some six thousand years,
> All nations have believed that from the dead
> A visitant at intervals appears ;
> And what is strangest upon this strange head,
> Is, that whatever bar the reason rears
> 'Gainst such belief, there's something stronger still
> In its behalf, let those deny who will."
>
> 'Don Juan,' canto xvi. stanzas 6, 7.

These lines, though indicating, as in the case of the gentleman formerly mentioned, a contest of theory against feeling, yet exhibit a strong conviction, and clearly prove the impossibility of any one, however reckless, being able to crush a sense of that evidence for the existence of superhuman power which is merely a superstitious form of belief in a God, and which, as will afterwards appear, results from the very constitution of the mind in connection with the circumstances under which we actually exist.

There have, however, been not only individuals, but nations, as in the case of the French during their great Revolution, which in paroxysms of passionate frenzy have denied this primary faith; but they have found it impossible for any length of time to adhere to their theory, even in form. Nay, the very extravagance of the language in which it was expressed, and the violence with which these professing atheists assailed all who presumed to differ from them, gave undeniable proof of their unconscious and unwilling belief in the very doctrine which they professed to repudiate. They thus showed a painful feeling that their theory was inconsistent with their real though unconscious convictions. It is always so with those who allow themselves to assume such a position. Men persecute in proportion to the violence of their professed belief, *as contrasted with the measure of their unconscious doubt of its validity.*

Under any other assumption, atheists could have no object in persecuting, nor even in affecting to underrate or depreciate, those who differ from them. It could do them no harm that others believe in a God, nor could they have any object in making converts, were it not that the opposite opinions of others press them with a sense of their own real convictions, and of the wickedness and danger of the theory which the excitement of passion had induced them temporarily to assert. The French atheists, however, could not long endure this war of conviction against passion. In order to have something to worship, they deified a prostitute, who, after all, although they might be little aware of it, was really, like the Bacchus or Venus of the ancients, a symbol of that worthlessness and those worldly passions with which men, unacquainted with the true God, have in all ages clothed the superhuman power or powers in which nature compels them to believe. But the symbol adopted by the French, or rather, perhaps we should say, by the offscourings of a Parisian mob, was too monstrous to be allowed for more than a moment to occupy its place. The Parisian Goddess of Reason became an object of universal mockery. Such a manifestation of the idiotic atrocities into which selfish and sensual passions will hurry men, aided materially in strengthening that revulsion of feeling which had already begun. Accordingly, when Robespierre induced them, a few weeks afterwards, formally and nationally once more to recognise the God of nature, his decree seems to have been received willingly or rather joyfully by the great mass of the people, as the first step for bringing them back to a faith which they felt to be irresistible, inasmuch as all their efforts, even during times of the wildest excitement, had not been able to extinguish it.

There never could have been a better opportunity for testing such a theory, and yet it utterly failed. As if from a sort of reaction, the French from that time became infinitely more religious than they had been before the Revolution began. Thus every consideration combines in proving that a belief in superhuman spirits exists under some form in every individual of our race, and that it *cannot be eradicated*. Nor could it be otherwise with respect to creatures such as we are, and placed in such circumstances. For we are conscious of a dependence on the assistance of others, which the qualities appertaining to our fellow-creatures do not enable them to afford, and we are conscious of a continual desire for security and happiness which the powers of our fellow-creatures do not enable them to gratify. On the other hand, we perceive an adjustment and order in the works of nature for which no material energy can account, and a regularity in the ways of Providence which nothing save the assumption of a superhuman intelligent agency can explain.

Hence originated that widespread belief which once existed, and which to some extent exists even now, in a plurality of gods. Men beheld an organisation and an energy displayed everywhere around them, which mere matter could never of itself have generated, because we know enough of the nature of mere physical matter to be assured that it is incapable of any spontaneous energy. To each of these phenomena of activity, therefore, it was naturally enough supposed that a special spiritual power was attached, which originated its action, regulated its operations, and determined its practical relations with all beings and objects which came within the sphere of its influence. To each of these powers, again, a certain respect, worship, or reverence was paid by individuals to the extent to which each seemed capable of affecting their interests. We say respect, reverence, or worship, because these, as offered to inferior beings, are all mere degrees of the same thing. Worship only differs in kind from the others when offered to the Supreme Power, from whose decisions there is no appeal, and who acts in every instance throughout the universe according to His own good pleasure.

Such was the origin of polytheism, which, however wide a range of subordinate deities it embraced, seems invariably to have recognised over them all a supreme power under the name of Fate, or some similar term, more or less intelligent, although in many cases, it is true, such power was only recognised in the most shadowy form, rather as a feeling than anything else. It was only as intelligence progressed, that thinking men began to discover polytheism to be altogether destitute of evidence under even the purest form in which it could exist, and that in any form in which it actually did exist it was distinctly contrary to evidence.

For though the existence of separate powers which preside over each law of nature or each phenomenon of the universe be without proof, it certainly is a possible theory, on the assumption that such powers derive their authority from the Supreme Spirit. But that polytheism, under *any* of the forms in which it has been actually found, is contrary to evidence, appears from its being invariably in some respect inconsistent with the attributes of the Supreme Being. There are in all instances mixed up with it forms of anthropomorphism. The heathen deities, instead of being morally identical with the attributes which reason and providence teach us to ascribe to the Supreme Being, are found to be imbued with the grossest forms of human passions, originating in an abuse of that constitution which nature manifestly intended to be the guide and governor of our race. Had such beings really presided over the phenomena of nature, the result in a very short time must have been universal disorganisation and confusion.

It seems to have been in the development of this argument that the relationship betwixt the science of religion, and those of morals and politics, as branches of the same subject, became by degrees more and more appreciated. Experience showed what is in so far evident from the very nature of the case, that the moral nature of intelligent beings must necessarily identify itself with the moral attributes of the deity which they respectively worship. From this appeared the pernicious consequence of men worshipping immoral gods. Hence, as we are compelled from the very constitution of our minds to believe in some form of deity, philosophers were led more carefully to inquire into the real character of the divine attributes. This was done by all the Greek philosophers, and especially by Plato, which accounts for the decided superiority of his religious and moral views. Thus it was that natural religion grew into a science, though still in certain respects complicated and imperfect. Theoretically, in so far it rested on logical proof which was absolutely unassailable. In its practical working, however, there were difficulties and anomalies found connected with it, which it seemed impossible to obviate or reconcile. Specially the moral attributes of the Supreme Being, as generally discoverable from the feelings and sympathies of the human mind, as well as from the arrangements of providence, seemed inconsistent in certain particulars with the artificial conditions and circumstances of human society. For the moral laws of God, as logically deducible from the relations of intelligent beings, were violated systematically through the influence that selfishness had acquired over every other tendency of the human mind. As a consequence, much sorrow and suffering had resulted, and were resulting, while there seemed no means provided under which the balance of our moral constitution could be restored.

The great primary relation of man, on which all the others depend, had indeed practically ceased to operate, for man had become alienated from his God, and put no trust in Him; nor did there appear to be any instrumentality by which the creature and the Creator might be brought again into mutual communication, and restored to mutual confidence. This is manifest from the consideration that, while we would be perfectly relieved from fear, did our deliverance from any danger depend on a relative or friend in whom we reposed confidence, we feel no such relief under ordinary circumstances from that trust which we profess to repose in the Supreme Being. We can trust more truly in a comparative stranger among our fellow-creatures than in Him whom we pretend to regard as the holy and benevolent God. The conclusion does not admit of dispute. The relation connecting us with our fellow-creatures still continues more or less in operation; but that connecting us with our God seems to have lost its power. Now, if there be such a relation—or, in other words, if there be a God—this must obviously be a most unnatural and anomalous state of things, striking at the very foundations on which high and permanent happiness can alone be rested. A sense of this alienation from God necessarily tended in a great measure to obliterate the impressions which feeling and reason generate in favour of the immortality of the soul. Immortality does not even seem desirable to him who has no trust in the only Being that can bestow happiness here, or assure it hereafter. While, therefore, the evidences of natural religion were felt to be in so far irresistible in theory, the effect of them was counteracted by the doubts and uncertainties which complicate its practical working.

Hence arose a conviction, which has been found universally to prevail, that the Deity would probably intervene by some direct proof, under which such doubts and uncertainties would be removed. Men felt a want which there was apparently no provision in nature to supply. They had no assurance of what might happen to them even the next moment, and still less of what should happen to them through eternity. This, in its fulness, trust in God alone could afford; and nature gave them no such trust. As we have seen, the relation betwixt the creature and the Creator had ceased to operate.

Thus human beings were necessarily led to expect some reunion with God through a revelation; and the eagerness and intensity of the desire, as in all such cases, striving after its own gratification, generated from the beginning that mass of assumed revelations resting on traditions which overspread every portion of the world.* Where people had not a true revelation, in other words, they gradually invented a false one. The identity of principle which in so far characterised all these varied forms, whether of supposed or of real revelations, amidst their innumerable diversities, flowed from the common belief in natural religion, which, to a greater or less extent, must be realised by every human being. Natural religion must be the foundation of every form of revelation, for natural religion is the primary revelation which the Supreme Being has made known to His creatures in the very constitution of their minds. With this it is manifest that no subsequent and

* That the expectation of a revelation may have been primarily derived from tradition is perfectly possible, but this of itself would not account for the universal belief in a revelation extending over all ages and countries. A felt necessity for some further information with respect to the relation betwixt God and man pressing itself even on the most uncultivated minds, can alone explain this extraordinary phenomenon.

supplementary revelation could be inconsistent; and hence, had men retained the primary constitution of their minds in its purity, they would have possessed an infallible test of the authenticity of any revelation. But be the cause what it may, men have become alienated from God, and thus their primary and intuitive feelings as to His nature have been modified. In this way their notions of the divine attributes necessarily took an anthropomorphic tendency. They confused the nature of God with the nature of man, and from this consideration we have an insight into the source of the main errors of false revelations. The false gods of each nation are distinguished by the peculiar tendencies which specially discriminate their respective worshippers. While, therefore, revelations to this extent differ—for we say nothing of their mere historical theology, as of no importance whatever to our personal subject—they must yet all assume such primary truths of natural religion as *the elementary reason is capable of deducing.*

A true revelation, therefore, may correct errors, and may add to the amount of knowledge which natural religion affords, but no true revelation can be inconsistent with natural religion. The doctrines of a true revelation cannot even imply anything away from the precise end which the Supreme Being seeks to realise in natural religion, since there can be no change in the purposes of the immutable God. In this way, natural religion must, up to a certain point, be THE INTERPRETER OF EVERY TRUE REVELATION. The principles of true revelation must be explained by it, and the sense of the terms employed in revelation must in so far be defined and limited by it. There could otherwise, indeed, be no definite meaning attached to them at all.

Having thus ascertained, in the first instance, what we have to do, and to a certain extent the mode in which our object is to be accomplished, we are directly brought to an investigation of the evidence for the existence and attributes of a God.

CHAPTER I.

ARGUMENT FROM OUR SENSE OF WEAKNESS AND DEPENDENCE; OR, A PRIORI ARGUMENT FOR THE EXISTENCE AND ATTRIBUTES OF A GOD.

EXPLANATION OF THE NATURE OF THE ARGUMENT A PRIORI, AS CONTRADISTINGUISHED FROM THE ARGUMENT A POSTERIORI—DOUBTS CONNECTED WITH A PRIORI ARGUMENTS AS HITHERTO ADDUCED—PROOF THAT THERE MUST BE AN A PRIORI ARGUMENT OF SOME KIND, SUFFICIENT TO CONVINCE EVERY ONE OF THE EXISTENCE OF A SUPREME POWER, OMNIPOTENT, OMNISCIENT, TRUE, JUST, BENEVOLENT, AND ETERNAL—RELATION OF THIS A PRIORI WITH THE A POSTERIORI PROOF—ITS CHARACTER AND LIMITS INDICATED.

AN argument *a priori* means an argument prior to experience, and arising from the constitution of the mind; as an argument *a posteriori* means an argument derived from experience, and concluding from effects to causes. The argument *a priori*, therefore, assumes that there are feelings born with us, which constitute a direct relationship betwixt us and a Supreme Being, and would compel us to believe that there is a Supreme Being, even were there no proof that could be discovered from the arrangements of Providence. There have been many such arguments proposed, most of them founding on what have been called innate ideas, or assumptions which are supposed to be intuitively known. Not a few of them have exhibited great ingenuity, and from their plausibility have commanded considerable attention for a time. But there is not one of them, notwithstanding their demonstrative form, which would appear to have produced permanent conviction. Hence we never find any one appealing to them as sufficient *in themselves*, which of course would have been the case had they been really demonstrative, but merely as a sort of supplementary proof, depending for its validity more or less on the conclusions of the argument from experience.

Indeed, in more recent times these arguments *a priori* seem to be repudiated almost altogether. Nor is this wonderful, when we consider that innate ideas are by philosophers of the present age more and more decisively ignored. Accordingly, even Clarke's argument, which is by far the most ingenious of them all, is now rarely alluded to. This is not merely because it is too metaphysical, but because its very primary assumption, that Eternity and Infinity are modes of the existence of a being, is an assumption to which no accurate thinker nowadays would be prepared to give an unqualified assent. That intelligent beings are inclined to repudiate the notion of time and space existing without any being existing during the one or in the other, is probably true. That such a proposition, however, would involve an absolute contradiction, or indeed that any proposition would imply a contradiction, where the subject is expressed in words that involve considerations beyond the range of human apprehension, will not, we presume, be maintained.

No argument, therefore, can be valid which founds on innate ideas, or which embraces considerations so entirely beyond the range of human apprehension that we cannot positively be assured whether they be true or false. Yet we have no hesitation in saying that there is an argument *a priori* for the existence and attributes of a God, which is involved in the very nature of our feelings, and which therefore tells upon the faith of the whole human race, even when they are altogether ignorant of it logically, as existing in the form of a proposition. It makes no appeal, however, to profound metaphysical speculations, and is consequently plain and intelligible to any one capable of exercising reason at all. It rests on the principle which both our feelings and our experience demonstrate to be true, that every primary and essential desire of the human mind has a co-relative—or, in other words, a something to gratify it—existing in the nature of things. The mode in which the development of this principle constitutes an argument *a priori* for the existence and attributes of a God we now proceed to explain; and it would be difficult, we think, to conceive an argument more simple or more unanswerable.

Every human being feels from the moment in which he comes into existence, and through his whole subsequent history, that he is in himself a weak, helpless creature. As we have said, this feeling begins from the very beginning of our conscious existence. The appeals of the infant for aid are made continually. We do not indeed assert that the infant, in these more or less instinctive appeals, knows its own weakness and helplessness *as a proposition*. This is quite a different question, with which at present we have nothing to do. No one, however, will dispute that it *feels* its own helplessness, nor will it be disputed that the appeals which it makes, if not conscious appeals, are, at all events, instinctive signs which nature has provided, in order that through them its feeling may be made known to those on whom, in the first instance, nature has made it dependent.

Accordingly, persons actually exist recognising this claim, and on whom nature has farther bestowed the means and the inclination effectually to respond to it. As we advance to childhood, youth, and manhood, our sense of power gradually increases. We are conscious that under certain circumstances we can do something for ourselves.

Yet this capability, we are also conscious in its very exercise, does not depend on us for its continuance. We cannot preserve to ourselves fortune, health, or even life, for *a single moment*. Yet all these things we desire,* and desire with the utmost earnestness, and desire as a primary tendency of our minds. We may not indeed always clothe such desire in words; we may not put it into the form of a proposition; but that it exists in every mind as a feeling, and practically operates upon every individual, is as certain as our existence itself, and is indeed manifest every moment in the efforts which we make to preserve these and all other forms of what we believe to involve happiness.

In this desire, consequently, we have the voice of nature speaking, and commanding us to use

* It is hardly necessary to say that when we speak of desires in this chapter, we mean primary desires implanted in us by the very constitution of our natures, or necessarily flowing from the constitution of our natures in the circumstances under which we are. The word, therefore, as thus employed, has no reference to mere wishes, accidentally or capriciously formed under artificial causes. I may wish or desire, in a certain sense, to see a golden mountain. Nature is under no obligation to provide a co-relative for this. Our argument simply implies, that if nature has implanted in us certain desires by the very constitution of our minds, then nature must have provided the suitable gratifications for such desires, or else she is deceiving us. Unless this be the case, we must, by the very constitution of our minds, be making continual efforts for procuring objects *which it is impossible that we can ever realise, because, by the supposition, they have no existence.*

such efforts. Of ourselves we know that they would be insufficient. The results depend upon causes over which we have no control. Our own efforts, we are conscious, are only means which nature has appointed us to employ, but their success depends on circumstances altogether beyond our power. It is, as has been said, the voice of nature telling us that each of our desires has a co-relative, through which it may be *fully* gratified by the use of the proper means. This co-relative, in the case of intense and permanent happiness, it is self-evident, can only be found in the existence of a God, omnipotent, omniscient, true, just, benevolent, and eternal, *in whom we repose entire confidence.* No other assumption could by possibility satisfy our desire for the highest and permanent happiness now and for ever. For to realise thoroughly the argument, it is to be observed that our desire is for the highest and permanent happiness. It is not imperfect or temporary happiness merely which we desire, though we may be compelled to be content with this, if we cannot procure more. It is the highest happiness possible for our natures, and that without end.

Now, if such happiness is to be attained at all, it can only be obtained through a God possessed of the attributes which we have enumerated. The moment we put full trust in that God, the object is accomplished. We can no longer fear that any evil will overtake us, since no conceivable power could injure those who are under the protection of an omnipotent and omniscient God. The desire can have no other co-relative. Unless He were omnipotent, we could not be sure of His ability to bless us. Unless He were omniscient, He might be ignorant of our precise circumstances, or of the means by which our happiness was to be secured. Unless He were true, we could have no confidence in His promises. Unless He were just, we might doubt as to the impartial execution of His laws. Unless He were benevolent, we should fear lest His rigour might neutralise His mercy. Unless He were eternal, our happiness must come to an end. Unless we trusted in Him, His attributes, whatever they might be, could be of no importance to us, because we could have no assurance that they applied to us.

All this, it is manifest, does not merely imply a high probability. It is absolute certainty. The only possible reply to the argument must consist in a denial of the principles on which it rests. It must either be affirmed that men do not desire the highest and permanent happiness, which we all feel to be absurd, or that a primary desire does not involve the assurance of a co-relative, which amounts simply to an assertion that our natures deceive us. This is certain, because if it be conceded that all men desire intense and permanent happiness, and that in every primary desire there is implied an assurance of nature that a suitable co-relative to it exists, all doubt upon the subject is at an end. If we are to believe nature, the conclusion is as certain as any demonstration of mathematics. There is a power omnipotent, omniscient, true, just, benevolent, and eternal, co-relative to the human desire for intense and permanent happiness, whence, therefore, such intense and permanent happiness is to be procured, if we choose to comply with the means *which have been provided for the purpose.* We must use such means, of course, just as we must use the suitable means which nature has provided for the purpose ere we can procure the adequate gratification of any other desire. It is indeed obvious that the exercise of inquiry and diligence in procuring the gratification of our desires, is the very object on account of which we have been placed in this world. So much is this the case, that through our whole lives *we never are and never can be engaged about anything else.* But if we do use the means which are provided, the gratification of our desires is procurable, or else our natures have deceived us; and nature, in that case, is only another name for a deception and a lie.

It may indeed be replied, that this argument would prove the lower animals to be also entitled to look forward to intense and permanent happiness. But the assumption is founded on a misconception. We know, indeed, that the lower animals desire *present* happiness, but we know nothing whatever about their *ulterior* expectations. This, however, is certain, that if the lower animals do desire intense and permanent happiness as involved in their primary feelings, then either means are provided for its gratification, or their natures are false and deceptive, and nature has created them so for the very purpose of deluding and deceiving them. There is no possibility of getting over the argument. It is simple and demonstrative; and if it be untrue, no rational conclusion can be depended upon.

Brief, clear, and demonstrative, however, as this argument seems to be, it is to be observed that the conclusion which it enables us to attain is exceedingly general, as indeed must be the case with respect to every demonstrative argument. It simply proves that, if nature speak the truth, there is a power existing and operating possessed of certain attributes co-relative to the universal desire of intense and permanent happiness in man. We can thus perfectly understand the origin of that universal belief in a supreme power which we have found to pervade all nations and tribes and individuals. It originates in a universal feeling, and therefore cannot be absolutely bid away. But as it is the *feeling* in which it originates, and not the *argument* derived therefrom, which is universally appreciated, and forms the universal ground of belief, so it is manifest that the mere feeling can never give us a precise and definite conclusion; and hence we may fall into such errors in detail as almost to neutralise its practical importance. Yet even the argumentative conclusion, as we have said, is very general; and although, no doubt, if thoroughly understood, it would obviate gross errors in regard to the Deity, yet even in that case our notions of His attributes would be wanting in the perfect clearness and fulness which are so desirable with respect to a subject of such infinite importance.

In order thoroughly to determine the nature and attributes of that power in which our sense of entire dependence compels us thus generally to believe, and to ascertain the modes of its operation, we must appeal to experience, so as thereby to discover the exact character of its dealings with the human race. This is called the argument *a posteriori*, with which it will be found that the argument *a priori*, as has been indicated, interweaves, and by which, indeed, it will be found that it is perfected.

CHAPTER II.

ARGUMENT FROM THE ARRANGEMENTS AND ORGANISATION OF THE UNIVERSE; OR, A POSTERIORI ARGUMENT FOR THE BEING AND NATURAL ATTRIBUTES OF A GOD.

OUR PROOF FOR THE EXERCISE OF INTELLIGENT AGENCY IN CONTRIVING AND CONSTRUCTING THE UNIVERSE, IS PRECISELY THE SAME AS OUR PROOF FOR THE INTELLIGENT AGENCY OF OUR FELLOW-CREATURES IN CONTRIVING AND CONSTRUCTING ARTIFICIAL ARRANGEMENTS—IT CONSISTS IN OUR ASSURANCE FROM THE KNOWLEDGE WHICH WE HAVE OF THE NATURE OF OUR OWN REASON, THAT INTELLIGENCE ALONE, OR SOME EQUIVALENT ATTRIBUTE, IS COMPETENT TO CONTRIVE AND CONSTRUCT ADJUSTED ARRANGEMENTS—THE POSSIBLE ETERNITY OF THE PHENOMENA OF NATURE DOES NOT AFFECT THE QUESTION AT ISSUE—A POSSIBLE POWER OF DEVELOPMENT IN THE PRODUCTS OF NATURE DOES NOT AFFECT THE QUESTION AT ISSUE—THIS STILL FURTHER REALISED IN THE NECESSITY OF SUPPOSING THAT THE ELEMENTS OF THINGS MUST HAVE BEEN ENDOWED WITH THE PRECISE PROPERTIES COMPETENT TO WORK OUT THE PHENOMENA—ACCORDING TO THE DEVELOPMENT THEORY, THESE PROPERTIES MUST HAVE BEEN INFINITELY NUMEROUS, IF NOT CONTRADICTORY, IN EACH MOLECULE—THESE CONSIDERATIONS OBVIATE EVERY FORM OF DIFFICULTY WHICH CAN POSSIBLY ARISE FROM THE ASSUMPTION OF THAT THEORY, OR OF ANY OTHER THEORY—EXTENT AND APPLICATION OF THE PROOF TO THE POWER, WISDOM, AND IMMUTABILITY OF GOD—SUMMARY OF THE ARGUMENT.

WE have now seen that a demonstrative proof of the existence of a Supreme Power, omnipotent, omniscient, true, just, benevolent, and eternal, arises from the constitution of the human mind. We desire intense and permanent happiness, and we are perpetually struggling, from the beginning to the end of our lives, to realise it in the highest measure which our faculties enable us to attain. *Not for one single instant are we employed about anything else.* If, therefore, in this ceaseless desire we have the voice of nature speaking and commanding us thus to struggle in seeking such happiness, as lying within our reach, if our pursuit be conducted in a suitable spirit, and according to the proper manner—and it seems impossible that this can be denied—the conclusion is demonstrably certain. There must be a God with the attributes enumerated, on whom we can depend as a friend and a father. Under any other assumption the object cannot be attained, and therefore our natures must be a delusion and a lie.

We can, however, arrive at the same conclusion under another equally demonstrative argument. The proof, indeed, *is identically the same as that under which we believe our fellow-creatures to be intelligent beings.* The real foundation of the argument from design has, we cannot help thinking, been misunderstood by theologians.

Some of them have been content with assuming that, as matter of fact, organisation does imply design, and therefore have done nothing but accumulate instances of organised existences in the universe. They have thus succeeded in proving what no one disputes, but have really settled nothing; since the question is not whether there are organised existences in the universe, but whether these organised existences prove the being of a God.*

Others of them have merely replied to the objections of sceptics. They have proved that the explanations which sceptics have offered with reference to the origin of organised existences in the universe are unsatisfactory, but they have substituted nothing in their place. In this way matters have remained much as they were; all systems of atheism have been disproved, but we

* There is a form of the argument for the existence of a God, however, which requires little more than an analysis of existing phenomena, and which, though by no means neglected, yet does not appear to have been dwelt on to the extent that might have been expected by those who did not appreciate the precise nature of the principle which connects adjusted arrangements with the intelligence of a creating God. We refer to the phenomena of instinct. The knowledge implied in instinct is not, and cannot be, a deduction of reason, since *it needs no experience.* Unless, therefore, we suppose that instinct implies a peculiar species of intelligence, giving some of the lower animals a sort of prophetical knowledge *in connection with innate ideas*, we must hold those phenomena which are the result of instinct to be generated under the direct action of a higher power, or, in other words, to be in a certain sense *new creative arrangements*, in which the animals themselves are merely the physical instruments. There seems no other theory conceivable. The notion that mere physical desires and properties could of themselves explain the phenomena of instinct, seems to be given up as altogether untenable.

F

are still left to labour under the painful feeling that some other system may be proposed which cannot be disproved.

A third class of theologians, however, for the praiseworthy purpose of supplying this deficiency, have argued that our belief in all organised existences, being referable to intelligent causes, arises from the experience which we have of their origin in the doings of our fellow-creatures. So far as our experience extends, they say, all organised existences have been contrived by our fellow-creatures, whom we know to be intelligent. Hence they conclude—under the principle universally conceded, that identical effects can only be produced by identical causes—as a necessary consequence, that all organised existences have been contrived by intelligence.

The argument, however, is false in its premises. We have no means of knowing that our fellow-creatures are intelligent, *except by inferring it from our observation of those very organised existences which we know them to have constructed.* We cannot discover the spiritual nature of our fellow-creatures *a priori*, as these parties seem to suppose. We cannot see it, nor hear it, nor smell it, nor taste it, nor touch it. We cannot, in other words, in any form perceive it. Nor can we be conscious of it. We can only discover it by inference.

Accordingly, it is in this way alone that we are

assured of our fellow-creatures being intelligent agents. As has been said, we know no more of their spiritual natures *a priori*, by any act of perception or consciousness, than we do of the attributes of the supreme spiritual power that exists in and around us. We perceive, however, certain acts which our fellow-creatures do, identical with certain acts of our own, *which we know that the intelligent portion of our natures could alone have enabled us to contrive or to execute*. We entertain no doubt upon the subject, and can entertain none, because we know from the constitution of our minds the relation betwixt design and intelligence, and are therefore not only assured from experience, but *intuitively feel that the effect could be the result of intelligence, or some similar quality only*.

The grounds of this conclusion are manifest, and are precisely the same as those under which we infer the existence of a spiritual agency superior to man. There is not the slightest conceivable difference. We perceive certain phenomena, identical with certain others resulting from our own intelligence, and which we know that our intelligence alone could have enabled us either to contrive or to execute. We therefore conclude, not merely as a matter of experience, but from our *rational knowledge of the nature of intelligence*, that such phenomena could only have been contrived and executed under the agency of an intelligent being. There is not a single particular in the one case which is not identical with a corresponding particular in the other.*

It is indeed true that our fellow-creatures may tell us by words or signs that they exist, and that they possess the same tendencies, feelings, and faculties as ourselves. But words and signs are themselves only effects, and certainly not more convincing effects than actions, which are the most satisfactory of all signs. We should not be less convinced of the intelligence of a fellow-creature who contrived and executed an adjusted machine, because he did not tell us in words that he had contrived it and executed it under the guidance of his intelligent nature. On the contrary, so convinced are we of the instrumentality under which he had attained his purpose, through the knowledge which we possess intuitively of the relation betwixt adjustment and intelligence, that we should never think of putting a question to him on the subject.

It has been said, however, and said by one of an extremely acute metaphysical mind, that we see our fellow-creatures contriving and executing adjusted machinery, but men never saw any spirit of a superior order contriving or making a world, or any of the parts or products of a world.†

* Appendix A.
† 'Dialogues concerning Natural Religion,' by David Hume.

The argument has been received with unbounded applause, and rested upon as an invincible objection to the proof *a posteriori* for the existence of a God. It will now, we trust, be obvious that it does not imply even the shadow of an objection to that argument, but, on the contrary, originates in utter ignorance of the principle under which we conclude that organised existences must have been contrived by intelligent agency. It assumes that we have some *a priori knowledge, some personal consciousness of the intelligence of our fellow-creatures*, and that it is by our experience of their power of contriving and executing adjustments in some cases, that we conclude intelligent beings to be alone capable of contriving and executing adjustments in any case.

This, however, it will now be manifest, is a perfect delusion. We know nothing about the intelligence of our fellow-creatures *a priori*, nor have we any personal consciousness of it. As we have seen, we discover the intelligence of our fellow-creatures solely from its effects. It is our personal consciousness of *our own intelligence, and our rational knowledge of its nature*, which enable us to infer the intelligence of our fellow-creatures; and this knowledge, involved in our very feeling of intelligence, applies as minutely and as stringently to phenomena of a similar kind beyond the competency of our fellow-creatures, as to those within their competency. Of course, the measure of the wisdom and power of the agent must in each case be determined by the relative magnitude and complication of the phenomena. Hence our belief in the operation of intelligent agency, wherever we discover adjusted arrangement, is equally full and valid, whether we do or do not perceive the phenomena in the actual process of construction, because the intelligence contriving the mechanism, and guiding physical power in practically executing its adjustments, is *as much concealed from us in the one case as in the other*. In either we infer its existence from the effects, as proving the existence of an intelligent being from results which we know by our own feelings that intelligence alone could have produced.*

In the same way, when we perceive the complex machinery of the world, each part constituting in itself a whole, and these uniting together to constitute a farther series of wholes, which again are summed up in a perfect universe, complete and regular in all its parts, and adapted minutely to the working out of manifest, harmo-

---

* Accordingly, when we see a machine, of which the parts are so adjusted as all to work together for the production of a definite end, we conclude that it is the work of an intelligent agent, not because we have previously witnessed intelligent agents making such machinery, but because, from our knowledge of the nature of intelligence as felt by ourselves, we are certain that *nothing but intelligence* could have contrived, or enabled its contriver to execute it.

nious, and important purposes, we conclude, *on the very same grounds as those on which we ascribe intelligence to our fellow-creatures*, that spiritual agency must have been there. In this argument we do not consider it in the least necessary to investigate the arrangements of the world with a view of proving that it implies and comprehends organised adjustments. It is infinitely less necessary than to investigate the arrangements of a watch or a steam-engine in order to prove that they imply and comprehend organised adjustments. Such an investigation is a mere waste of time. Indeed, we are convinced that the many minute investigations of this kind which have been made, as in the 'Bridgewater Treatises,' apart from any satisfactory determination of the principle connecting in our minds adjustment with intelligence, have led to misapprehension, by suggesting some doubts as to the reality of a fact which required so much scientific knowledge to prove and to appreciate. Attention has been in this way distracted from the only particular which needs an argument to another, which no sane man can regard as admitting of a question. We doubt if the man who has made himself intimately acquainted, for example, with the anatomy of the human hand, has any higher idea of its mechanical organisation than he who only knows such organisation in its practical working. It is at all events very singular that there seems to be at least as large a number of sceptics and pantheists among medical men as among the professors of any other science. If there were truth in the notion that a mere knowledge of the details of organised adjustments in the universe constituted a stronger proof *in itself* of intellectual agency in their contrivance and execution, this could not be the case. The same remark holds true of all naturalists. The reason is obviously to be found in their attention to the mere physical mechanisms drawing away their thoughts from the spiritual agencies in which they must originate, and generally, indeed, from spiritual considerations of every kind.

He who denies that the world is full of organised adjustments, or that it is itself an organised and adjusted machine, with its parts respectively corresponding to each other, and all arranged so as to operate in harmonious combination, is quite incapable of being convinced by argument. We never indeed heard of any one who ventured to take up such a position. It would be too manifestly absurd even for the most extravagant of sceptics to assume. On the contrary, instead of denying the organisation of the universe, sceptics *assume* the universe to be a most perfectly organised system, and *all their efforts are directed through science to explain the organised relations of its parts to one another.*

We repeat, therefore, that when we perceive the

universe in all its parts and as a whole so beautifully adjusted, we conclude in the very same way, and on the very same grounds which force us to ascribe intelligence to our fellow-creatures, that spiritual agency must have been there. On a superficial consideration, indeed, it would appear that there must have been many spiritual agencies at work. Just as in seeing an immense assemblage of various mechanisms before noticing their mutual bearings as parts of a complete whole, we naturally suppose that each must have been the contrivance of a different individual, so in seeing the vast multitudes of mechanisms in the universe, we at first assume that each is the effect of a separate cause. But when we come to discover that all these mechanisms interweave with one another, having a common object, to which they are all so essential that were any one away the whole would be imperfect, the conclusion is forced upon us that all must have been the contrivance of a single mind. It is here that science becomes specially useful in theology, by proving the unity of God through the universality of the relations which it is gradually discovering among all the various parts of the universe.

It by no means follows from this, however, that the great Contriver may not have employed distinct and multifarious agencies in the execution of His work. This is perfectly possible, but we have no proof upon the subject one way or the other. We have only the phenomena from which to judge, and, as in all other cases, we are not entitled to assume more causes than are sufficient to explain the phenomena. Such is the real process under which, by the *a posteriori* argument, we determine the power, the wisdom, and the unity of God; and if we argue from the phenomena of nature as we argue from artificial phenomena, the conclusion is inevitable. It is, again, as demonstratively proved as any proposition of mathematics.

It is said, however, that we are not entitled to argue in the same way from natural phenomena as we argue from artificial phenomena. There is, at any rate, this distinction, we are told, betwixt natural and artificial phenomena, "that the former *may be* eternal, while we know that the latter had a beginning; and that if the universe be eternal, it may have a power in itself of spontaneously generating all kinds of products; higher forms gradually developing themselves from lower forms; while anomalous and monstrous forms necessarily perish from their want of inherent power to preserve life in opposition to the counteracting influences assailing it."[*]

It will be admitted that the argument is fairly stated, and we have pleasure in stating it in the clearest form, because it is the last, and, we believe, the dying argument of pantheism. It is panthe-

[*] Appendix B.

ism pushed to its legitimate result, and although beyond all doubt extensively recognised during the present age in a variety of more or less confused and indefinite forms, yet we are convinced that it will not bear the slightest examination when thus precisely stated, under the principles which, in the previous part of this chapter, we have endeavoured to establish.

For, in the first place, the assumption that the world is eternal is altogether away from the question at issue. There is an infinity of artificial mechanisms which we have never seen in the act of being constructed, and which, therefore, may be eternal in so far as we have any direct knowledge of the matter. Even if we have seen similar mechanisms constructed by our fellow-creatures, it proves nothing, because we discover that our fellow-creatures are intelligent *from the very fact of their being capable of contriving and executing these mechanisms.* We could not have known that they were intelligent by any other means. To say that we have experience of intelligent creatures contriving organised adjustments, is absurd. *It is the organised adjustments, on the contrary, which they contrive, that prove those that contrived and constructed them to be intelligent creatures.* The proof arises from our identification of the effects which they produce with the effects which our own intelligent natures produce, and in connection with this, from a feeling made known to us through the operation of reason, that nothing but intelligence could have produced them. It is under this argument alone that we can know our fellow-creatures to be intelligent.

Hence our conviction of the adjusted world being the work of an intelligent Agent does not in the least depend on our experience of artificial adjusted arrangements having been contrived and executed by our fellow-creatures. On the contrary, except from our knowledge of the rational faculty, or of intelligence *as felt in and thus known to ourselves*, we should not have known these arrangements to be the work of intelligent creatures at all. As we could have had no *a priori* means of knowing how they were constructed, none of them could have been ascribed to any definite origin. In other words, we could not have told whether they had been made in time or lasted through eternity, any more than we can tell whether the world was made in time or lasted through eternity. The only evidence we have is identically the same in both cases. The knowledge which we have of our own intelligent natures assures us that both artificial and natural arrangements were contrived and constructed by intelligent beings, or under their direction, these beings having powers proportioned in each case to the magnitude and complication of the phenomena. Our belief that the artificial mechanisms around us, so far as we have not seen them constructed, have been constructed in time, is the effect of habit, or is assumed as a probability. *We have nothing to call proof* upon the subject. All our proof ends with the assurance of our intelligent natures, that they must have been contrived and constructed under the guidance of natures like their own.

This brings us back to the point from which we started, by showing how entirely the objection is away from the question at issue. That question does not regard *the time* when the world was created, but the agency through which it exists. The question is, Was the agency through which the universe exists intelligent or non-intelligent? It is no reply to this question to say that the universe may not be the work of an intelligent agent because it may be eternal, any more than it would be a reply to an inquiry as to the agency in contriving a house, to say that it may not have been contrived by an intelligent agent because it has lasted a hundred years. The eternity of the world, even supposing it to have been eternal, only relates to the length of its duration, and has nothing to do with the cause or causes under which its parts have been adjusted and combined. If it has existed throughout eternity, therefore, its intelligent cause must have existed through eternity also, assuming that intelligence is essential to the contrivance and construction of it; the intelligent agency and the phenomena must thus have existed as cause and effect throughout eternity.* It signifies nothing, so far as this conclusion is concerned, whether the universe came into existence by a fiat of a Creator's power, or continued throughout eternity under the eternal operation of such a power, or, having originally existed—created or eternal—as an apparently confused mass, gradually developed itself by a sort of self-expansive power communicated to it, whether in time or from eternity, into that exquisite and complicated structure which is now an object of admiration to intelligent beings. In this last case, a still larger amount both of wisdom and power would seem to be indicated in the primary conception and construction of such a wondrous mechanism. In all other respects the conclusion must be identically the same.

Nor does it make any difference to say that "the world *may* have the power in itself of spontaneously generating all kinds of products." The question again recurs, Whence did it procure the

* We are so accustomed to find the cause preceding the effect, that at first sight the idea of cause and effect being contemporaneous seems inadmissible. But the difficulty arises from our considering causes and effects as always existing in time. It is, however, evident that so long as the cause operates the effect exists. If, therefore, a cause has operated throughout eternity, *its effect must have been produced throughout eternity;* and there is no more difficulty in conceiving a cause to operate than a cause to exist throughout eternity. Wherever the word eternity is introduced into any proposition, there must always indeed be an idea involved in it beyond our grasp, but the argument, it will now be seen, *in so far as our object is concerned*, is perfectly demonstrative.

power of generating organised mechanisms? If nature tells us in the very knowledge of intelligence which our conscious feeling of the rational faculty involves, that this could only have been through the agency of intelligence, and intelligence proportionate to the magnificence of the result, as we have seen to be the case, then of course there can be no farther difference of opinion on the subject. The conclusion is settled and certain. To say that " the world may in itself have the power of spontaneously generating adjusted arrangements and organisations " in any other sense, is simply to say in other words that adjusted and organised machinery may be generated *without intelligence.* It just comes to this, therefore, that we either do not attribute the contrivance and construction of adjusted and complicated machinery to intelligence by the essential constitution of our nature, or else that the teaching of nature is not entitled to belief. Now the former of these propositions is opposed to every man's experience and conscious feelings. This is proved by the indisputable fact, that unless we attribute the contrivance and construction of adjusted and organised machinery to intelligence *by the very constitution of our rational natures*, we could never attribute it to intelligence by any process of the human mind, nor could we indeed form any conception of the principle in which such contrivance and organised construction originate.

The notion that we know something of the nature of the intelligence of our fellow-creatures *a priori*, we have seen to be false and absurd. We are neither conscious of it, nor can we perceive it by any of our senses. We know as little about the spiritual nature of our fellow-creatures *absolutely*, as we do about the spiritual nature of our God. We know both solely from our knowledge of our own spiritual natures, by recognising phenomena in certain of their doings, which we are assured spiritual feelings and faculties similar to our own, and specially the faculty of intelligence, *alone could have produced*. When, therefore, we understand distinctly the grounds under which we attribute intelligence to our fellow-creatures, we also understand the grounds under which we attribute intelligence to that power which contrived and constructed the world and all that it contains.

The argument is so plain as hardly to admit either of doubt or of misapprehension. There is no other possible mode of accounting for our universal belief that adjusted organisation proves intelligence in any one case. If, therefore, from our knowledge of what intelligence or some equivalent attribute alone can do, we attribute the formation of artificial machinery to our fellow-creatures, it is a mathematical demonstration that we must attribute the more exquisite and complicated machinery of the universe to an intelligence proportionally greater.

This brings us to the only other possible assumption, to the effect that the teaching of nature is not entitled to belief. Now this assumption has been already dealt with. It is a practical absurdity. Whether the teaching of nature be true or false, it must be true to us, since we have no other means of ascertaining truth. If, therefore, we deny the validity of the teaching of nature, there can be no argument, no conviction, and no opinion even about anything. The very objection itself implies a contradiction and an extravagance. There can obviously indeed be neither sense nor weight in an objection which *founds on the very assumption that it repudiates*.

But though the argument from the adjusted organisation of the universe and its products appears to be thus so clear and so precise as to admit of no reply, if the teaching of nature is to be trusted, yet there is still another mode of stating it, which it is worth while to outline for the sake of exhausting the subject. For adjustment requires that materials should exist suited to its realisation. The universe and its products could not have existed in an organised form, unless the elements of which it is composed had possessed the properties under which it was possible for them so to combine, as to constitute the various mechanisms which the universe and its products exhibit, and these again all so related to each other as to form harmonious portions of an apparently infinite whole.

The pantheistic disciples of the hypothesis of development argue that the universe and its products may have been gradually formed by the operation of the laws of nature alone. The "laws of nature" are, in their eyes, a sort of magical or mysterious power altogether unknown to man, but capable in themselves of working out definite results. It is a theory exceedingly unintelligible, but it does not seem to be true even to the limited extent that a meaning can be attached to it. The "laws of nature" do not in any degree imply a magical or mysterious power. A "law of nature" is simply the name which we give to the qualities or properties of existences, so related to each other as to produce certain definite effects through their mutual action. It is a "law of nature," for example, that the qualities of fire have such a relation to the qualities of paper, that if they are brought into a position where they can act upon each other the fire reduces the paper to ashes. These relations, consequently, must practically realise themselves when they are placed in a position wherein the several qualities which they possess can act upon each other, for otherwise the relations in which they stand to each other would *at once be the same and different.**

---

* The "laws of nature," as usually employed, is therefore just another name for the constitution of nature as inferred from

The result in each case, therefore, is manifestly certain. The same qualities or powers cannot work out different effects. The elements of things must possess those properties by which they combine together, and act upon each other; or, in other words, they must possess inherent relations to each other, under which they can constitute phenomena, or else there could be no " laws of nature." These elements might have been imbued with any other of the infinite variety of properties which are conceivable, so as to have stood to one another in relations which would either not act on each other at all, or would not act in the forms and according to the degrees essential for the production of phenomena. Had they not stood to each other in the exact relation in which they actually exist, therefore, there could have been no " laws of nature," or, at all events, *there could not have been the laws of nature which we now find operating.*

How then do the elements of the universe and its products come to possess those precise properties in the precise degrees which enable them so to combine and *regularly* operate as to

the properties or qualities with which nature has invested the various elements or essences which exist *in their relations to each other.* As used by pantheists in their cosmological theory, the " laws of nature," though it may be unknown to many of themselves, is, on the other hand, either merely another name for INTELLIGENT AGENCY, or to us it is self-contradictory, and can have no positive meaning at all.

constitute what are called "laws of nature"? How do they come to possess those precise properties, in the precise degrees, which enable them to endow each mechanism of which they are the parts with qualities not only conservative of themselves and other existences, but also developing into more extensive relations by becoming more perfect organisms? The development hypothesis does not fully explain the theory of phenomena, *even assuming that they originated with an intelligent being*; but it does not even pretend to explain in any way the still more striking manifestations of design which necessarily precede phenomena, by accounting for the elements of things being endowed with those precise properties which could alone have rendered such phenomena possible. This can only be done by a reference to that "law of nature" which connects organised adjustment with intelligence. The elements of things might have existed under an infinity of other forms, and with an infinity of other properties, or, for aught we can tell, without any relative properties at all; and no theory, save the assumption of the contrivance and action of an intelligent power, can give us even the most shadowy conception of the means under which they could have been so constituted, and so related, as to form a universe complete in all its parts, harmonious in all its proportions, and exquisitely adjusted in all its relations. If our intuitive knowledge of the nature of reason, as involved in the very feeling of it, assures us that adjusted arrangement in any case can only be the result of intelligent agency, still more—if there can be a more or less in regard to such a conclusion—still more does it assure us that the properties of those elements, without which there could not be such a thing as adjusted and *mutually related* arrangements, must be the result of intelligent agency.*

To say again that the elements of things are so constituted as to form every possible variety of phenomena, of which, however, only the most perfect survive, so as that the system and its parts are continually developing into higher and higher perfection, which, as has been said, is the last, and we believe the last possible, *development of pantheism*,† is only to illustrate the evidence. What, indeed, could be conceived more perfect

---

* Just as human beings know and select and shape the parts suitable for constructing artificial mechanisms, must the supreme power have known and constituted with suitable properties the elements suitable for constructing the mechanisms of the universe. This must be our conclusion, unless we assume that these suitable elements existed, and *no others*,—an assumption which would just lead us back to our former conclusion, though by a circuitous process.

† This is not necessarily a pantheistic theory. It is only pantheistic when the development spoken of is assumed to be a *property of matter*. We call it pantheistic, therefore, because it is usually understood in this sense, though our argument in truth demonstrates that it really leads to a conclusion the very reverse of pantheism.

than the intelligence which imbued every element with every property, *except those that are contradictory*, and in such a manner that, when they began to operate, the resulting phenomena would essentially and necessarily have the power of purging themselves of all that is imperfect, so as ultimately to generate an infinite progression of farther phenomena leading continually to higher perfection *without end?* There is at least so much to be said in favour of this theory, that it certainly seems to involve an effort of wisdom and power so enormous as to afford us something like a practical notion of infinity. If a mechanism at once so minute and so magnificent, so exquisitely organised and so inconceivably complicated, could exist under the action of physical causes, what a deception must those natures of ours be, which compel us to believe that intelligence, and no small measure of intelligence, is essential to the contrivance of an egg-cup and the construction of a pin! But if our natures are to be trusted and the laws of nature to be believed, how incredible and pitiable, on the contrary, must be the folly of those who attribute the mechanism of worlds and their products to physical causes! Assuming that our natures are to be trusted, and what, indeed, is felt intuitively to be true, *that we cannot help trusting them,* it will be admitted that this theory of development, involving the operation of even more stupendous intelligence than any other which has been proposed, seems a not unsuitable finale to that mass of wild guesses which modern pantheism has originated, and of which each has been successively found on examination to be more destructive of that very pantheism than any of its predecessors.

Under these views, we hardly think that our conclusion will be contested, *at least by the use of reason.* There may be difficulties with respect to some of the attributes of Deity, and these we shall consider afterwards; but that this universe, in its elements and in its adjusted arrangements, is the contrivance and the work of an intelligent agency, is so intuitively certain from the knowledge which we have of our own intellectual nature, that if it admit of dispute, all confidence in the teachings of nature must be at an end. We have no conviction more precise and more indisputable than that "adjusted organisations, with their elements, originate in intelligence." The proposition, indeed, is a mere expression of the intuitive assurance which our mental experience from the first exercise of reason gives us of the nature of intelligence.

We have now examined everything which has been proposed deserving the name of an objection, for the purpose of even suggesting doubts as to the being of a God; and we respectfully but confidently submit, that these very objections have only served to give the argument more thoroughly the character of a demonstration. We admit that it does not prove the *absolute* omnipotence and omniscience of the Supreme Being—*a posteriori*. We can only prove a power and a wisdom sufficient for the contrivance and construction of the universe, so far as it falls under our observation with all the existences, organic and inorganic, which it comprehends. Even *a priori* we can only prove infinity of any kind as a something of which we cannot conceive the limits. But *a posteriori* our proof is farther narrowed. We can only prove a vastness of wisdom and power, of the limits of which we can realise some conception, although from its very immensity our conception of it must necessarily be vague. Yet this is more than enough for our purpose, even apart from the *a priori* proof. It is all that finite creatures, indeed, can even in a measure appreciate upon such a subject. Anything farther, as with respect to the infinity which the *a priori* argument teaches us, is merely negative. It is at this point, accordingly, where the combination of the arguments becomes available, were it necessary for a still ulterior proof. The negative assurance, that the attributes of the Supreme Being can have no limits, demonstrates that the power which operates within the sphere which we know must be the same Being that operates beyond it wherever space or time is to be found.

The immutability of God follows from the

premises already established. It is impossible, and indeed involves a contradiction in terms, to suppose that a perfectly wise Being can doubt either as to His plans or the modes in which they are to be realised. Accordingly, this attribute is ascertained by our unvarying experience, in so far as the phenomena are submitted to our cognisance. Every law of God we find to be steady and permanent in effecting its purpose, *so far as its realisation has been reserved to Himself.**

The sun, for example, retaining all his properties, rises and sets with such perfect regularity at the appointed times that each of them can be mathematically calculated. The stars, in the same way, pursue their several courses in an undeviating order. The spring, the summer, the autumn, the winter, recur in unchanging succession. In a word, all the arrangements of nature, in so far as they depend upon the Creator, are so uniform, consistent, and harmonious, as in every particular to confirm the general principle, that He who fixed and decreed them is in the strictest sense of the word immutable. This we believe so firmly that we act upon the conviction every moment, and without a hesitation as to the result. We have no evidence upon the subject, *except the assurance that a perfectly wise Being cannot change;* and yet so deeply is the conviction stamped upon our

---

* The nature and effect of this exception will be fully explained afterwards.

minds, that no persuasion could induce us to believe that the sun will not rise to-morrow, or that any of the arrangements of nature will deceive us. In believing the phenomena of nature immutable, therefore, we imply a substratum of belief that their cause is immutable, and that He will never consequently change them, until He show those whom He has made dependent upon them, by some unquestionable sign, that His purpose in sustaining them is perfected.*

Such, then, are the proofs demonstrating the existence of a God, in connection with His natural attributes, as derived from natural theology, and we do not hesitate to say that they are perfect. We do not believe that any objection having the appearance of plausibility can even be proposed to them. We admit that hitherto the proof has been too much rested on the mere experience which men have of the contrivance and construction of adjusted arrangements by their fellow-creatures. This, however, it will now be seen, cannot strictly constitute an argument for proving that other adjusted arrangements must also have been contrived and constructed by intelligent beings, because we do not perceive the intellects of our fellow-creatures contriving and construct-

* This intuitive feeling of the permanence of natural laws, as flowing from our conviction of the immutability of the Supreme Being, evidently results from that sense of dependence on an *omniscient* and omnipotent power, which constitutes our proof of the natural attributes of God.

ing, any more than we perceive the Spirit of our God.* The two conclusions depend upon *exactly the same evidence*, and we consequently just as much require to prove that the adjusted arrangements contrived and constructed by our fellow-creatures are the result of intelligence, as that the adjustments of nature are the result of intelligence. To make two conclusions, therefore, which depend on precisely the same evidence, probative of one another, is evidently to argue in a circle. The proof *in both cases* originates in our intuitive knowledge of the nature of intelligence as felt by ourselves and discriminated by our reason, under which we are assured by the voice of nature *that adjusted arrangements, as well as the construction of the elements or parts which effect adjusted arrangements, can only be the product of intelligence, or of some equivalent attribute.*

No doubt, if any one denies that the voice of nature gives us an assurance that adjusted arrangements can only be the product of intelligence, he meets our argument for the being of a God; but HE ALSO MEETS ANY POSSIBLE PROOF FOR OUR BELIEF IN THE INTELLIGENCE OF OUR FELLOW-CREATURES. The argument which proves the one is *the only argument* which proves the other. Hence, he who denies or doubts the intelligent agency of a God in

---

* On the contrary, the misconception which originated this form of stating the argument has mainly given rise to modern pantheism.

contriving and constructing the universe, must of necessity, as matter of logic, *deny or doubt the intelligent agency of man in contriving and constructing the artificial arrangements and machinery which exist in the world.* There is not one particle of evidence proving the one, which does not also prove the other. Now, if this be true—and we cannot help thinking that it has been demonstrated— THERE IS AN END, WE PRESUME, TO ANY FORM OF PANTHEISM. Men may still, indeed, allow themselves to be more or less practically deluded, through ignorance or prejudice; but any theoretical objection to the *a posteriori* argument for the being of a God having even the appearance of plausibility seems impossible. Such an objection must assume the form of absolute scepticism, in denying that we have any means of knowing whether our fellow-creatures be mere acting and speaking machines, or intelligent creatures like ourselves. There is no conceivable argument which will prove them to be intelligent beings, which will not with the very same certainty prove the universe to have been contrived and constructed by an intelligent God.

CHAPTER III.

ARGUMENT FOR THE MORAL ATTRIBUTES OF GOD.

DEFINITION AND CHARACTER OF MORALITY—GOD CANNOT BE AN IMMORAL BEING—PROVED FROM THE POSITION AND RELATIONS OF MAN TO HIS FELLOW-CREATURES AND HIS GOD—THE DIFFICULTY ARISING FROM THE RIGOUR OF GOD'S JUSTICE OBVIATED—NO DIFFICULTY EXISTS ON THE SUBJECT, EXCEPT IN SO FAR AS ARISES FROM THE LIMITED NATURE OF THE HUMAN FACULTIES —CONCLUSION.

MORALITY is a general name for the feelings with which intelligent beings must regard each other in order to secure their highest individual happiness, and the highest happiness of the whole; and ethics is the name of the science which teaches morality. These feelings, or attributes, as they are usually called in reference to the Supreme Being, necessarily imply happiness in themselves.

Farther, feelings which have in view the happiness of others must evidently, *in so far as they gratify ourselves,* realise their gratification in their exercise, because there is no other source from which it can be derived. No doubt the gratification will be intensified when the feeling actually attains its purpose in promoting that happiness of others which is its ultimate aim. This, however, is simply a portion of the same gratification, *so far as we are concerned*, since another man's happiness cannot absolutely and in itself gratify us.

The happiness which we ourselves realise in the process from first to last, therefore, arises from our enjoyment of the primary feeling of love, since the welfare of another cannot possibly constitute in any accurate sense a source of selfish gratification. To call our delight in the happiness of another selfish, is a mere abuse of terms. We could not be moral beings unless we delighted in the happiness of others. Hence the happiness which we derive from actually benefiting another, is merely an intensification of that moral feeling of love in which our efforts to be useful originated, as more closely binding us to him whom we have benefited. Apart from all external considerations, therefore, moral feelings are blessed in themselves; and no feeling can be truly moral which does not in this way more or less bless us in itself, even though no other advantage should accrue from it.

We discover the same thing from the evidence of our personal experience. Every moral feeling, we are conscious, is *in itself* an agreeable feeling; while, on the contrary, every immoral feeling, *so far as it is immoral*, is *in itself* painful; the pleasure which it may involve not consisting in anything in the feeling itself, but in our anticipation of the satisfaction to be derived from its ultimate gratification. Every form of malignity is consequently painful, as arising from perverted desires, which, involving violations of natural laws, must be in themselves painful,—such as envy, jealousy, hatred, revenge, and the like.

We admit, indeed, that there may be immoral desires which do not in themselves necessarily imply malignity, as in the case of sensual desires; but if they do not imply absolute malignity, they imply, when in excess, more or less of that selfishness which we also know from experience crushes the spirit of love, apart from which, man's nature is hateful to himself as well as to others. It is obvious, therefore, that malignity cannot in the nature of things be predicated with respect to an omnipotent and omniscient Being. Such a Being could have no object in malignity, as being unsusceptible of the weaknesses in which it originates. He cannot be envious, nor jealous, nor influenced by hatred and revenge, because all things are His, and all beings are at His command. It is impossible, therefore, that such perverted desires could be felt by Him. It is almost more absurd to suppose moral than to suppose intellectual weakness in the Supreme Power. The supposition, indeed, seems to imply a contradiction in terms.

In the same way, and under the same principles, do we conclude that an omnipotent and omniscient

Being must realise in Himself perfect blessedness. An omnipotent and omniscient Being must, from the very nature of His attributes, have the means of blessedness in His own power, and must know how to use them. From the constitution of His existence, therefore, He must be perfectly blessed. A contrary supposition would, again, imply a contradiction in terms. No doubt, creatures such as we are can argue but very imperfectly with regard to the nature of Him who reigneth for ever and ever. But here there seems no difficulty in the matter, if reason imply universal principles, and the conclusions of reason consequently be of universal application. The omnipotent and omniscient Being must be perfectly blessed in the exercise of His own attributes, *or else He must prefer suffering*, which reason teaches us to be impossible. The conclusion seems nearly an identical proposition. God, therefore, must possess every attribute of moral excellence, because these constitute the only perfect blessedness, as being dependent on no external thing, but being blessed in their own enjoyment. He consequently must necessarily be a God of love, truth, and justice. These form the law, if we may so speak, of His nature, and must be obligatory on all His intelligent creatures, as involving the principles under which they are related to Him. By these alone can they be united, consequently, with God, and enabled to participate according to their measure in His blessedness.

PROOF OF GOD'S MORAL ATTRIBUTES. 113

But this conclusion, which, even thus generally stated, seems altogether indisputable, is further demonstrated by a consideration of the very nature of man, although not, we think, under the mode which has usually been adopted. To understand this argument thoroughly, we must ascertain in so far, in the first instance, the precise position and constitution of human beings in relation to the object on account of which they have been placed in this world. It is to a misconception with regard to this matter, we are inclined to believe, that difficulties connected with the argument are almost exclusively to be ascribed. We say of human beings, not only because we know too little of the position and constitution of the lower animals to be enabled to determine anything positively with regard to them, but because, so far as we can discover, man is the only moral being that exists on the face of our earth, and therefore the only being capable of appreciating moral attributes.*

---

* We by no means intend to affirm that the lower animals are altogether devoid of moral feelings. On the contrary, they show great affection to their young, sometimes are seen to sympathise with each other, frequently manifest affection towards those who are kind to them, and in many instances can be taught certain duties required of them by those on whom they are dependent. In all these cases, however, the feeling seems rather the effect of a moral instinct than of any appreciation of natural relationship; and we cannot in any instance trace among the lower animals an approach to that more perfect morality which connects creatures with their Creator.

From the position, then, of human beings in this world, taken in connection with their mental constitution and character, it is perfectly certain, as we have already seen, that they are here for the purpose of seeking for happiness. All men, in all circumstances, are perpetually seeking for happiness, *and for happiness only*, and that the most intense and permanent that they can procure. The desire has no limit. It is perfect and endless happiness that they seek; and if they are content with less, it is only because they cannot see their way to attaining more. They will even make a sacrifice for the time, for the purpose of securing more intense and permanent happiness subsequently. In seeking happiness, indeed, different individuals take often entirely different methods, according to their respective characters and circumstances, but the general end is invariably the same. There are no exceptions. Now in this universal pursuit of happiness there is a continuous struggle between our selfishness and our moral feelings. Each is perpetually, though we may be more or less unconscious of it, striving for the

Except under the guidance of pure instinct, indeed, we cannot discover that they have any idea of futurity, or make any provision for it. In a word, as we have said in the text, the nature and constitution of the lower animals are too little known to us to ascertain with any measure of accuracy the precise object on account of which they have been placed in this world, or almost anything farther in regard to them, in a spiritual point of view, than the general relations which connect them with the human race.

mastery; and as this cannot possibly be avoided, we must conclude that it was the purpose of nature that it should be so.

These propensities and feelings, however, are not absolutely inconsistent. We may enjoy both selfish and moral gratifications without the one counteracting the other, and that even more intensely than when either is enjoyed singly. This, however, is only possible when selfishness is kept in a subordinate place. When in the slightest degree it acquires a mastery over the mind, the sensibility of our moral feelings becomes proportionally blunted. From the usual character of our early training, however, and from the constitution of human society, it is extremely difficult to exercise the necessary control over our selfishness, so as to enjoy with any measure of fulness both classes of tendencies. We are almost educated in selfishness, and the effect of education, of course, passes into more advanced life, on which we have no sooner entered than we find almost all around us having their whole souls apparently concentrated on the interests of themselves and their families. The desire of sensual indulgence, with the corresponding love of admiration and lust of ambition which it engenders in youth, adds enormously to the evil, by chaining us, as it were, to the earth, and so assimilating us to the lower animals that we can hardly look forward to ulterior consequences at all, except in so far as regards the means by which worldly suffering may be avoided, and our passions and worldly purposes may be gratified.

Now there are no doubt various modes provided by nature, under which men may subdue their passions and habits, and recover the use of their reason, so as more or less fully to ascertain wherein the most intense and permanent happiness is to be found; but as matter of fact we know that this result is usually and mainly effected by suffering. The difficulties, calamities, and fears which occur to us in life, constitute, in the great majority of cases, the instrumentality by which we discover that selfishness and sensuality are not the means of securing intense and permanent happiness. This is most thoroughly realised, at all events, when disappointments trouble us, when misfortunes sadden us, when pain racks us, and when the prospect of death terrifies us. These are the grand means which nature has provided for leading us to meditate on our true position, and on the *only* mode in which our increasing desire for happiness can be realised. It is consequently an utter error to suppose that our Creator is benevolent in the sense of His desiring His creatures to be free from all kind of suffering in this present world. On the contrary, His benevolence is frequently displayed in causing that very suffering, if it be rightly applied, to work out for us a far higher and more permanent happiness than we could otherwise have procured. The afflictions of life, therefore, under this view, may become eminent blessings. Indeed, they are never sent except for the sake of blessing those who are visited by them; and hence, if they are not blessings to us, it is because we refuse to recognise in them the message of God, and the purpose of His all-perfect providence.*

An entire suspension of suffering, moreover, seems from the very nature of things impossible, even were it desirable, with respect to creatures enjoying free will, and at the same time possessing not only a very limited intelligence, but an intelligence in its development so dependent upon experience. Supposing them even to have been created happy, and *with the means of realising the highest happiness*, it is yet obvious that any error

---

* Afflictions, however, are only sent by reason of the hardness of the human heart. The Supreme Being would choose rather, we are assured, to sanctify us through indulgence than through suffering. He sends suffering as *the only remedy under the circumstances*. Let us receive the gifts of God with gratitude, each of them augmenting our love for Him, and leading us to a closer union with Him, and every step in this direction will diminish our worldly sufferings. We never, indeed, in this world, can arrive at that degree of perfection which would render all suffering useless, but the nearer we approach to it will our sufferings be less and less. This, however, though it appears to be conformable to the attributes of God, is only to be determined by evidence, and we have no hesitation in saying that the evidence is strongly in favour of the assumption. Let a man only make the trial, and he will be satisfied by his own experience, which is the best of all evidence.

in judgment, or any sudden impulse, might at once alter their condition, and subject them to evil. Nothing save a continuous miracle could prevent this, and a continuous miracle would manifestly interfere with free will, so as to subvert the very system of discipline which God has decreed for the purpose of determining character. Experience directed by reason can alone constitute the guide of such creatures, under which, having been taught the only means of securing intense and permanent happiness, they are induced under the practical convictions thus attained to realise them.

The object of the Supreme Being, therefore, in the creation of such beings as we are, must have been to direct them to happiness *through experience,* so that, becoming acquainted experimentally both with good and evil, they might learn to choose the good and eschew the evil. Thereby men necessarily become imbued with a *character,* which, depending on no incidental or external objects for happiness, realises such happiness in itself as essentially involved in the very nature of their feelings.

Such is, accordingly, the actual condition of the human race. However men may have been created, it is certain, from the existing constitution of human society, that we are *now* in a state of moral discipline. Born as infants into the world, without the capability of distinguishing betwixt that which is or is not calculated to secure our highest and most permanent happiness, every one is appointed to engage in the struggle betwixt selfishness and love, and to determine thus in his own experience *the character* which will most assuredly realise the object of his existence. In other words, we are here in a state of discipline, to be exercised by ourselves, under the influence and through the faculties which God has constituted and given us. It is not, therefore, selfish enjoyment or indulgence with which the Supreme Being intends or proposes mainly to bless us, but moral happiness *constituting a character*, so as to be not only permanent, but permanent in the sense that it cannot be taken away from us, as having become of the very essence of our natures, and which, when once begun, circumstances will not only not deteriorate, but will enhance and purify. Circumstances, and especially suffering, become the very means through which the character is thus more thoroughly perfected, until a time arrive, when, the character being established, circumstances as means will be comparatively unnecessary, except in so far as our changed natures may be more entirely gratified in the opportunities which they enjoy of its practical realisation.

This argument seems really to consist of a series of almost identical propositions. It is just a description of the actual position in which man exists. In other words, it is a development of the manifest laws of nature, in so far as man is concerned, by which his conduct must be regulated for good or evil. Nor can the effect of this argument fail to be enhanced, when we consider that it explains the long-disputed problem of the origin of evil, demonstrating that both physical and moral evil are *implied in the plan of God's government*. It shows that physical evil is absolutely essential to the working out of His purpose, and indicates that moral evil must necessarily arise under it, from the very gift of free will conferred upon creatures born and trained under such a condition of society as that which, from whatever cause, actually exists among men.

Thus far our conclusions, we presume, as matter of logic, can hardly admit even of difference of opinion. What the intense and permanent good is, in its precise form, which the Supreme Being thus calls upon us by the voice of nature to seek, and what the evil which He calls upon us to eschew, is a different question, which comes next to be more particularly determined. Of course such determination will enable us, under still another form, to ascertain the moral attributes of the Deity.

With this view, then, it is to be observed in the first instance, that moral feeling, speaking generally, is, as we have seen, the only condition of mind which implies happiness in itself. All our other feelings depend for their gratification on externals, which are incidental and occasional. The pleasure derivable from our other feelings, therefore, can only last while such incidental and occasional gratifications are in our power, and while our desire for them continues to exercise an influence. We say while our desire for them continues to exercise an influence, because it is an imperfection connected with all such gratifications that there not only comes a time at which they cease altogether, but that in all pleasure derived from such sources the desire in a great measure ceases in the very act of gratification. Supposing us even to have the means of gratification in our power, the indulgence of these desires after a time becomes indifferent, if not offensive, to us. This is especially the case with reference to mere sensual desires, which, if gratified to excess, actually generate results destructive of our bodily health and of our mental energy. There is here, therefore, a distinct practical precept taught in the laws of nature that we are bound to regulate and control such desires.

With reference to other selfish passions, such as ambition and the like, they, if carried to excess, not only after a time cease to afford anything beyond a mere negative gratification, but necessarily interfere with the operation of our moral feelings; as indeed is also the case with sensual desires carried to excess; and the moment that either of them does this, they begin both to generate moral pain on the one hand, and to subject us to the dislike and vengeance of our fellow-creatures on the other. In this, again, we have a practical precept in the law of nature, to the effect that we are bound to regulate and control them.

The laws of nature are, however, the laws of God, for they are a mere name for the relations under which He has constructed and arranged the universe. In these precepts, therefore, we have an expression of the will and the design of God to the effect that there is a point at which our selfish tendencies are to be regulated and controlled, even for the sake of our selfishness itself, because beyond that point our selfishness overreaches itself, and generates an amount of suffering, directly and indirectly, which ultimately exceeds, and may far exceed, any amount of enjoyment which the farther gratification of our selfish propensities could afford. In this manifestation of the will and design of God, we are in thus far of course made acquainted with the moral attributes of God, which originate, if we may so say, His will, and thus are assured that God is in the highest sense a moral Being, who allows us to enjoy the pleasures of the world in which He has placed us, but strictly under subservience to that moral nature, in the exercise of which He thereby shows it to be His purpose that our higher and more permanent happiness should be found.

This, however, clear as in so far it may be, is only the very elements of the argument. For our selfish gratifications, *and just in proportion to the degree that we are intelligent,* become embittered by the uncertainty of our future fate. We may not only be deprived of all our external enjoyments, but plunged in misfortune, sickness, and pain, with the prospect of death before us, and we have no possible means of protecting ourselves even for a single moment. Of all this we have continual experience. Every day we hear of such vicissitudes in human affairs. Every day we hear of persons of all ranks, ages, and degrees of strength being cut off when they least expected it; and in addition, we have the prospect before us of a future world, as to our condition in which, we are, if possible, still more helpless. We may be condemned to eternal misery, and we have no means of avoiding it. No man can altogether get rid of such considerations. We can only elude them by banishing them from our minds, so far as is in our power. For this purpose, those who cannot bear such thoughts—and, in truth, none could bear them if they dwelt upon them, for they would drive us mad—plunge into the business, and amusements, and indulgences of life, that these may occupy their attention; or, in other words, may as opiates deaden their mental sufferings and fears. We say deaden, because no one can entirely supersede them. As the criminal condemned to death can never altogether stifle the thought of his approaching doom, even though he have an opportunity of partially deadening it by intoxication, or other similar indulgences—and the sting involved in the prospect does, as matter of fact, perpetually more or less torment him—so is it with all men whose whole trust is in this world. We are all as surely condemned to death as he is, and the only difference is the possibility of a short respite. There is no difference whatever, except in point of time, and this is not very material, since the time to us is altogether uncertain. Like him, therefore, we cannot, do what we may, altogether supersede the horror which we feel under such circumstances at our approaching fate. We may be *hardly conscious of it*, and yet it is no less certainly qualifying our state of mind. This wretchedness is aggravated just in proportion to the degree of our selfishness, and the hopelessness of its farther gratification.

We have known not a few, and one in particular, in whom we were sincerely interested, who was reduced under such circumstances to absolute despair. He had been guilty of no particular crime, but, on the contrary, had been greatly respected, and was indeed in his general character a very lovable person. But he had been absolutely trained to selfishness, for every wish that he had indicated was anticipated almost before it could be expressed. He professed religion, and with an ordinary measure of sincerity, but he had never been practically taught that religion requires us to exercise self-control, specially with a view to the promotion of the happiness of others. Accordingly, his whole life was spent in a round of amusements. He was perpetually in society, and delighted in the attention and admiration which his qualifications both of body and mind secured him there. From his peculiarly youthful appearance, he maintained his position amongst the gay and the worldly till a comparatively late period of life. Then, however, misfortune began to overtake him. His relations died. His fortune—although he still possessed the means of comfort—was seriously impaired. His health in some degree gave way. It was then that he deplored to us the condition to which he was reduced. He avowed his hatred of those who were in more favourable circumstances than himself. It was with a sort of horror that we heard him express his anguish that a worthy person had recovered from the disease of which his own nearest and dearest relation had recently died. He had not a hope of further happiness on earth. His sufferings were intense, because he saw no prospect of their being alleviated. He would willingly have died, if he could have been assured that death was annihilation. But a consciousness of his own engrained selfishness made him afraid to die. It was hell begun.

Nor is this by any means a solitary case. We have known several in much the same condition;

and from the very nature of man, there can be no doubt that there must be thousands. Every one, indeed, who is the slave of selfishness, must feel this, and just in proportion to his intelligence, when overtaken by calamity or disease, specially if accompanied by bodily anguish, so that there is no means of using those opiates for deadening spiritual pain to which we have adverted. Different men, no doubt, according to the strength of their nerves and the degree of their mental energy, will suffer more or less; but no mortal man, under such circumstances, can fail to suffer, and to suffer severely, however much strength of nerves and mental energy may enable him to conceal it. Moral feelings *of the highest class* can alone help to sustain us, for they depend upon no external thing, and cannot be taken away.

But they may do much more than help to sustain us, if rightly understood. This will be obvious from a farther development of the argument. For hitherto we have mainly spoken of our moral feelings in the most restricted sense, as relating us to our fellow-creatures only. They have, however, a far more extended range. It is indeed the erroneously narrow range within which they have been usually limited, that has left the moral attributes of God rather proved than demonstrated. For our moral feelings not only connect us with our fellow-creatures, but constitute the essential link by which we are also connected with our God. It is impossible, indeed, to conceive that the all-perfect God should have created beings who were to have no practical relation to Himself, and who must therefore be altogether indifferent with respect to Him. Still more impossible is it to conceive that He should have created beings for the purpose of hating Him. This is to us incredible. We cannot imagine that the very devils could have pleasure in being hated. The idea of any intelligent being having pleasure in being hated is to us an absurdity. We could just as well imagine a sentient being having pleasure in pain.

That the Supreme Being, therefore, should have pleasure in malignity, or should be gratified by the indifference or hatred of His creatures, is perfectly incredible. It is an assumption not only inconsistent with the moral feelings of our natures, but, judging from the laws of our natures, is inconsistent with itself; and we must in this, as in all similar cases, argue from the laws of our natures, because *there is nothing else from which we can possibly argue.* But these laws are the laws of God, and consequently are the outgoings of His attributes and the declaration of His will. We could not have other or better evidence, unless we were capable of knowing the essence of the Divine nature in our consciousness. It is the evidence under which we judge in every instance, and the very same, in a more irresistible form, under which we ascertain the feelings and dispositions of our fellow-creatures.

It is under these considerations that the teaching of nature guides us again with a firm hand to a still fuller assurance of the moral attributes of God. For as we feel that we are related to our fellow-creatures by moral laws, which in themselves and in their effects generate our most intense happiness on earth, so that were we left solitary and alone *we should be utterly wretched*, in the same way do we feel that we are in a still closer degree related to the Supreme Being.

In fact, we are every moment made conscious of our entire dependence upon God. With the prospect of possible misfortune, which we have no means of averting—of possible sickness, which we have no means of relieving—of death, which we have no means of evading—of everlasting misery beyond the grave, which we have no means of escaping, our fellow-creatures being utterly unable to preserve us,—*apart from trust in God, it is impossible that we could be happy*. Is it not, on the contrary, manifest that under such a prospect nothing save continual engagements and amusements distracting our thoughts could preserve those who are capable of reflection from a sort of protracted despair?

Hence it is, as we have already indicated, that men so often have recourse to engagements and amusements and indulgences, without which even the most senseless and inconsiderate, and still more intelligent men, would be forced by very weariness of spirit to think, and to think in bitterness of heart, on their prospects here and hereafter. Such is the position in which human beings stand whilst they are away from God; and assuredly it is difficult to conceive any condition more awful, or more agitating.

The moment, however, that we begin, under such circumstances, to realise our sense of dependence on God, and thence to feel a trust in Him, which is *manifestly the moral relation that ought to connect intelligent beings with their Creator*, all this is and must be changed. The slightest hope that we may be protected by Him who is omnipotent and omniscient, at once infuses a balm into our souls, which, in proportion to the degree of its strength, soothes all our sorrows and alleviates all our fears. We are conscious that no power can injure us if He be really our Father and our Friend.

Thus peace begins, and as our trust grows our happiness is still farther and farther enhanced, because thorough trust in God necessarily implies perfect happiness both here and hereafter. A conviction of the immortality of the soul is therefore, from the very nature of the case, involved in it. We have in this way our grand and increasing desire for permanent happiness fully assured, and that under the most intense force of which our natures are susceptible. Nor, in the first instance, does it signify whether our belief be or be not well founded. The belief, apart from everything else, blesses us at once, and in itself. The inconveniences and even the sufferings of the world become actual sources of blessedness to him who believes that they are mere means of procuring glory through eternity, just as a few months of toil and even suffering would be welcomed by the worldly man who believed that he was thereby to secure to himself rank, wealth, and fortune.

In this, indeed, we have an irresistible evidence for the truth of our belief. For our natures must be worse than a delusion if the only belief which can realise the unceasing object of our whole lives is to be regarded as a falsehood. We have, consequently, in this belief, something more than even the voice of nature; it is almost as if we literally heard the voice of God calling us to Himself, and proclaiming, in language which cannot be misunderstood, that in a union with Him we have the whole purpose of our natures satisfied, and the ultimate object of our natures realised. There can be no other means. If it cannot be thus effected, the end for which we live, at which we are perpetually striving, and apart from which our very creation would seem an abortive effort of nature, must be hopelessly disappointed. We cannot conceive this to be possible. To us the very proposition implies again a contradiction in terms.

Our union with God, however, involves the most entire consummation of moral excellence. It involves a trust pure and unfeigned, since the omniscient God cannot be deceived; and this again involves the realisation of a love equally pure and unfeigned, for perfect trust cannot exist without love and respect and reverence. These, however, cannot again be realised in exceptional cases. They *imply a character*, and consequently it is to the attainment of such a character that we are led, if *we have given fair-play to intelligence*, by the impulse which, as we have seen, directs our whole lives, and can alone enable us to realise the end and aim to which they exclusively direct us. It is indeed true that, under the influence of selfishness and passion refusing fair-play to intelligence, we may allow ourselves to be seduced from the way. That, however, is not the question. For if we listen to reason, we cannot miss the way; or, at all events, it seems impossible to maintain that there *is any other way* of procuring intense and permanent happiness. If, consequently, we allow ourselves to be seduced from that way, it must be at our peril. Nature thus tells us that we ought perpetually to follow after love, trust, and truth, as the sole means of uniting us with God, and by such means assuring our highest and everlasting happiness. In this assurance the perfection of the moral attributes of God is demonstrated, so far as any absolute fact is capable of demonstration. It is the voice of nature telling us under the most explicit form that God seeks our love in truth, and will reciprocate our love in truth; and here the *a priori* and *a posteriori* arguments for His moral attributes interweave and confirm each other.

If our conclusion be untrue, then the nature of man is a lie, and his unceasing desire for the most intense and permanent happiness is a lie, since that desire is by the supposition a deceitful tendency innate in our souls, impelling us at every instant to seek a gratification which it is impossible to realise, because no such gratification exists. The man who can bring himself to believe this *can believe nothing else,* because he repudiates the only authority for belief. He is impervious to argument, because he must have settled down into dogged *a priori* scepticism.* To him, the evidence of his

---

* It is indeed difficult to conceive how a man under such circumstances can, with any show of reason, pretend to believe in his senses. They are just feelings, with the same evidence as any other feelings, *and no more.* The matter, however, is not worth discussing, because, whatever they may profess in words, men in reality recognise the valid authority of all their primary feelings. They cannot help it. Hence, if any one admits the validity of mental feelings in one case, and denies it in another, because it does not suit his theory, or his prejudices, or his passions—if, for example, he recognises the legitimacy and universality of reason as applied to mathematics, and denies its legitimacy and universality as applied to morals—he must take the consequences.

PROOF OF GOD'S MORAL ATTRIBUTES.

senses, if he reason logically, must merely imply phenomena which warrant no conclusion, and involve no faith.

We have thus a higher proof for the moral attributes of God than we have for the sympathies and feelings of our fellow-creatures. But it may be said, or rather it has been said, that we know the moral feelings of our fellow-creatures by experience, but we have no such personal experience of the moral attributes of God. Those who thus argue fall into the very error, previously exposed, of assuming that we have some *a priori* knowledge of the intellectual and moral nature of our fellow-creatures. It is, however, an utter delusion. *We never saw, nor by any of our senses perceived, either the intellect or the moral feelings of our fellow-creatures, nor have we any personal consciousness of them.* We know them in the relations which we feel towards our fellow-creatures—*i.e.*, in our sense of dependence upon them for happiness; but this is only after we have discovered their moral qualities from their acts, precisely as we discover the moral attributes of God.

There is not the slightest difference, therefore, in the process, except that we have a clearer consciousness of our dependence upon God, and more manifest proofs of His love, than we can have with reference to our fellow-creatures. For God might have doomed us to hopeless misery. Giving us a love of life, He might at the same time have made every morsel of food nauseous, and every breath of air painful. But, on the contrary, He has blessed us with a thousand blessings, having constituted us with no one tendency or property of which *the natural effect is not to produce happiness*. Above all, He has given us an assurance in the very essence of our feelings, that if, as freewill creatures, we realise our obligations to our fellow-creatures, and to Him on earth, we shall also realise eternal glory by our full moral union with Him in the world that is to come. He who denies the moral attributes of God must therefore, as we have said, be prepared *to deny the moral qualities of men;* for God has practically, in our experience, evidenced to us far more certainly than any of our fellow-creatures have done the existence of His moral attributes in attaching an *absolute* happiness to every moral feeling, which progressively increases as our moral natures continue to improve. He thus assures us, by the very testimony of our feelings, of the most intense and permanent happiness in a moral union with Himself, when our moral natures have attained such perfection as to be capable of thoroughly realising the relations in which intelligent beings and their Creator stand connected with each other. It seems impossible even to imagine a more irresistible argument. It *must* be sound and true, unless God and nature have contrived a scheme purposely to deceive us.

But though our conclusions in thus far seem indisputable, it may perhaps still be said that our argument only regards the subject under one aspect. For though it may be clear, so far as reasoning can demonstrate anything, that under the view of the subject which we have now taken God is a God of love, yet it would appear, on the other hand, that His justice is rigorous, and that a neglect of His laws must, *under the very same argument*, lead to misery. Now, this is neither to be denied nor doubted. A breach of law, of any kind, must of necessity incur a proportionate penalty. Unless this were the case, law would be a mockery. But let it be observed that the relations of nature, which we usually call the laws of God, are *from their very perfection made to vindicate themselves.* The penalty, therefore, of moral guilt is necessarily involved in the commission of sin. In its very essence it implies moral suffering, partially deadened, it may be, for a time by opiates, but *becoming greater and greater as worldly employments, amusements, and indulgences cease to act as opiates, and we are left to the uncontrolled operation of spiritual law.*

---

* It must be kept in view, that while we argue, *as a matter of certainty*, that under the moral law of God immorality must *ultimately* work out its own penalty, we do not intend to maintain that all suffering in this world is a direct punishment of

From natural religion we can discover no ground whatever for supposing that there are arbitrary penalties attached to a violation of the moral law. As the realisation of our moral relations both to man and to God blesses in itself both in the direct feeling and the indirect consequences, so the breach of these relations curses in itself. Not only is there no objection, therefore, which can be taken upon this account to the love of God, but there is an irresistible proof of the perfection of His love for *moral excellence* in a justice which necessarily flows from our very natures, and which we cannot avoid recognising as the most exquisitely adjusted that it is possible even to conceive.

No doubt there are many who seem placed from circumstances in a very unfavourable position for realising moral relations, but it must be remembered that the realisation of moral relations depends *upon the intention, and not on the mere external act*. It will be the intentions of such parties, therefore, in the voluntary exercise of free will, that will incur the penalty. From the very nature of the case, it is evident that their acts in

immorality. In the theological sense we do not even maintain that it is in this world a *punishment* of immorality at all. This subject seems excessively misunderstood, but we do not enter upon it at length, because it would necessarily lead to the introduction of considerations appertaining exclusively to the doctrines of revelation, which we desire entirely to avoid. As has been said, the conclusion in the text is positively certain as a doctrine of natural religion, and we have here nothing farther to do with the subject.

themselves can involve no moral pain, and therefore incur no moral penalty.* Nor, under natural religion, can we tell what may be the future position of such parties, nor what arrangements may be made when the things of time have passed away for redressing evils and compensating irregularities. Any knowledge on these points can be derived from a revelation only, and must be considered in relation to its other doctrines, under the condition that all such doctrines must be conformable to the principles of natural religion, and therefore specially consistent with that love, justice, and truth, which natural religion determines, beyond the possibility of rational dispute, to be attributes of the Supreme Being.

It, however, will no doubt be maintained by some who are little accustomed to think about anything except the external affairs of the world, that however difficult it may be to reply to this argument, abstractly considered, yet as matter of

---

* Man is a developing creature, both as an individual and a race. What may be the effect of death in the case of infants, natural religion cannot determine, because we necessarily want a knowledge of the state of their minds. But all *men*, however low in the scale of civilisation, are developing under a system of dicipline. Many of them, in the lowest stage of civilisation, exercise great self-control. Their fate in futurity must depend, therefore, on their efforts and intentions; or, in other words, on the state of their minds. The higher, however, they rise in civilisation, it is obvious that they enjoy the greater advantages for rising high in spiritual excellence, and therefore for attaining a more elevated position, both in this world and the next.

fact the most moral men are not always, nor perhaps generally, the happiest. This assertion manifestly, though tacitly, implies a theory, that the spirit of selfishness may afford greater happiness *in itself* than the spirit of love, and that, consequently, a man may be happier in repudiating all moral connection with his fellow-creatures and his God, than in loving his fellow-creatures and his God, and being beloved by them. No one, we presume, will maintain the theory in this extreme form, which, however, must necessarily be true if the theory in any form be logically defensible. In fact, that any one should maintain such a theory at all, arises from an almost voluntary, if not intentional, confusion of ideas. Men confuse the external gratification of selfishness with its internal and essential character. Such external gratification may afford pleasure, but it cannot, from the very nature of the case, afford happiness, which arises from no external gratification, but from *the nature of our feelings themselves*. Pleasure is a temporary, and happiness a permanent, state. No one, therefore, could prefer pleasure to happiness, even though the pleasure were more intense than the happiness, as a matter of reason, still less where the happiness, from beginning to end, is more intense than the pleasure, which, as we have seen in the case of those who realise the love of God, must be the case. It is obvious, therefore, that where human beings satisfy themselves with temporary pleasure at the expense of happiness—*for it is quite possible that they may enjoy both*—it is because they overlook their relationship to God, and, consequently, the happiness which a realisation of that relationship must secure for them. The assumption that the most moral man is not always the happiest, proceeds evidently, therefore, on a mistake, or rather a series of mistakes. It confuses pleasure with happiness, and ignores the decisive fact in the controversy. On the supposition that there is a God, omnipotent, omniscient, just, holy, merciful, and true, or, in one word, a God of love, with whom the realisation of our moral nature unites us as a father and a friend, there can be no controversy upon the subject.

While, therefore, there is no doubt a point at which our knowledge stops, and beyond which, consequently, we cannot proceed with our argument as to the divine attributes, because their perfection is higher than our mental faculties can comprehend, yet, so far as our capacities can reach, it seems equally complete and simple. It does not appear liable to any form of objection. For to rest objections on supposed facts, which are admittedly beyond our capabilities to ascertain, is absurd. It is a mere begging of the question to argue from what we do not know, and cannot know. To attain a legitimate conclusion, we must argue from what we do know, and know with certainty. Thus arguing, it is demonstrated, if ever there was a demonstration, that the Supreme Being realises the perfection of every moral attribute, and hence, delighting in the exercise of these attributes by His free-will creatures, blesses these creatures by a very necessity of nature, in exact proportion to the measure in which they realise them. We have in all this a most exquisitely adjusted process; and the very perfection of its beauty, in the love of moral excellence which it displays, seems to direct us of itself to the love and the wisdom of the great First Cause.

CHAPTER IV.

RELATION BETWIXT GOD AND MAN.

GOD HAS CREATED US FOR THE PURPOSE OF SEEKING INTENSE AND PERMANENT HAPPINESS, THROUGH VICTORY IN THE STRUGGLE BETWIXT SELFISHNESS AND LOVE—THIS CONSIDERATION NECESSARILY OPENS TO US THE PROSPECT OF AN IMMORTALITY—THE VOICE OF NATURE HEARD IN THOSE LAWS WHICH ASSURE US OF AN IMMORTALITY — THIS IMMORTALITY WILL BE INTENSELY AND PERMANENTLY HAPPY TO THOSE WHO SEEK IT IN THE WAY WHICH NATURE INDICATES— SUCH HAPPINESS INVOLVED IN TRUST IN GOD—THIS TRUST IMPERFECT OR WANTING IN ALL MEN UNDER ORDINARY CIRCUMSTANCES—MODE IN WHICH NATURE INDICATES THAT IT IS TO BE SOUGHT.

HAVING ascertained the perfect moral excellence of the Supreme Being, in so far as the extent of our knowledge enables us to reach, we have next to determine the relationship which ought to be realised betwixt Him and the creatures whom He has endowed with intelligent and moral natures. This relationship is substantively made manifest under those principles which have been already ascertained. For we have found that men are created with only one object in view. They seek intense and permanent happiness, and they are unceasingly engaged in seeking it. This object can only be attained by the assurance of God's protection as our Father and our Friend. Assured of this, the prospect of eternal glory opens to us. Our very desire of living gives us indeed some belief of immortality, and, in connection with it, some hope of intense and permanent happiness. We have the same belief in immortality, *naturally*, as we have in the continuance of life for a time upon earth, and it is founded on the same evidence. There is no more ground for believing that we shall live for a day, than there is for believing that we shall live for ever. Both beliefs proceed from our desire of life, and our consciousness that this desire is the voice of nature speaking to us. Accordingly, there is no proof whatever that we shall live in the body for another day. Our belief of continued life applies really to the mind. We rarely think of the matter, indeed, under this aspect, because we rarely attempt to analyse the more subtle states of our minds. It is no less true, however, on that account. That other people live in the body under the same circumstances apparently as ourselves, is no rational evidence that we shall continue to live in the body likewise. On the contrary, it frequently happens that men, under apparently the most favourable circumstances, are suddenly and unexpectedly summoned to the grave. Our hope of continued life really rests on a conviction *which has no limit in time*, and which cannot almost in the most desperate state of disease be shaken away. Perhaps the phenomenon is most strikingly manifest in children. They have no idea of dying; and indeed, through our whole lives, the fear of death requires to be forced upon us. Of itself, it never seems to occur to any one, and so far is our experience with regard to others from leading us to believe that our lives will be prolonged, that it is only our experience with respect to others which *compels* us to believe that we will die. A belief that we will continue to live, is our natural and normal state, and specially anything like annihilation is a possibility perfectly abhorrent to our feelings. This manifestly implies that there is happiness in the very act of living, and consequently, from the nature of the case, a desire of continuing to live. In this, again, we have the voice of nature telling us that by using the suitable means we might live for ever, seeing that the annihilation or death of the soul must at once put an end to permanence of happiness by closing existence itself. *

* We are quite aware that many believe the doctrine of an immortality to be discoverable from revelation only. We trust that the argument in the text will show this to be a complete mistake; and a most pernicious mistake it is, though we believe it has been encouraged from excellent motives. Nothing can show more clearly that truth, and truth alone, ought to be our object in all investigations. If the laws of nature are to be believed, the doctrine of an immortality, as we trust has been proved in this chapter, is *demonstrable* under natural

Nor is the conclusion less certain if drawn from a consideration of the apparent design of the universe. All things are therein arranged, so far as we can discover, under a scheme of the most perfect wisdom. Every creature has its distinct part to perform, and adequate means are provided for the realisation of the natural tendencies, and the gratification of the primary desires of each. Over the whole, man has been appointed, in respect of his intelligence, as the lord and sovereign. All things are subjected to him, and he is impelled by a desire which never leaves him to improve continually his position, in endeavouring to secure the most intense and permanent happiness. But if this desire be a delusion and a lie; if human beings be destined to perish with their bodies; if, like moths, they are to move a brief moment upon the earth, and then to disappear for ever; if, notwithstanding the desire which incessantly impels them to pursue intense and permanent happiness, they are, do what they may, condemned to be contented with those wretched scraps of pleasure which this world can afford, mixed with the sorrows and sufferings of which all human beings participate,—then never was there a more perfect burlesque than creation. It is a system splendidly contrived and exqui-

religion. What Scripture has really done in "bringing life and immortality to light," it is not of course our business to discuss here.

sitely adjusted up to a certain point, but left imperfect and unfinished. Nature becomes a ludicrous and monstrous absurdity, which employs the most gigantic machinery to work out absolutely nothing. The constitution of the human mind presents a magnificent theory, complete and harmonious, and true in all its parts, until it comes to a result, and then all is found to be a falsehood and a mockery. The thing is impossible. We cannot believe that such an anomaly could have existed in nature, apart from every consideration of a God. When, however, we know in addition that there is a God, omnipotent and omniscient, and whom our very desire for intense and permanent happiness, in connection with the position which we occupy and the relations in which we feel ourselves to exist, proves to be a God endued with every moral excellence, our conclusion becomes *a matter of feeling* as well as of intellect. In truth, we have all the evidence which is possible. As we have seen, it is the very same evidence on which we conclude in every case where we deem our conclusions the most certain. It is the formal assurance of our natures; and if we be deceived by that assurance, there can to us be no such thing as truth.

Hence it appears that the very same argument which assures eternal life to those who seek it in the way which God has provided, assures also intense, or at all events growing and permanent, happiness to those who seek it in like manner. In fact, the one conclusion is evidently involved in the other. For it is the desire for such happiness, as the never-ceasing object of our aspirations, which is the voice of nature assuring us that it is attainable. If, however, the voice of nature be worthy of any confidence at all, it must be worthy of confidence in a case where it not only never ceases to speak, but absolutely impels us to struggle every moment after an object which it thus declares to be the end and consummation of our existence. In this, consequently, we have our relationship to God clearly developed, since this, as we have already seen, can only be attained by trust in God. If we thoroughly trust in Him, then, as invariably happens with respect to the laws of God, the law, *in its own working, vindicates itself.* We are blessed, in other words, in the very nature of our feeling. Fear vanishes, suffering is soothed, anxieties are annihilated. All the events of our history become sources of happiness. We have peace here, and in that peace a foretaste of intense and permanent glory for ever.

The relationship in which we stand to God, therefore, implies trust in Him, as the only means of securing the ultimate end of our being. This follows, as we have seen, from a consideration of that end itself, but is no less manifest from the very essential character of the relation which must exist between creatures and their Creator.

From the very nature of the case, we are bound to put our trust in Him, on account of the many blessings which He has already bestowed upon us, on account of the farther blessings which He has put it into our power to procure, and on account of that entire dependence in which we have lived, and must ever live, upon Him, for anything which we can possibly desire or enjoy.

To suppose that He will deceive us, that He will still withhold from us those gifts which He has promised in the very constitution of our natures, is not only to repudiate the authority of reason, but to exhibit the vilest spirit of ingratitude. Such ingratitude involves the grossest possible breach of the laws of our spiritual natures, and thus will necessarily involve its penalty in itself. It is an infinitely greater breach of those laws than any violation of those moral relations which bind us to our fellow-men. A breach of either must lead to misery, though we may deaden our sense of it for a time by plunging into the business and amusements of life. Such misery, however, must ultimately overbear all our opiates, and will be intense in proportion to the degree in which the laws of our natures are violated. This we must believe, if we believe the teaching of nature at all. We cannot evade the conclusion except under the assumption either that trust in a Supreme Power will not secure our happiness, which is a contradiction in terms, or else that intense and permanent happiness is not our only object in life, which is inconsistent with every man's personal experience.

The only remaining question, therefore, regards the mode in which such trust in God is to be realised, and this is manifest from what has been already said. It is not to be attained by any direct effort of will, because the will is itself only practically determined in the case of a change of character through the gradual operation of motives. The ordinary condition of man is consciously known to himself as involving separation from God, and, consequently, a want of confidence in Him. This is proved, as we have already seen, in our constant experience. If we be exposed to danger, or subjected to suffering, from which a relation or friend, or indeed any fellow-creature whom we believe attached to us, can relieve us, we are at once full of hope, and generally feel no distrust in them whatever. But if we are exposed to danger or subjected to suffering from which no fellow-creature can relieve us, no one will pretend to say that by an effort of will he can, or that he does, repose the same confidence in his God. In fact, under ordinary circumstances, we repose more confidence even on the aid of a neighbour or acquaintance than on Him whom we call our Creator, our Preserver, our most bountiful Benefactor. Our professed confidence in God, it hence appears, is a matter of only half faith. We have a sort of intellectual conviction of our relationship to Him, but not a felt assurance of His love. Thus it is that the mass of human beings are in a perpetual state of anxiety as to their interests here, and, when they allow themselves to think upon the subject, as to their welfare hereafter. Did they trust thoroughly in God as a matter of feeling as well as a matter of intellect, there could be no such anxiety. How could that man be anxious as to his welfare either in time or in eternity, who knows and feels that the Supreme Being is his Father and his Friend? But we do not know and feel that God is our Father and our Friend, because we do not seek such assurance by the only means which He has provided for procuring it, either with respect to other intelligent creatures or with respect to Himself.

Trust in God, like trust in our fellow-creatures, can only be the result of manifesting our love towards Him in our conduct. This alone can constitute our practical relationship with Him, as it can alone constitute our practical relationship with them. In order to trust in Him, we must therefore be perpetually endeavouring to realise a sense of His presence in every event of life, until we become conscious that in each He is blessing us. As we subdue our selfish desires, and delight more and more in a spirit of love, a trust in Him who is the Framer of the laws of nature will, under the operation of those laws, necessarily grow upon us. We thus feel that we are becoming more and more thoroughly identified with the attributes of God, and more and more thoroughly the objects of His protecting care. Trust in God becomes an essential portion of our mental condition. We learn to trace the action of His providence in the course of our history. We discover all things working for our happiness, under processes so complicated that reason itself proves such results never could have taken place under the ordinary arrangements of providence. We no longer care for the things of the world, save in a very subordinate degree, for their own sakes. We only consider them important as means of improving our moral dispositions, and drawing us nearer and nearer to God. The kind of happiness which we seek is, in so far, altogether changed. We still enjoy the pleasures of life, and even more intensely than before, because they are no longer embittered by fears of that which is to come. Our great happiness, however, is sought within us in the growth of the spirit of love, which we feel to depend on no external thing, but to bless us in itself, and in a perfect union with our Father and our God. This is, it will be perceived, the growing attainment of the unceasing object of our lives. It is heaven begun on earth, and consequently involves in its very nature a foretaste of the glories of eternity.

That all this is absolutely certain as matter of mere abstract reasoning, seems to admit of no dispute. But in truth it is frequently realised in actual life, and to a greater or less extent probably in far more instances than is usually imagined. Whether it can be realised, however, by the mere use of ordinary means, or without a revelation, is a different question, with which here we have no connection whatever. All that we have to determine here is the nature of the relation betwixt God and man as Creator and creature, and the necessary result of that relation, if it be realised; and so far as that is concerned, the argument seems to be complete. The conclusion will admit neither of logical doubt nor difference, if it be admitted that the laws of nature, and the voice of nature speaking in those laws, are to be believed, and ought to be obeyed.

PART II.

ETHICS, OR THE SCIENCE OF MORALS

ETHICS, OR THE SCIENCE OF MORALS.

INTRODUCTION.

THE THEORY OF THE RELATION BETWIXT GOD AND MAN APPLIED TO HUMAN CIRCUMSTANCES—SUBJECT LITTLE UNDERSTOOD—DEFINITION OF ETHICS—THE VARIOUS MORAL THEORIES THAT HAVE BEEN PROPOSED, AND WHY UNSATISFACTORY.

WE have already seen that the grand object of human life is, the attainment of the most intense and permanent happiness which it is possible to realise. This happiness we are engaged in seeking, not now and then, but at every instant. Such is the constitution of our minds, that we cannot for a moment lose sight of it, nor can our attention even for a moment be directed to anything else. We hear in this the voice of nature telling us that such happiness can be procured, for nature must manifestly be a delusion and a lie, if she compel us by a law of our minds to seek perpetually that which is not to be found. It is however true, that different persons follow this object in very different ways. Nor need it be said, when we look around us on the world, that multitudes mistake the means by which happiness, and still more the highest and most permanent happiness, is to be attained. So far it is manifest, even on the most superficial consideration, that happiness must originate either in the gratification of selfishness, or in the enjoyment derivable from realising and reciprocating a spirit of love. THERE IS INDEED NO OTHER SOURCE OF HAPPINESS POSSIBLE.

Now, in our present condition, those two sources of happiness, selfishness and love, are perpetually contending against each other. Each of them has a certain power over the human mind, but each strives to gain the victory; and it is indisputably true, that under ordinary circumstances selfishness has the advantage. The process under which this usually occurs has been described in a former chapter. Still the spirit of love is not wholly eradicated. A certain amount of affection towards relatives and friends, in whom we put confidence, is left to exercise an influence. We find this exhibited even among the most degraded and worthless of our race. It is indeed essential to any measure of happiness that we should love and be loved, so that the very lowest forms of selfishness do not imply a wish that love should cease. To love and to be loved more or less by those on whom we depend, or at least to believe that we so love and are loved, seems essential to the very endurance of existence. Yet mutual love, to the very limited extent which could thus be generated, would hardly serve the purposes of individuals, or be sufficient to keep society together. Hence many directly or indirectly profess a kindness to their fellow-creatures which they do not really feel, or at all events do not feel to the extent that they profess it. Nor is this in every case hypocrisy. In many instances it is a sort of self-deception, resulting from the power which a sense of self-interest exercises in concealing from human beings the operations and condition of their own minds. In this way there is an artificial morality generated, which serves the purpose of founding hollow friendships, and thus binding society together by ties which, though weak in themselves, are yet sufficiently strong to prevent it from falling altogether in pieces.

Now there is no denying, however unsatisfactory it may appear, and the cause of it will be explained in detail afterwards, that this is the moral condition in which human beings usually exist, *and constitutes almost the only morality by which a multitude of them are influenced.* Yet people feel that the very necessity of thus substituting false professions of love in the place of real love, for the purpose of holding society together, proves, apart from all other considerations, that there is something wrong and anomalous about the moral condition of our race. They have it pressed on them, as manifest from the very character of the fact, that a manner of life cannot be conformable to the laws of nature which makes the relations in which we stand to our fellow-creatures a mockery, and the realisation of those relations a living lie. Thus there is necessarily impressed upon the human mind a tendency to seek some higher morality, by which the laws of nature may be reconciled among themselves, and that truth and consistency established amongst them, with respect to the relations of intelligent beings, by which they are distinguished in regard to the relations of physical things.

We arrive at the same conclusion, moreover, by another and equally convincing process. Men, as we have seen, quickly discover that mere selfish pleasures are in no way sufficient for realising our desire of permanent and intense happiness. Our enjoyment derived from them is not only of short duration, but after a brief indulgence becomes less and less in degree. Depending on external causes, they are farther liable to many contingencies. Accident, sickness, the death of friends, may not only modify the gratification which selfish pleasures afford, but may sweep it away altogether. The happiness generated by a spirit of love, on the contrary, depends on no external cause, but consists in the disposition of our minds, and therefore cannot be taken away. It grows, indeed, as we suffer and are afflicted under a process already outlined, *till it becomes a character*. As the disposition, moreover, increases in degree, the happiness augments in intensity; nor is there almost any limit, so far as we can discover, by which it is to be circumscribed. The conclusion, therefore, irresistibly follows, that there must be means under which this disposition or character may be fostered, so as to give it the control of selfishness. This is the only mode under which that which we feel to be the unceasing end and object of our natures can be realised. It is not, however, therein implied that our selfish enjoyments are to be repudiated, but only that they are to be indulged under subordination to the spirit of love, that thus they may be intensified in their combination with higher gratifications, *and a character formed* implying in itself a happiness which, as depending on no external thing, contingencies cannot modify, nor circumstances impair.

All this has been already indicated under our argument for the moral attributes of God, which, it will be perceived, is intimately connected, or rather interwoven, with the present subject. The moral attributes of God are indeed mainly proved from the moral condition of man, who, having been placed in this world with an unceasing desire for intense and permanent happiness, comes to find from experience that there can be no approximation to such happiness unless it be in a moral excellence uniting us through the spirit of love with our fellow-creatures and our God. Keeping this in view, as connected with the preliminary remarks contained in this chapter, we define moral or ethical science to be "the science which teaches intelligent beings the laws that must regulate their feelings, and through those feelings their conduct, so as to secure their own highest happiness, as well as the highest happiness of others."

The definition indicates the immense importance of the subject; and yet we may venture to say that there is no subject less understood,—at all events, in so far as its principles are concerned. No doubt some sort of a moral system is professed by all men, but nothing can be more unsatisfactory than such systems usually are; and indeed there is not one of them to which grave objections may not be taken, or which will in any full degree explain the phenomena. In fact, this science of ethics is in such a state of confusion, in so far as its principles are concerned, as hardly to leave a claim to it of deserving the name of a science. Of this every one may readily satisfy himself, who thinks it worth while to investigate the grounds on which moral principles are at present rested, and the obligations under which they are held to be enforced.

Nor is it almost possible to over-estimate the disastrous consequences of such a condition of things, especially in the present state of society. We attribute to it not a little of the immorality and irreligion of the present age. It is indeed true, that even where the philosophy of a science is unknown, necessity may compel some practical observance of its details. It is, however, equally true that when men *have discovered* their ignorance of its philosophy, such observance will be comparatively imperfect and desultory; and this must specially be the case with respect to a science which has less regard to external acts than to the state of mind in which such acts have their origin, and where, consequently, the obligation to a practical observance of its details *must depend in a great measure on a clear apprehension of its principles.* Hence we have perhaps the primary cause of the unsatisfactory character of these various systems of ethics which have hitherto been proposed. From a misapprehension of the nature of moral science, they look rather to external acts than to the state of mind which generates them. They give us rules of conduct rather than determine what ought to be our feelings, apart from which our mere acts neither fulfil the moral law, nor consequently realise the object on account of which the moral law has been prescribed to us. This will appear by an investigation of the character of those systems, the principles of which we shall endeavour as clearly as possible to ascertain and explain.

Among the ancients, morality never assumed anything like the character of a true science, because their religious theories involved considerations absolutely inconsistent with their moral speculations. There was truth, no doubt, in the moral theories of all the Greek spiritual philosophers, Platonists, Peripatetics, Stoics, and even Epicureans; but their ignorance of the relations of the Supreme Being to man prevented the possibility of their discovering how these theories— or rather that theory, for it was very much the same in essence—could be practically realised. Hence an additional reason for the superiority of moral theories since the publication of Christianity, though none of them has made our knowledge of the relation betwixt God and man suggested to us by Christianity sufficiently available, as will appear from our subsequent argument.

The Jews, indeed, among the ancients, had the details of a moral system singularly excellent for their special circumstances, and no doubt a system resting on perfect principles might have been deduced from the theory of the Jewish dispensation. This, however, was never done. The Jews rested the obligation of their moral law on revealed command, *as enforced by immediate penalties.* They were consequently at all times liable to error, even with respect to the details of morality, whenever questions arose which the revealed law had not precisely determined.

The heathen, however, were in a much worse position. They were conscious of the necessity of some kind of morality as essential to the welfare, if not the very existence, of human society. But they had no correct idea even of its details, and still less any clear notion of its principles, as having no conception of the real grounds of its obligation. The Jews, as we have said, rested their morality on the commands of God revealed in His word, and enforced by immediate penalties in case of disobedience. But the heathen had no such revelation, and their knowledge of natural religion was too limited to enable them accurately to determine either the details or the principles of morality for themselves.

Since the publication of Christianity, the details of morality, using the word in a general sense, have been better understood than they were even by the Jews; because Christianity has given us broader moral precepts, and these have been more or less borrowed from it, even by the very persons who have questioned its authority. But Christianity, while it gives us broader and more general precepts of moralty, and indicates unmistakably the principles on which they rest, instead of appealing to authority, has appealed to *natural religion* for their truth, and for a determination of the primary grounds of their obligation. Indeed, Christianity rests its claim to divine authority in no small measure on the perfect uniformity of its moral system with the conclusions which natural religion—or, in other words, enlightened reason—enables us to ascertain. It has thus left us—assisted, no doubt, by the doctrines which the Gospel has revealed—to work out the great problem which concerns the foundation of morals for ourselves. Hence the wide differences which still prevail even among Christians, both as to the motives sanctioning morality and the primary grounds of its obligation.

The lowest form of an ethical theory is that which rests the obligations of morality on selfishness. The necessity of assisting and benefiting others for the sake of securing their assistance and support for ourselves, is discovered, we are told, from the position which human beings occupy in the world. According to this theory, there is no such feeling as love or affection towards any of our fellow-creatures, and therefore all expression of such love and affection must be regarded as falsehood and hypocrisy. Morality is therefore merely another name for utility; and hence the system, if system it can be called, is denominated utilitarianism. There is no such emotion as we imagine binds a mother to her child, a brother to a sister, or a friend to a friend.

It is almost unnecessary to say that this is directly inconsistent with human feeling, which becomes more manifest from the consideration that a mere prospect of utility could have no effect whatever in generating a feeling of love or affection. A man may load us with gifts, and yet if we believe that they are bestowed from selfish and interested motives, we shall realise none of that love towards him which we feel towards those who can be of no worldly use to us whatever, but by whom we believe our love to be reciprocated.

It is farther of consequence to observe, because it has been singularly overlooked, that the theory of selfishness is in its very form impossible and self-contradictory. For as all profess to entertain feelings of affection and kindness towards each other, the theory implies that we attempt to cheat each other into acts of mutual utility by pretending to a feeling to which, under the assumption, *none of us could attach any sense whatever.** The expression of the theory manifestly involves the existence of this very feeling which it professes to deny. If there be such a feeling as love, affection, or benevolence in the human mind, *to however small an extent it may exist,* then this theory

---

* Although it is manifestly certain that this could not be the case unless both parties had *some* consciousness of the feeling to which one of them pretended, yet it is true that many make the consciousness of this feeling available for *pretending to a much greater love than they actually realise.* Hence the origin of hypocrisy, which being the means that we use to secure the love of others by pretending to a false measure of love for them, frequently becomes a tendency, which ultimately *unconsciously* influences us.

of selfishness is at an end. If there be no such feeling, then the word *can have no meaning*, and *the use of it could convey no idea.*

A theory, indeed, which makes human beings pretend to be actuated by a feeling which no human being ever did, or will, or can feel, and assumes that others may be induced to believe themselves actuated by such a feeling, is so manifestly absurd, that it never could have been proposed, had it not been necessary as part of a broader system. It is in truth an essential portion of the grossest form of materialism. Under such a form of materialism there can be no mutual love. For, that material mechanism, in the only sense which we can attach to the word material, could work forth *absolute* thoughts and emotions, is indeed a monstrous hypothesis; but that it should work forth feelings *connecting us relatively with others in a spirit of love*, so that we feel actual happiness in their happiness, and actual suffering in their sorrow, implies an extravagance of hypothesis which is repudiated even by the grossest materialists from their sense of its utter impossibility. There is, indeed, in this constitution of indirect relationships, such an evident exhibition of spiritual design and intelligent purpose, that to attribute it to any cause except intelligence, is felt too strongly to violate every principle of reason for any sane man to assert it. Hence the theory of selfishness or utilitarianism, and hence its adoption as a matter of necessity by all who avow the grossest form of materialism.

It has already been demonstrated, however, that the grossest form of materialism is not only to us impossible, but that to us the very terms in which it is expressed are unintelligible. Pure utilitarianism, therefore, it will now, we trust, be admitted, is to us an impossible theory also. That men are influenced by a spirit of selfishness to a large extent, is indeed too true; but that they are also influenced by a spirit of love, is as certain as that they exist. A conviction of this is interwoven with the whole character and conditions and habits of human life. It is as surely though less deeply stamped on the heart of the ruffian and the murderer, as on that of the fond mother and the affectionate child. The very selfish philosopher himself repudiates the selfish theory in practice and in private life, for he feels that of all curses the practical realisation of his own theory would be the greatest, leaving him a sad and solitary outcast, without a friend, without a relation, and without a God.

There is another form of this theory, which, rejecting the character of a mere system of utilitarianism, and admitting the existence of mutual feelings of love, tests morality by its effect in generating the highest happiness, under the assumption that men are benevolent as well as selfish. This theory, therefore, assumes the exist-tence of moral feelings in the human mind, and concludes that the highest happiness results from gratifying both social and selfish propensities, thus combining the theory of utilitarianism, which all admit to be in so far true, with the additional assumption of moral tendencies. The only difference betwixt this theory and that of utilitarianism is the introduction of the new element of mutual love, which also expresses a still further amount of truth, and gives the theory a plausibility which mere utilitarianism could never realise. Although true, however, so far as it goes, the theory is yet so deficient as human beings actually exist, that by a circuituous process it brings us back nearly to the purely selfish theory again, whenever its influence begins to be of *some practical importance*. For selfishness, or a desire of our own personal gratification, is so much stronger than our benevolent or moral feelings, while the argument is limited to the relationship of human beings among themselves, that *without some additional motive* these last are superseded, if not crushed, whenever our personal interests or passions are fairly brought into competition with them. In other words, as human beings actually exist, our benevolent or moral feelings are never strong enough to vindicate themselves, except where they are so interwoven with our selfishness, that we cannot violate the one without sacrificing the other. The cause of this manifestly lies in the fact that we do not love our fellow-creatures as we love ourselves; and consequently, whenever the promotion of their happiness counteracts the gratification of our own desires, *unless some other motive be brought to bear,* their happiness is necessarily sacrificed to what we believe, whether truly or falsely, to be our own. Our moral feelings, therefore, will be sufficient to keep us right, up to the point that they do not seriously interfere with our own desires, or what we believe to be our worldly interests, but beyond that they must be swept away under the action of the stronger power which is brought to bear upon us.

Whenever any one appears, therefore, to restrain himself beyond these bounds, *unless there be some other motive influencing him,* it must, according to this theory, be an act of hypocrisy; because, according to it, the love of others could only be an operative motive, so far as it did not interfere with what we believe to be a higher happiness. In this way a man would not appropriate the property of another, when, in addition to the pain which he might feel in injuring his fellow-creature, there was such a risk of detection as might expose his prospective interests to serious detriment. But, on the other hand, if he had the means of appropriating a large amount belonging to another, without risk of detection, he would under this theory be *morally bound* to avail himself of the opportunity, supposing him to expect more happiness from the possession of the property, than he would suffer pain from the injury which he had done to his fellow-creature. In like manner, a man who, in addition to the pain which he might inflict on a fellow-creature, foresaw imminent danger of personal loss and suffering to himself, would in any given case be induced to restrain his licentious passions. But if he foresaw little or no risk of ulterior loss or suffering to himself, it would be his *moral duty*, under this theory, to act as a seducer whenever his passions vehemently impelled him; and this just to the extent that his hope of immediate gratification should overbalance any pain which might arise from the possible injury that might be sustained by his intended victim.

Even under this modified theory of selfishness, therefore, it is evident, as has been said, that apparent self-restraint could only be hypocrisy, where a man believed that from any act which he had it in his power to realise he could derive greater happiness than he would suffer pain by refraining from realising it. He must inevitably in such a case be determined to self-restraint by the foresight of some evil consequence specially known to himself.

As men actually exist, this is practically, therefore, almost as much a selfish theory as the former. Yet, as has been said, it is theoretically nearer the truth, as admitting the element of mutual love, which the purely selfish theory repudiates, and which a materialist can never possibly allow. It is therefore also deficient, though in a lesser degree, as requiring still a farther element to give it efficient practical power. Deficient as it undoubtedly is, however, experience too truly proves that it is practically the *main* theory which, consciously or unconsciously, regulates the conduct of a great proportion of the human race. We say the main theory, because that all men are further influenced by another principle will be found to be certain, although it is too often unconsciously, and to a very limited extent.

It is only necessary to add, that this theory is further deficient, as being altogether incapable, *even were it fully realised by men loving their fellow-creatures as they love themselves*, of procuring us that intense and permanent happiness which is the great object of our lives. *It cannot, therefore, be true to the laws of nature in their full import.* This subject, however, will be subsequently illustrated in detail.

There is still another form of the selfish theory proposed, which originates in very different causes. It is the theory of Paley, who considers "everlasting happiness" to be the motive inducing men to be virtuous. Now we shall subseqently show that in a certain sense this is true, but it is not true under the sense in which the words are employed by Paley; for Paley means by "everlasting happiness" some form of *arbitrary* happiness to be realised in a future state of existence. Hence, while he investigates the comparative utility of actions as bearing on the general welfare, he strangely enough disregards our *present* spiritual happiness as a motive altogether. In fact, he does not consider morality to consist in a state of feeling, but in acts exclusively. He expressly defines virtue to be "the *doing* good to mankind, in obedience to the will of God, and for the sake of everlasting happiness." Paley's moral philosophy, consequently, is not really moral philosophy, but a system of casuistry nearly allied to jurisprudence, and which, though generally laying down true rules, yet rests on no definite principles. After innumerable distinctions, and divisions, and subdivisions, and limitations of subdivisions, it degenerates into a mere investigation of the particulars which, on the whole, are best calculated to promote or to injure the temporal interests of mankind. In this investigation there is much acuteness displayed, but even as a system of casuistry, which he confuses with moral philosophy, it is exceedingly imperfect. There is the absurdity further involved in this theory, that every act would be immoral, *even when proceeding from the moral principle of love*, unless it were done for the sake of an arbitrary "happiness."

Now this is subverting the principles of morality. It is absolutely reversing the truth, for if morality do not originate in the spirit of love, it must originate in the spirit of selfishness. We have here something worse, therefore, than a confusion of principles—we have practically a denial of the feeling of love altogether as the motive of moral conduct, and a substitution of selfishness in its place. Our intense and permanent happiness would be the result of external and arbitrary, instead of internal and essential, causes. Morality would thus be the law of an inferior being, not of the Supreme God, whose laws, originating in the arrangements of perfect wisdom, must be such as necessarily to vindicate themselves.

It is not, moreover, the least objectionable peculiarity of this theory, that while it mainly rests on Christianity as teaching us "the will of God," and assuring us of "a future state of rewards and punishments," it yet substantially cuts up the most important evidences of Christianity at the roots. For the evidences of Christianity mainly consist in the identity of its moral system with the morality taught by natural religion. But if morality itself can only be known from Christianity, and its effective motive can only be discovered there, then it follows that the appeal which Christianity makes to its morality in evidence of its truth, must be merely an argument in a circle, and the whole weight of what are usually called the internal evidences of Christianity is annihilated.

Farther, if we have no feeling of moral approbation, which it is impossible that we can have if our only motive to morality arise from the prospect of arbitrary future happiness, then it is difficult to conceive how we can prove the moral attributes of the Supreme Being at all. We must in such a case assume that we are created in a moral condition different from the moral nature of the Supreme Being, and under such an assumption a mass of difficulties crowd in upon us, not only with respect to the moral attributes of God, but with respect to God's relation to man, which there seems no means of obviating. Granting, as Paley maintains in his 'Natural Theology,' that "in a vast plurality of instances, in which contrivance is perceived, the design of the contrivance is beneficial," this would not prove the moral attributes of God. It would not even prove Him to be perfectly benevolent; for it is perfectly certain, as matter of experience, that however much happiness there may be in our world, there is also an enormous amount of suffering, while such suffering falls not unfrequently upon those who seem least to deserve it. Such an argument, therefore, assuming the omnipotence of God, can only prove His benevolence to the extent that the happiness existing in the world may exceed the misery. Apart, however, from the pleasure derivable from the consciousness and exercise of moral feeling, to which Paley does not even allude in this chapter on the goodness of God, it is a very questionable matter whether happiness or misery in this world will be found to preponderate. During the great proportion of life, apart from moral feeling, men seem rather to endure existence than anything else. The rest of our lives, in a large number of cases, may be pretty equally divided between trouble and enjoyment.

In one word, Paley's theory of morals is in principle very nearly identical with that of the Mohammedans, and hence a Mohammedan *would not object to his definition of virtue.* They recommend strict morality in this world, on the ground that it will lead to the most exquisite sensual enjoyment in the world to come, and thus actually deteriorate moral feeling by resting it on a false principle. They thereby fix the attention on an immoral, or at all events a mere physical, enjoyment hereafter, and thus necessarily detract from the excellence and inherent blessedness of the disposition which is to procure it; or rather they make morality consist in the mere act, and thus annihilate the inherent excellence and blessedness of the disposition altogether. Paley in like manner recommends morality on the ground that it will lead to some arbitrary enjoyment hereafter, *without telling us of what kind*, and thus his theory would weaken morality by withdrawing attention from that spirit of love which constitutes the essence of morality, and the true source of the highest human happiness, *wherever we may be*, and consequently would not only subvert the evidences, but directly contradict the principles, of Christianity.

Whilst, however, these theories attributing the origin of morality to selfishness are thus manifestly insufficient and unsatisfactory, it is not to be supposed that any of them is entirely devoid of truth. There can be no doubt that even selfishness, in the grossest sense, often procures its gratification through the observance of moral conduct; and it is certain that, apart from any kind of practical morality, human society could not be held together. The lowest theory of selfishness would therefore, to a certain extent, explain the phenomena of the moral world. Men would soon discover from experience that they could not exist even as a race, or at all events that they could only exist as wild beasts, keeping away from each other as much as possible, without some kind of morality. But it would be a morality limited by the narrowest bounds; and it seems very doubtful if, under a purely selfish system, mothers could even be induced for years to nourish and care for their children. What might be true of creatures regulated by unintelligent instinct, would by no means necessarily hold good with respect to beings, among whom instinct is superseded by a cold and utterly selfish intelligence. In the case of intelligent beings nothing save a feeling of the most devoted love, interwoven with a sense of duty, can account for such a phenomenon. At all events, there could be no mutual kindness among human beings, no truth, no real sociality even, or common sympathy, since it would be felt that every sort of friendly communication was a mere form of hypocrisy, and that there was only needed sufficient temptation and opportunity for individuals to plunder, defraud, and, if it could serve their purpose, to murder one another.

No doubt, the theory of a certain degree of mutual love combined with selfishness constitutes a wide step in advance. It implies a certain measure of common sympathy and mutual confidence, but in the actual condition of our race there would still be a great deficiency of motive. The power of selfishness would still overbear the influence of love, and no possible means could exist under which the harmony of the spiritual laws of our natures could be organised, or the grand object of our aspiration in the attainment of intense and permanent happiness could be secured and realised.

If, again, this demi-selfish theory were still farther modified as in that of Paley, so that morality were made to depend on authoritative laws sanctioned by the assurance of arbitrary rewards and punishments in a future life, it would no doubt still more effectually tell upon human conduct. But the principle would be equally wanting. It would in thus far be the selfish and not the benevolent tendency of our natures which would be strengthened. It would not, therefore, be a really higher morality which would be generated, but a series of external acts *imitating its results*. This is indeed the moral theory, and the moral condition, as has been indicated, of a great proportion even of the Christian world. We know it in our practical experience. As we have seen, it is literally the theory of Mohammedanism somewhat purified of its grossness. It implies an utter misconception of the true theory of morals.

The theory which approximates most closely to those now considered, is that of Adam Smith in his able and interesting work on the 'Theory of Moral Sentiments.' It may be expressed in a few words. Smith thinks that our love for others is not an absolute state of mind at all, but originated in our imagining other people's position to be our own, and thus sympathising with them, as if their joys were actually our joys, and their sufferings actually our sufferings. Sympathy, according to this theory, is a kind of delusion, under which for the time we unconsciously identify ourselves with others. Love thus becomes a sort of imaginary selfishness. It is indirectly a feeling for ourselves. Consequently, when we sympathise with and do good to others, we are really in imagination feeling for and doing good to ourselves. This form of selfishness is altogether different from that which is implied in any of the theories formerly mentioned. If we do and must, from the constitution of our natures, sympathise with and feel for others, the mode in which such sympathy or feeling originates is of little consequence. Indeed, to feel with and for others, as if they were in some sense a portion of our own personal existence, appears to identify them with ourselves almost by a closer connection than if we felt with and for them absolutely and directly.

Nor can there be any doubt that to a certain extent the theory is true. The transference, as it were, of other people's feelings to ourselves, is a phenomenon of which we are all occasionally conscious. It is scarcely possible, for example, to see a disgusting sore on another without feeling some uneasiness in the same part of our own bodies as is affected in theirs. In like manner, we cannot look upon a fellow-creature crawling with vermin without exhibiting a sort of imaginative sense of their transference to ourselves. We mention these as examples of which almost every one has had experience, but there are many similar cases, of which we are more or less conscious, as we observe more or less carefully the nature and modifications of our states of mind. But though this theory be also to a certain extent true, yet, like those which we have previously examined, it does not express the whole truth, nor does it touch at all the great principle of moral obligation. The very measure, indeed, in which we sympathise with others, demonstrates the imperfection of the theory, since our sympathies are not the same, *even under the same circumstances*, with respect to every individual, but are modified according to the degree of kindness or affection which we feel towards the individual whose condition has called them into exercise. This consideration, which is attested by universal experience, is of itself fatal to the completeness of Smith's theory. For as our sympathy with others, according to this theory, is really a feeling for ourselves, and has nothing to do with the character or relationship of the parties towards whom it is felt, so it manifestly must be measured by the intensity of pleasure or pain which we believe them to realise in each instance, and could neither be increased nor diminished by any other cause. If indeed we were to assume that it was increased or diminished by any other cause, then that cause would necessarily constitute a new element introduced into the theory. As, however, the phenomenon cannot be explained without the assumption of another cause, it follows beyond question, that there must be a moral feeling, or, in other words, a principle of love, existing in the mind *antecedently to any sympathy which may be generated by a transference of other people's feelings to ourselves,* which such sympathy, so far as it exists, only strengthens and vivifies. Thus it becomes stronger just in proportion to the increased degree of affection which we bear towards those with whom we sympathise. This is an *experimentum crucis* if the facts be conceded, and they are too simple and notorious to admit of being denied.

Smith's theory, consequently, can only be partially true, so that we are left once more as ignorant of the primary principles of morality as ever. Nor is it to be overlooked that he has himself felt so strongly the imperfection of his theory, that in various instances, though probably unconscious of it, he has changed his ground. He again and again appeals to general rules of morality, and to moral faculties as implanted in us by the Deity, regarding sympathy in such cases as a mere measure of the extent to which we realise those rules and obey those faculties. At this point, however, his opinions become so confused and complicated, that it is impossible clearly to understand his principles; nor is it necessary to attempt investigating them farther, because each particular which he thus introduces as supplementary to his theory is more fully developed by other writers.

The next theory of morals which presents itself for our consideration is that which assumes a mental power or faculty, usually called "conscience," or "the moral sense," which sanctions that which is right, and condemns that which is wrong. Now, that there is no such power or faculty determining the nature of our *actions*, does not need any proof. It is a conclusion perfectly certain from the notorious fact, undisputed and undisputable, that actions are neither right nor wrong in themselves, but are right or wrong according to the character of the feelings which generate them. Hence the same action may be right in one case and wrong in another. Right, indeed, simply means a feeling that involves *happiness in itself*, and is therefore conformable to the spiritual laws of our natures. Wrong is a feeling that involves *suffering in itself*, however many incidental pleasures may coexist with it, so as for the time to conceal such suffering even from ourselves, and is therefore inconsistent with the spiritual laws of our natures. Right and wrong, therefore, are terms which, strictly speaking, are not applicable to actions at all, but to our feelings and intentions only.

When, therefore, it is said that there is a faculty teaching us what feelings are right and what feelings wrong, it must be meant that this "conscience" or "moral sense" is something in addition to the pleasure or pain involved in the feelings themselves, and indicating their rightness or wrongness—*i. e.*, their conformity to, or inconsistency with, the spiritual laws of our natures—by some wholly different process. But unless this "conscience" or "moral sense" be confused with intelligence, it is extremely difficult to conceive what it means, or how it is to be discovered. If we speak of the sense of sight or hearing, and of the faculties of perception, or memory, or reason, and of the emotions of gratitude or sympathy, every one immediately realises corresponding ideas. But when we speak of the faculty of "conscience" or a "moral sense," except in so far as we are conscious of certain feelings blessing us in themselves, and certain others implying suffering in themselves, we not only have no corresponding idea, but we have no precise notion of the results with which such faculty is said to make us acquainted.

It is argued, indeed, that the existence of such a faculty is proved by a sense of approbation or disapprobation which invariably accompanies its exercise. The assumption is founded on a mistake. There is no sense of approbation or disapprobation, though there may be a sense of pleasure or pain, in any *absolute* state of mind whatsoever. It is the moral effort which a man puts forth for the purpose of realising that which he believes to be right or conformable to the higher spiritual laws of his nature, which is the object of our approbation; and the cowardly yielding to selfish desire in respect of that which he believes to be wrong, or inconsistent with the higher spiritual laws of his nature, which is the object of our disapprobation. Hence we do not feel any sense of approbation for a kind temper, or a chastity which proceeds from coldness of constitution. We only approve of those who regulate the impetuosity of temper, or control the impulses of irregular desire, under the conviction that in doing so they are obeying the higher spiritual laws of their natures.

In like manner, we do not disapprove of acts, however mischievous they may be, which originate in *irremediable* ignorance of their character and bearing, in so far as the individual committing them is concerned. We only disapprove of them in so far as they are purposely mischievous, or in so far as the person who commits them had, or might have had, the means of knowing their ultimate effects, and the inconsistency of the feelings from which they may have originated with the higher laws of his spiritual nature. Any disapprobation which may be felt in such a case regards, *not the individual,* but the character of the feeling which actuated him as not sufficiently regulated and controlled. It is, in other words, the act, and not the individual, which is condemned. It is therefore manifest, under whatever view we take of the subject, that the theory of "conscience" or "a moral sense" is only true as expressing an *unknown* cause of certain spiritual phenomena, and can consequently never afford any satisfactory explanation either of the principles of morals, or of the obligation under which we are bound to realise them. Accordingly, this theory has neither given us any additional means of distingushing betwixt right and wrong, nor any additional motive for pursuing the one or avoiding the other. It is of no practical value, nor could it consequently be made available for any practical purpose. The hypothesis that there is a faculty which teaches what feelings are right and what wrong is perhaps the only one which, being pure verbiage, conveys no precise information, and involves no absolute truth whatever. The pertinacity with which it has been adhered to by a large proportion of the religious world, has had a great effect in giving currency to the most imperfect but still partially true theories of selfishness.

There is still another theory of morals closely connected with that which we have just considered, and which deserves to be mentioned, because it has derived some character from professing to regard morality as a feeling entirely disinterested. According to this theory, the obligation to morality consists in its constituting "the will of God," and concludes, therefore, that it is to be realised apart from any "hope of reward or fear of punishment." It seems strange that the disciples of this theory do not perceive the inconsistency of its terms. Delight in the exercise of the spirit of love, apart from any personal or selfish gratification, is in itself the most pure and perfect disinterestedness. Mere obedience, apart from any pleasure in obedience, would rather be the virtue, if it could be so called, of an automaton, than of an intelligent being. In the case which we are considering, however, such disinterestedness as is contemplated is impossible in the nature of things. To suppose that obedience to the will of God should not imply happiness or a reward involved in itself, and disobedience suffering or a penalty involved in itself, is to suppose that the laws of God are mere arbitrary arrangements, without any excellence in themselves, or any suitability to the creatures whose conduct He has appointed them to regulate. From this it is obvious that under such a supposition we could have no means of discovering what the will of God is. It has been shown that there is no special faculty which can discover the spiritual laws of God, or, at all events, no faculty which can discover them with such precision as to be practically available. If they do not, therefore, discover themselves by the intense and permanent happiness which they are calculated to generate, it seems evident that we never can discover them at all.

No doubt it may be said, and is usually said by those who hold this theory, that God might discover His spiritual laws to us by revelation. But, besides that, under this assumption, they could only be *binding on those who had received a revelation*, the assumption would in a great measure annihilate the evidence of a revelation itself. For while we are far from desiring to underrate the external evidences for revelation, yet their importance, whatever value we attach to them, must mainly depend on their connection with the internal or moral evidences. In their own place they are perfectly satisfactory, but apart from the internal evidences they would be worthless, since of themselves they could only at the utmost prove wisdom and power. Their validity, as probative of a true, benevolent, and just God, must depend upon their harmonising in themselves, and in their effects, with those attributes of truth, benevolence, and justice, which we know from anterior evidence to appertain to Him, and thus necessarily to originate the laws which He has decreed for the purpose of regulating the feelings and principles of His intelligent creatures.

It is indeed farther said, that as morality, were it universally realised in human conduct, would effect the highest happiness of our race considered as a whole, so this of itself proves that it is "the will of God" that we should cultivate it. But, besides that this introduces a new element, distinct from mere obedience to the will of God, Paley has clearly seen, and strikingly shown, that the highest happiness of the whole *in this world* would neither prove that morality was "the will of God," nor would constitute a sufficient motive for inducing men to cultivate it. On this account, he added, as a motive and obligation to morality in his own system, "happiness in another world," and his error lay in not understanding the nature of that happiness. Instead of regarding it as a happiness involved in the very nature of morality itself, and thus constituting happiness everywhere, he wrote of it as some sort of arbitrary happiness, and thus undermined our proof for the attributes of God on the one hand, and identified his theory with a principle of selfishness on the other. Nor could it be otherwise, since, if the happiness resulting from morality is limited to this world, or to mere arbitrary, and therefore selfish, happiness in another, it is clear that our own personal happiness, and not the spirit of love, must be our great motive, and thus imply the strongest obligation. Consequently, it would follow that any man would, and in a certain sense ought, to secure his own highest happiness, altogether away from any consideration of others, except in so far as their happiness bore upon his own, and this he would be justified in believing to be the "will of God." For the "will of God" can only be ascertained by a determination of the means best calculated to attain the great end of our being, under the circumstances in which we actually exist. As selfishness, however, may be regarded under most

INTRODUCTION.

plausible arguments to be the best means of securing the highest happiness of individuals under the circumstances in which we exist, and without hopes of living in another world, so it would farther follow that selfishness is the true principle of morals, and the true motive and obligation by which our conduct should be regulated. If, again, we add Paley's motive of arbitrary happiness in another world, we *must* conclude, as has been already shown, that the Supreme Being actually proposes selfishness as a motive to morality; and thus the very principle of morality is subverted at its foundations.*

Now, in all these theories of morals, with the exception of that which rests our knowledge of morality on a special faculty, there is a certain amount of absolute truth. Yet, as we have seen, they are all imperfect. No one of them, nor indeed all of them taken together, will explain the phenomena, nor afford us sufficient motives

---

* The selfish theory of morality, under whatever form, has for its motive limited and temporary *pleasure*. The true theory of morality *must* have for its motive intense and permanent *happiness*. The theory which proposes "the greatest happiness of the greatest number" as the principle of morality has no *definite* test, and no motive of any kind, *except in so far as it trenches on one or other of the theories above mentioned*. For there is no desire in the human mind for "the greatest happiness of the greatest number." We may desire the happiness of individuals, or of the whole human race; but to desire the happiness of a *majority*, as a primary feeling, is ridiculous, *for it might in many cases imply the unhappiness of the minority*.

for cultivating moral dispositions. There is clearly something wanting in order to constitute anything like a science of morality. We shall now, therefore, endeavour to ascertain what that something is, so that the fundamental principles of morality may be fully and demonstratively determined.

ETHICS, OR THE SCIENCE OF MORALITY.

CHAPTER I.

SPIRITUAL LAWS OF NATURE.

DIFFERENCE IN CHARACTER BETWIXT THE PHYSICAL AND MORAL LAWS OF NATURE—DIFFERENT KINDS OF HAPPINESS—WE HAVE IN THIS A DISTINCT INDICATION OF THE MODE IN WHICH OUR CONDUCT SHOULD BE REGULATED—IN THE STRUGGLE BETWIXT LOVE AND SELFISHNESS, SELFISHNESS CONQUERS IN THE FIRST INSTANCE—PROCESS DESCRIBED—POWER OF HABIT AND ASSOCIATION—ONLY MODE IN WHICH LOVE CAN BE GENERATED—IT MUST BE STIMULATED AND STRENGTHENED BY THE SAME MEANS AS SELFISHNESS IS STIMULATED AND STRENGTHENED—THE OBJECT CANNOT BE ATTAINED APART FROM RELIGION—THIS PROVES THE TRUTH OF RELIGION, EVEN IF IT HAD NO OTHER PROOF.

THE physical laws of nature, we know, immediately vindicate themselves. They on the instant work out their purpose to the full extent that they are brought into operation. A sufficient force applied to machinery at once puts it in motion, and to the precise extent that the force and the machinery stand related to each other. It is altogether different with respect to spiritual laws.* They do not of necessity vindicate themselves immediately in proportion to their relative importance. Their effect, on the contrary, is modified by the will of the agent, *as well as* by an infinity of incidental motives. These motives originate in the amount of happiness which each individual may suppose at the moment his conduct likely to realise. No doubt it might appear, judging from physical laws, that in this men acted wisely, and that the degree of happiness expected in each instance would constitute a just measure of the importance which nature attaches to the mental state under which each law is realised. This is by no means the case, however, because human beings frequently judge under the influence of impulse and ignorance, as will manifestly appear from a somewhat more careful consideration of the subject.

As we have already seen, the object which all human beings are continually seeking is happiness. We seek literally nothing else at any mo-

---

* That there is such a difference in character betwixt the physical laws of nature and the spiritual laws of nature as that mentioned in the text, cannot be disputed. *It arises from the different characters of the existences to which they apply.* The one is suitable to the nature of inanimate, the other to the nature of the intelligent and moral, beings. *Hence the difference of their sanctions.*

ment of our lives. But, as we have also seen, there are two sources from which happiness may be derived. The one is realised in our own personal gratification exclusively; the other is realised in the love which we feel for others, combined with that which we believe them reciprocally to bear to us, so as to constitute both, as it were, one being in the intimacy of a moral union. Now a desire for these two kinds of happiness exists in our natural feelings, and in such a way that if the gratification of either be extended beyond a particular point, it necessarily comes into collision with the legitimate gratification of the other. Hence in this we have a distinct direction given by nature as to the manner in which our desires in these respects ought to be regulated. At the point of collision they are to be controlled, so that, the one never interfering with the other, we may thus enjoy the unalloyed happiness resulting from both. Did the laws of our spiritual nature immediately and fully indicate themselves as is the case with physical laws, it is obvious that this result would be forced upon us. But in that case human beings could only be a species of automata, without any exercise of free-will. As free-will creatures, however, we soon find that spiritual laws do not immediately vindicate themselves, and that the result in each case is materially modified by the action of that free-will itself which as rational beings we enjoy.

In order to understand the mode under which free-will operates in such cases, we must attend to the gradual development of the spiritual character in man, in connection with the causes which are found to modify that character. Nor is the process difficult. Infants and children are in the first instance invariably selfish, as we know from experience. It must be so, indeed, because they realise the happiness resulting from personal gratification from the first moment of their existence. Everything presses the value of this kind of happiness upon them; while there is nothing to teach them practically the happiness derivable from love. All the care profusely lavished upon a child by the most affectionate mother is necessarily received by the infant *as if it were the result of a physical law*. It could not, indeed, be otherwise, since infants have no means of distinguishing the spiritual qualities of their fellow-creatures from the physical qualities of a machine. The infant never can do this till it feels conscious of its own spiritual qualities, and is thereby led to attribute the same qualities to others by a regular process of reasoning.

Even when the spiritual qualities of others are in so far in this way discovered, it can only in the first instance be very partially. The infant, and even the child during its earlier years, can have no full conception of the motive of a mother's care, and therefore cannot by possibility appreciate it.

Such care must appear to them a mere matter of course, as being utterly ignorant of the anxiety, and weariness, and even suffering, which it involves. Yet at a very early age a child will exhibit some faint reciprocation of a mother's love. This partakes, no doubt, of the selfish element; but yet the element of love can also be discovered clearly enough to preclude any question of its existence. Anything like a high indication of the spirit of love is, however, very rare among children. They, on the contrary, seem to show almost indifference to suffering. This often proceeds from a very imperfect idea of what suffering is. They have themselves never been subjected to suffering, or have forgotten their sufferings, and thus cannot appreciate suffering in others. The very injuries which they inflict with apparently the greatest recklessness upon animals, seem indeed in many instances to be inflicted in a spirit of thoughtlessness, or even of mistaken kindness. But admitting this to the fullest extent, it is certain, from what has been already said, and what is attested by universal experience, that children never come to realise love in a high degree till they learn to appreciate their dependence upon others, and the high degree of love which others manifest towards themselves by experiencing intelligently their care and kindness, and comparing it with the little which they themselves have done in return. After that, as in all other cases, they learn to measure it by its effects; and if their education has been conducted in a spirit of kindness, they usually manifest a warmth of affection such as is not equalled at any other age. This arises from their feelings being as yet in their normal state, and uncorrupted by those causes which, as we shall subsequently show, come to operate deleteriously on their purity.

In thus far, however, we have only considered the case of those who are most favourably circumstanced, for a vast number of children are actually trained to selfishness. When their moral education is not neglected altogether, it is too often a mere form. The effect of this, and specially its bearing on their subsequent characters, cannot be doubted. For when they come to more mature years, and the struggle between the spirit of selfishness and the spirit of love fairly and formally begins, it cannot fail, under such circumstances, that selfishness should gain the victory. Of course, we do not mean to say that love towards our nearest relatives, or those with whom we are in any way intimately connected, may not overrule the grosser forms of selfishness. In our feelings towards them, and all whom we trust, there is real love, but at the same time there is usually a large measure of selfishness combined with such love. Their interests are so interwoven with ours that our mutual welfare depends upon each other. We only mean that selfishness is the ruling principle, and that therefore to our own personal gratifications and personal interests, directly or indirectly, the principle of love is subordinated.

Nor is this wonderful, since, as has been already indicated, men are frequently, if not always, trained in selfishness. They have an example of it in the conduct of all around them, and that growing more and more manifest as, leaving their domestic circles, they mix in the active world, and become acquainted with its ways. They find few in whom they can put confidence, and consequently few that they can love; for without confidence there can be no true love. Sometimes they even find that there are persons possessed of keen worldly intelligence, who violate by treachery and ingratitude the confidence which truth and love had reposed in them. Under such circumstances, suspicion and selfish prudence are almost forced upon those· entering the world, till exclusive attention to our own interests becomes a habit. With this the influence of sensual desire—which, though often incidentally generating noble impulses and acts, is in its own nature essentially selfish—combines to confirm and extend the power of selfishness in a multitude of different directions. All this becomes still farther complicated by new and secondary desires which growing habit produces under the influence of association. For if we accustom ourselves to think of any object which in itself involves neither pleasure nor pain, in constant connection with another which does involve pleasure or pain, the feeling which appertains to the one will by degrees be transferred to the other ; and thus a secondary desire is constituted, which in time may become so strong as to assume all the appearance of one that is primary.*

This process is perhaps in no case more strikingly developed than in the growth of avarice. Avarice is evidently no primary desire of the human mind. No one from any primary desire cares for bills, or bank-notes, or pieces of grey or yellow metal, *for their own sakes.* We seek them *at first* merely as means, through which primary desires may be gratified. But as we continue for a length of time to seek those means without almost thinking of the end, except in so far as the desire involved in it continues steadily to be our impelling motive, that desire gradually connects itself with the means, which thus assume in our minds the place and character of the end, and in this way a new or secondary desire is constituted. This desire ultimately becomes so strong in many instances, that it could not be discriminated from

* It will be obvious that in this there is no new feeling. *There is only a direction of the old feeling to new objects.* The power of association merely transfers the primary feeling which strictly belongs to one object, to another object *that has coexisted with it.* The nature of the process is obvious. Association cannot originate a new feeling absolutely ; the very idea of such a thing is absurd.

a primary desire, save from the consideration that its immediate object affords no gratification of itself, but could only have primarily gratified us as the representative and means of securing an ulterior object or objects of which it has assumed the place through habit and association.

There is another very striking development of the same process in that love of dress which often acquires so much influence over the minds of persons who in their youth are anxious for personal admiration. In the first instance they seek for elegant and expensive dress, only for the purpose of gaining such admiration. The idea of the dress, consequently, is always interwoven with the desire, so that it comes to be connected intimately with the pleasure with which the expected gratification of the desire is contemplated. Hence the pleasure involved in the prospective gratification of the desire continues connected with the dress when the gratification of the desire itself is hopeless. The means through habit and association have, in other words, taken the place of the end; and such persons consequently delight in the dress, when every expectation of personal admiration, and almost every wish for it, has from advancing age or other causes entirely faded away. The primary desire has disappeared, and a secondary desire, growing out of the means which we had used in endeavouring to realise it, has taken its place.

But if habit and association thus generate absolutely new desires and passions,* still greater is their effect in intensifying primary desires and passions. This is specially marked in the growth of that selfishness under its various forms which no doubt exists to a certain extent as a primary condition of the human mind, but which, from being so often uppermost in our thoughts, under the influence of the various causes already enumerated, gradually becomes more intense through the influence of habit and association. So much is this the case, indeed, that, unless carefully guarded against, it ultimately supersedes every other consideration, so that all the links of love which naturally bind us to society are loosed or broken. Thus also by the same means may any primary feeling, desire, or purpose be intensified. We have only to allow any one of them to be perpetually in our thoughts *seeking gratification*, and its influence in time will become overwhelming. It will reach a species of moral insanity, under which every object acquires a new character, being tainted more or less deeply with the colouring which the prevailing feeling, or desire, or purpose affords.

It is precisely in the same way that our desires, consequently, are directed to particular objects. Thus a young man or woman, under the influence of passions appertaining to their age, having their attention directed to an individual of the oppo-

* In the sense of "new" previously stated.

site sex under suitable circumstances, by dwelling on their qualifications in connection with their own feelings, gradually form an attachment, which for the time supersedes all counteracting considerations. Hence it is that difficulties, as in all other cases of desire, add fuel to the flame of sexual love. The effort to overcome the difficulties keeps the parties more incessantly in each other's thoughts, and with a more overbearing impression, so long as there is any hope of success, while the time is prolonged during which the growing passion is either flushed by hope or exasperated by disappointment. The effects of all the arts of flirtation, it is obvious, are, as forms of difficulties, reducible to precisely the same principle. Those who exercise them do, though for the most part very unconsciously, act on the most philosophical principles in thus alternating hope and disappointment. They are stamping their own image on the hearts of their admirers by the most effectual process which they could employ; and if they be cautious in not going too far, so as to bring counteracting principles into operation, they will seldom fail of success, because they are really following the laws of nature. All this is because, the qualifications of the individuals being associated with pleasing prospects and favourable inclinations, these individuals come ultimately through habit and association to be invested with attributes which exist only in the imagination of the admirer, and a happiness is thus anticipated from a union with them, which it is unlikely that even these attributes, if they actually existed, could realise.

In the same way once more, we may by habit and association generate a species of affection for animals, localities, houses, furniture, or anything else. It is unnecessary, however, to dwell at greater length on the application of these principles, because every one has it forced upon his attention in his own experience.

Hence it will be obvious that the conduct of men is frequently regulated by motives in which considerations of their ultimate welfare have little or no share. Long habit and association have in a large number of cases so strengthened one class of desires and weakened another, that there hardly can be a struggle between them. Thus, under the process described, our thoughts become so steadily and continuously fixed on the world, and the gratifications of the world, that we never think of our moral relations at all. Love for others, except in so far as it is a modified form of selfishness, almost ceases to influence us. Now this certainly seems an unnatural state. It makes human beings monsters of one-sidedness, the authority of the higher and nobler part of our nature being swept away. The happiness of persons in this frame of mind becomes purely incidental; of essential happiness flowing from the very condition and character of their minds, they can have no notion whatever.

Under such circumstances there is no possibility of restoring the balance of our natures, and thus attaining in any measure the ultimate purpose of our existence, except *by reversing the process*. We must renovate the spirit of love, in other words, in the same way as we had previously stimulated the spirit of selfishness. No mere act of will can at once change our tendencies. The ambitious man, for example, cannot will effectively and at once to renounce his ambition; nor the sensual man his sensuality; nor the selfish man of any kind his selfishness. By the constitution of the mind, it requires a struggle; and the more deep-seated our habits, the more earnest and continuous must the struggle be. This is the ordinary law of humanity, and in this, consequently, we discover the purpose of God. But to set about realising such an object, requires a sufficient motive. We must feel a want, we must be thoroughly conscious of an evil, ere in earnest we can be induced to seek a remedy. Hence, though such a consciousness may be suggested to us by many causes, yet the most effective of them, as formerly indicated, is to be found in a sense of suffering. It is through suffering specially, as is manifest from the very nature of the case, that the utter insufficiency of selfishness to secure happiness is pressed, and indeed forced upon us. We are thereby taught by the most effectual lesson our own weakness, and our dependence upon others. We are made to feel in our experience the need of sympathy, and from the intuitive assurance in such feeling that sympathy can be procured, we necessarily are induced to call in the aid of reason for the purpose of discovering more precisely the means through which it may to the fullest extent be realised.

Nor is the investigation in this case difficult. All experience teaches us, the moment we direct our attention to the subject, that to secure the love of others *we must ourselves love*. Indeed, our very desire for sympathy seems to generate a principle of love, or rather to vivify the spark of love that lies latent within us; and we are made to feel at once, that in the very consciousness of its existence such consciousness blesses us in itself. Under this influence, steadily realised, it grows and grows in an increasing ratio, as we are made more and more sensible of the blessedness of mutual love resting on mutual confidence. The approbation of our conduct too, both as felt by ourselves and as expressed by others, gives from the beginning an energy to our efforts. We feel that the object which we have in view is higher and nobler than any which we had previously sought. Our very natures become elevated, and the power of selfishness is thus subdued under a reversal of the process by which it had been strengthened.

Yet it is perfectly impossible that our efforts can be successful in realising fully the spirit of love apart from religious considerations, simply because we have no approach to any sufficient motive. It is from overlooking this that all theories of morals are found so unsatisfactory. No doubt, during the season of calamity or suffering, the exquisite sweetness of sympathy, and our consciousness of solitary wretchedness apart from it, will in a great measure for the time subordinate selfishness, and bind us to others by the cords of love, as all have felt in their own experience. But we soon discover that there is much more wanted than the utmost affection of our fellow-creatures can supply. They, at the best, can only very imperfectly remedy our ills, and they can give us no assurance whatever for futurity. Not for a day nor an hour can they secure our health or our welfare. We are conscious of this; we cannot *thoroughly* repose confidence in them. Our sense of dependence demands another co-relative. Our love for them, consequently, cannot be of that intense kind which alone implies *a realisation of the principle of love*, because we do not entirely trust in them. It is perfect trust alone, as we have already seen, and as indeed we all feel in our own experience, which can realise the principle which thus becomes *entire in degree and universal in application.* We can only in an imperfect degree love those whom we do not perfectly trust, because the very want of trust implies not merely our knowledge of their want of power to bless us as we desire to be blessed, but a doubt of our love being fully reciprocated, which must ever be felt with respect to dependent and imperfect creatures. Love, therefore, without any mixture of selfishness, can only be felt in its fulness towards one whom we know to be altogether devoid of selfishness, whom we know to be able to bless us with the most intense and permanent happiness, and in whose willingness so to bless us we repose unlimited confidence. The moment that we realise our relationship to such a being, love *as a principle* necessarily follows, and must consequently embrace every intelligent being in so far as they are not absolutely selfish. We say *absolutely* selfish, because to love any being *as selfish* is impossible, and would imply a contradiction in the nature of things. It would imply love for that which is the opposite of lovable, and consequently is the natural object of abhorrence. Yet for such a being, the man who realises a spirit of love will feel pity mixed with indignation, which is the only form that abhorrence can assume in him who has realised such a character. He cannot hate, for hatred is a painful feeling, and he who has the principle of love thoroughly uniting him to his God can have no spiritual pain. He is blessed in his God, and the nearer, therefore, that he approaches to full spiritual communion with Him, the higher, of course, his happiness rises.

Whether such a state of mind as this can be attained solely through the knowledge which natural religion affords, is, again, an entirely different question. We only desire here to show, under the laws of nature, the only possible mode of procuring intense and permanent happiness. As, however, such happiness is the object of our whole lives, from instant to instant, and from the cradle to the grave, it will not be disputed that it is an object which nature directs us to seek; and that therefore it must be attainable by some means, unless God and nature be purposely deceiving us.

CHAPTER II.

NATURE AND OBLIGATIONS OF MORALITY.

THERE IS IN ALL HUMAN BEINGS A CERTAIN FEELING OF LOVE FOR OTHERS—THIS THE SOURCE OF A HIGH MEASURE OF HAPPINESS FROM THE BEGINNING, WHICH GROWS GREATER AND GREATER — MORALITY ESSENTIAL TO THE EXISTENCE OF OUR RACE—THIS PROVED FROM OUR RELATIONS TO ONE ANOTHER, OUR SENSE OF APPROBATION AND DISAPPROBATION, AND OUR PROSPECT OF A FUTURE LIFE—HOW A SENSE OF RELIGION OPERATES ON THE HUMAN MIND — THE OBLIGATIONS OF AND MOTIVES TO MORALITY DEFINITELY STATED, AS DISCOVERABLE FROM THE PRECEDING CONSIDERATIONS—MODE UNDER WHICH WE DISCOVER RIGHT AND WRONG IN EACH CASE — MODE IN WHICH WE CAN REALISE RIGHT—CONCLUSION.

THAT men have a feeling of mutual love towards each other, under the very constitution of their natures, is manifest from the tendencies and conduct of every human being. We do not speak merely of the love which all feel more or less towards relatives, and those who, as they believe, love them, but of the kindness which all human beings manifest in a certain measure towards those of whom they know nothing, in so far as they do not interfere with the gratification of their own selfishness. Indeed, the very fact that we desire the love of others,* proves that we have the feeling of love in ourselves, *or else we could form no idea of it.* We cannot have any idea of a primary feeling, unless we have actually felt it; and as love is a primary feeling, if it be anything, it follows as a matter of certainty that, unless we felt it ourselves, we could not have the least notion of what it could mean; and that, therefore, to speak about love for others, or their love for us, would be as unintelligible as if we were to describe a new sense, or to imagine a new feeling of any kind.

The desire of being loved further gives us the voice of nature enjoining us to seek love in using the suitable means of procuring it. In other words, it enjoins us to love others, and to realise such love so far as we can in our conduct, under the assurance that this is the only means through which we can procure their love in return. That selfishness must be subordinated to this love, appears not only from our experience that as the power of selfishness is diminished the love of our fellow-creatures towards us is increased, but

---

* It will not be disputed that we delight in the admiration and love even of a stranger. This is the cause of *real* courtesy, and of that desire to oblige which every one feels in the normal state of his nature. No doubt, there may be many other causes in operation, but this principle must be the fundamental motive. Under any other assumption, there neither could be real courtesy, nor a sincere desire to oblige. Admiration in itself necessarily implies a feeling of deference, and deference as necessarily implies a form of respect or love.

specially from the application of the principle to the Supreme Being. We all would wish to secure for ourselves the love of God, and His protection, because we should thus secure everything that we could desire; for all things are His, and He can give them to whomsoever He pleases. That we do not, however, *in earnest* seek His love, is just because in doing so we must entirely subordinate selfishness to the attainment of it. This we know in our knowledge of the nature of God, since it is obviously impossible to conceal one grain of our selfishness from Him who is omniscient, and who therefore knows every process that is in progress in our souls. Yet till we do in earnest seek the love of God and His protection we cannot realise the principle of love in its fulness and its purity, and consequently cannot begin to realise even the first traces of that intense and permanent happiness which we all continually and exclusively seek as the end and perfection of our existence.

The same argument, however, may be stated in another and no less satisfactory form. For it is evident that morality in some shape is essential to the welfare, and even the very existence, of society. If every man considered his fellow-creatures as enemies, whom he was entitled to injure and put to death wherever he could find them, and if every man actually carried this theory into effect wherever he had an opportunity, it will be admitted that society could not exist. We have, therefore, the voice of nature proclaiming the laws of morality in so far. It may be said, indeed, that to restrain ourselves thus far is a mere form of selfishness. This to a certain extent is true, but the principle implies a great deal more. For did we believe that every one, instead of feeling kindness, felt hostility towards his fellow-creatures, and was only restrained from gratifying it by selfish motives, or a sort of tacit paction founded on the necessity of mutual forbearance, which would be precisely the condition of intelligent beings without any spirit of mutual love, the effect on society would be little better. All would require to be perpetually on their guard, since no one could tell when an impulse of passion, or an outburst of hatred, or the influence of personal interest, might induce a breach of paction, and expose people to insult, or injury, or death, without any means of meeting the danger. Society only exists under the mutual conviction that men have naturally a feeling of kindness towards each other, and that so strong as to prevent the chance of its violation, at all events under any ordinary circumstances.

If, again, all human beings were deceivers and liars, so that no one could put any confidence in the assurance or pledge of his neighbour, it is equally manifest as in the former case that human society would be dissolved. Nor would it be much better if truth and faith had no foundation in mutual love, but were only binding as a sort of tacit understanding among men, for the sake of their mutual advantage. Such an understanding could have no foundation in itself on which to rest, and consequently would be violated without scruple whenever our selfish interests might overbear the expectation of advantage to be derived from its observance. When, therefore, we find men, while perfectly aware that they are injuring their selfish interests, yet steadily maintaining truth and good faith even where they are exposed to no risk of discovery, we have a proof that a sense of right is exercising its influence over their minds. They indicate, in fact, thereby, that there is a law of nature requiring them to love their fellow-creatures, which is directly opposed to the law of selfishness, and of higher authority.* No doubt many violate this law, but not without a struggle, or at all events the power of habit and

---

* It may indeed be said that this is not a primary but a secondary feeling, generated by habit and association, inasmuch as men, being trained from infancy to believe that falsehood and treachery will call down upon them the wrath of God, come ultimately to adopt the assumption as a principle. This, however, brings us back to a still more advanced conclusion, since, if a belief in the superintending providence of God be the motive to truth and good faith, it proves, *from whatever source the belief may arise*, that we have got at the true explanation of the phenomenon. The existence of such a belief under the assumption demonstrates its absolute necessity.

association must have become exceedingly strong in an opposite direction ere such a result could have been produced, and even then not without a consciousness that a higher and holier law had been violated. In this, again, we have the voice of nature proclaiming still farther the laws of morality. We say *the laws* of morality, though, strictly speaking, it is only *the law* of love. Deceit and falsehood would be perfectly harmless, or rather there could be no such thing, if they neither directly nor indirectly injured our fellow-creatures.

We arrive at precisely the same conclusion with respect to the superior obligations of the moral law, in the case of such acts as bear more directly on our personal character and condition. He who eats or drinks to excess, not only injures his own worldly happiness to a greater extent than present enjoyment can compensate, but he renders himself an object of contempt and disgust to his fellow-creatures. He as well as they feel that in impairing his mental energies and superseding his mental faculties he is degrading himself, and violating the spiritual laws of his nature. Hence, he and they are conscious that he is doing wrong, for right is acting in conformity with the laws of our spiritual nature, and wrong is violating them. We have here again the voice of nature proclaiming the obligation of moral law, which, as in all other cases, is really the law of love. To wallow in selfish gratifications and indulge in sensual desires would be of little importance in themselves, did they not materially interfere with our capability of realising those relationships by which, under the law of love, we are bound to our fellow-creatures and to our God.

The assurance, however, of morality being a realisation of the laws of our spiritual nature, in practically recognising the superior obligation of the spirit of love, is perfected in that sense of approbation and disapprobation which a successful or unsuccessful struggle against our selfishness respectively generates. Self-approbation is merely a species of happiness, distinguished from other forms of happiness as a sort of elation originating in the feeling of having conquered our selfish tendencies in a moral struggle. There is indeed a sense of elation wherever we succeed in any object in regard to which any serious difficulty has been encountered and overcome. The special peculiarity in the case of moral elation lies in its originating in a success over ourselves, and in opposition to our selfish propensities. It has, consequently, nothing to do with any external result, except in so far as our mental triumph may be vindicated therein. The gratification would be the same, or might even be more intense, where there was no external manifestation of any result whatever. Self-approbation is, therefore, blessed in its own nature as a result of the feeling that we have vindicated the supremacy of the nobler part of our natures, in subjecting their lower and less worthy laws to the higher and more perfect. The voice of nature is, therefore, here specially precise, and in the language which she employs announces emphatically that it is the voice of God.*

But it is not merely self-approbation that we realise from the success of such a struggle. Wherever it is known, it commands the approbation of our fellow-creatures too. We find that they are so created as to sympathise with us, and that, so far as they admit the existence of the struggle and its success, they cannot avoid doing so. Even the lowest and most degraded can in some measure appreciate the grandeur of the moral struggle in

* We have here the grand deficiency of the ancient moralists, whether Platonists, Peripatetics, Stoics, or Epicureans, for they all held the same principle, that *virtue is its own reward.* But they all failed in making good their theory, because they overlooked the necessity of trust in God as the highest virtue and the source of all moral duty. Without trust in God, virtue, though realising much happiness even in its subordinate forms, would not constitute a motive sufficiently strong to control our selfishness, because it would only imply love, and consequently happiness, of a secondary and inferior character. There are hints of the principle to be found in the writings of some of the ancient philosophers, especially of Plato, as if he were dreaming in delight on some conceivable and glorious possibility; but not one of the ancient writers give it even a prominent place in their theories, and no one of modern philosophers, so far as we know, has made even an approach to a full appreciation of it. Yet it lies at the foundation of moral science, which, apart from it, as we have seen, can have no solid foundation at all.

which selfishness is subdued by love. Perhaps, indeed, their own knowledge of themselves increases their admiration. But with them, *while there is yet a spark of rivalry*, selfishness, under the guise of vanity, mingles with their sympathy. Hence we have, in so far as this matter is concerned, the origin of envy and jealousy. Those who are conscious of their own comparative baseness hate while they admire. They consequently attribute all manner of unworthy motives to those whom they feel superior to themselves. They cannot bear the sense of their own comparative degradation. Here, again, surely, we have the voice of nature loudly proclaiming that the moral law, or the law of love, is the law of nature and the law of God.

But whilst we are thus certain that the moral law is of the very essence of our natures, and that the law of love implies a superior obligation to the law of selfishness, yet the power or motives involved in it, we find from experience, would be altogether insufficient to overcome our selfish propensities, were our moral relations limited to those which connect us with our fellow-creatures. Without the prospect of higher happiness flowing from the realisation of a higher relationship, there must be a drop of bitterness mingled in the cup of life, which would poison its sweetness, however exquisite otherwise might be the draught of which, for the time, we were permitted to participate.

Hence there is no desire, however strong, no temporary enjoyment, however delicious, which we would not be prepared to repudiate for the purpose of realising what we believed to be more permanent happiness at a future time. Were every one, indeed, at once to yield to his impulses, our world would be one universal scene of anarchy and confusion. Here then, again, we have the voice of nature telling us what we should do. In giving us an unceasing desire for intense and permanent happiness, it assures us that such intense and permanent happiness is to be found. In compelling us, from the very nature of our condition, to be continually engaged in controlling our present desires for the sake of attaining ulterior and more permanent happiness, it shows us how the object is to be accomplished. Finally, in pressing upon us a sense of our own weakness, and the dependence in which both we and our fellow-creatures incessantly live upon God, it teaches us the quarter to which we are to look in order that this grand object of our existence may be realised, while it assures us that, if we act on the lesson thus given, our efforts will not be in vain.

At the same time, it must be a clear and decided conviction which will induce men to waive present pleasure for the sake of prospective happiness. When the happiness suggested to them is distant, or seems less desirable, present enjoyment exercises a paramount power. Nor is this wonderful, since, apart from religion, there seems no assurance that ulterior objects will ever be realised at all. It is not only that we are not sure of long life, but we cannot be sure of fortune, health, or anything else which belongs to us, even for a single moment. Present gratification must consequently exercise a predominating influence over us in the first instance. When, therefore, any prospective compensation is distant and uncertain, or, above all, *when we do not thoroughly appreciate its excellence,* the influence of such prospective compensation on our feelings must be proportionally diminished. From this we can readily discover the cause or causes of the collision of the spiritual laws of our natures, and hence of the preponderating influence of selfishness, in cases where the phenomena clearly indicate that the spirit of love ought to preponderate. For, away from religion, our assurance of that which *may* happen in futurity is not such as to balance the realisation of present, or the hopes of comparatively early gratification. This also holds true even when religion exercises some influence, but where our religious expectations are vague, in contradiction to a well-defined and eagerly-desired selfish enjoyment, either at the moment in our power, or which we seem to have a certainty of securing at a comparatively early period.

That the influence of religion may be available, consequently, it must in so far, at all events, be practically in operation. We must have actually realised such love of and trust in God as will enable us to engage with earnestness in the struggle against selfishness *strong in the prospect of immediate indulgence.* In this view, we must believe in a future and eternal state of being, where the most intense and permanent happiness of which our natures are susceptible is to be realised. It is, however, impossible availably to believe in this, unless we more or less practically realise a union with God in our *present* state, and rejoice in His love, as, *at this present time*, blessing us with peace. A mere intellectual belief in a future life, resting on indirect evidence, though essential as a foundation, could never give us that trust in God's love which can alone render such belief practically operative, if God in the mean time manifested no spiritual love towards us, however earnestly we might seek Him. The belief that God, though He may at some distant time bless us, yet does not manifest any personal love towards us *now*, would be almost destructive of anything like full practical trust in Him, because it would imply that He was neglecting the relationship which *now* connects us with Him. Accordingly, it would be quite insufficient for enabling us to contend against selfishness rioting in the prospect of immediate gratification. A full practical trust in God, on the contrary, resting on *an actual sense of His presence with us as a father and a friend*, infuses into us a power more than sufficient to control all our selfish propensities.

It is self-evident that it must be so. Experimental trust in an omniscient, omnipotent, and righteous Being must overbear every other influence from the very nature of the case. We have here, therefore, the voice of nature again calling upon us to strive after that love of God, *under a sense of His perpetual presence*, which can alone work out the grand end of our being and the object of our unceasing desire, in assuring us of a growing happiness here, and an ultimately intense and permanent happiness hereafter. In this we have the nature of morality developed, and the obligations to morality completely vindicated. It is, as we have said, once more the voice of nature, and in the voice of nature the command of God, loudly calling on us to realise the spiritual laws connecting us with Himself, as the only possible means under which our spiritual natures can be perfected, or the grand and unceasing desire of our lives can be gratified. It is, in other words, commanding us to live perpetually under a sense of the divine presence, as a means of uniting us with the divine nature, in inducing us to strive continually at the realisation of His will. As in this struggle we feel our union with the divine nature, and our happiness in the assurance of divine love, continually growing, a consciousness of the purpose of our existence being attained becomes more and more fully ascertained. It is heaven begun on earth, involving in itself the assurance that heaven thus begun will be perfected in eternity. It is no reply to this to say that practically such a state of mind never is attained. If such a state of mind is not attained, it is because it is not sought with sufficient earnestness, or not sought in the right way. Nature tells us, and God in nature tells us, that it is attainable, and it is a mere absurdity to argue that they may be deceiving us. *We could not believe it even if it were true.* To us the proposition that God and nature deceive us implies an impossibility.

Morality, therefore, is simply obedience to the spiritual laws of our nature, under which we are related to our fellow-creatures and our God. The obligation to such obedience consequently arises from the happiness which it at once and permanently realises from the very constitution of our minds, and the misery which, on the contrary, disobedience necessarily generates while we continue disobedient. Perhaps it would be still more strictly correct to say that the obligation consists in the fact of laws existing which imply happiness or misery in the very act of observing or violating them, as well as in the consequences resulting from observing or violating them respectively.*

* The motives to morality and the test of morality are co-relative. The test of morality is the realisation of its mo-

That the obligation is not, however, sufficient for enabling us to realise perfect morality *under mere worldly considerations*, we have already seen, and all experience proves. From the very fact of our coming into existence as infants, and thus being necessarily to a greater or less extent trained in selfishness ere we have the means of appreciating the highest motive to morality, it is evident that in our present state it was not intended by nature that it should be so. Connecting this early training, again, with the history of man's subsequent life, it would appear that we cannot perhaps expect to attain entire moral perfection, nor, consequently, a realisation of the most intense happiness, in this present world. It is, on the contrary, beyond all dispute the purpose of nature and of God that we should, *under ordinary circumstances*, be striving after it through our whole lives. The very position which we occupy in this world demonstrates that there is a disturbing element *purposely* introduced into our moral natures. Hence it follows that in determining the difference betwixt right and wrong—or, in other words, in determining what in each instance is conformable to the spiritual laws of our natures—we must call in the aid of reason

---

tives. When we have the test, we have the motive; and when we have the motive, we have the test. The motive to morality, therefore, being a disposition constituting happiness here, and *involving in itself* the assurance of permanent and intense happiness hereafter, the realisation of this disposition is the test of its reality.

for the regulation of our conduct. Nor is it by any means certain that reason will always prove an unerring guide as to the effects of our acts on the welfare of our fellow-creatures, because not only may circumstances deceive us, but prejudice and habit may unconsciously overrule its decisions. We may in all cases, however, attain a sound *general* conclusion even as to our conduct, if we use our reason in a sincere and honest spirit. At this point, however, we strike away from morality in the strictest sense, which regards the mental state only, and therefore we here allude to conduct merely as constituting the means through which such mental state may be attained.

In this view we are bound to *do* in every instance that which we believe to be right, even when that which we believe to be right is unpleasing to us, because it is through our acts mainly, in the first instance, that our states of mind are constituted. No mere act of intellectual will, as we have already seen, can of itself change our tendencies. This can only be effected in any case by a struggle in which we first realise that which we wish to be in act, and then our struggle in act, steadily maintained, will gradually modify our mental tendencies. When a change of mental character is thus effected, the acts suitable thereto will afterwards, of course, follow without a struggle. The struggle is past, and all will now flow on placid and pleasing. This is illustrated in our whole lives under principles already explained. Any tendency may be generated and all counteracting influences subdued, through persevering efforts practically to realise it, *under a conviction that it is for our ultimate and permanent good.* A man who in the first instance dislikes the profession which circumstances have compelled him to adopt, by persevering in the study of it *as essential to the welfare of his future life*, often becomes not only fond of it, but devotes himself to the prosecution of it with such enthusiasm and success as to illustrate it by his discoveries to an extent frequently far exceeding the mass of those who may have at first selected it of their own free will. The very triumph which he has gained over his own inclinations has given him, under a law of nature, a deeper interest in his subject. We have observed examples of this specially in the medical profession, where we have repeatedly known persons who had entered on their medical studies with a certain degree of repugnance, prove the greatest ornaments of that profession in after life.* Instances of the same thing are, however, known to almost every one, as occurring in their own history, or within their personal experience. The principle holds equally true with reference to the subject which we are now discussing. We all love to seek the things of the world, and the pleasures of the

---

* On this subject there are some excellent practical remarks in the 'Autobiography of Sir Benjamin Brodie.'

world, in the first instance, in preference to that happiness which a strict self-control and attention to the moral laws of our being can alone ultimately procure. It is a tendency which is very strong, from causes already mentioned, and can never, consequently, be subdued, save by an earnest endeavour to realise moral sentiment in the strict and persevering performance of practical duty, under a growing assurance of the happiness which it will enable us both at the time and through eternity to secure.

Such an assurance is absolutely essential, as otherwise there are and can be no motives which would induce us to pursue such a line of conduct in good faith. That we may be persuaded to do so, we must be convinced that our efforts at self-control, and at the attainment of moral rectitude, painful as they may be for the time, will yet procure for us an amount of happiness, present and prospective, more than sufficient to compensate for the voluntary repudiation of pleasures and objects within our power, and promising immediate gratification. Now, as was formerly indicated, this can never be assured so long as the gratifications of the present life are all that we *practically* expect. The very supposition of such a thing is felt to be absurd. Even were the kind of happiness which morality ultimately has in view earnestly desired by us, it could hardly be expected that we would sacrifice present pleasures for what, at best, would be only a possibility. The kind of happiness which morality has in view, however, consisting in the realisation of a spirit of love, is by no means desired earnestly by creatures who are all, in the first instance, under the influence of selfishness. It is doubtful, indeed, as has been said, if it really would be desirable to any one, at the expense of a perpetual struggle, and sometimes of a sacrifice of the most intense present pleasures of life, *were this world our only place of abode, and therefore the attainment of perfect love altogether impossible.* It is, indeed, perhaps too much to say that it is even doubtful, since under such an assumption morality would really be a delusion; for such an assumption would imply the falsehood of nature, and consequently distrust in God; and such being the case, there could neither be right nor wrong, the laws of nature themselves being deceptions, and their precepts, therefore, an utter mockery. Hence were the happiness involved in self-approbation our only motive to morality, we do not go too far in saying that under such a theory it would be instantly swept away—weakened as it would be by the conviction of its being merely part of a system of moral fraud—under the hope of gratified passion and the prospect of successful selfishness.

No doubt the approbation of our fellow-creatures would exercise some influence, but it would rather be on our acts than on our principles. Hypocrisy, which is the worst form of immorality, would in almost all cases serve our purpose as well, and in many instances even better, than sincerity. Not unfrequently, moreover, the opinion of the world would rather encourage us in immorality, as in duelling, gaming, sensual indulgence, pandering to popular passions, and even in personal selfishness, *when it proved successful.* The only motive which can effectually induce human beings to seek by persevering self-control the acquisition of a moral character, is trust in an omniscient Being, giving us assurance that by such means we shall realise peace here and glory hereafter. From such a Being no thought can be concealed, and with Him, consequently, no hypocrisy can be available. Apart from this belief and this trust, there could be no such thing as moral sentiment, farther than mere instinctive good feeling might extend. This, however, as we have seen, would go but a very small length in checking the impulses of passion or the influence of selfishness. In a short time, indeed, under the habit of yielding to these, the power of instinctive good feeling would rapidly disappear, as is manifested continually in the history of human life. Men would become the mere slaves of passion and of selfishness, except in so far as they might be coerced by human laws.

That such a result is not realised invariably, arises from some sense of God's presence, and some fear of His judgment, *that still continues to linger in the minds* EVEN OF THE MOST DEPRAVED.

Take this away, and earth would become a species of hell to those that inhabit it. But it cannot be. Every event of life, and every feeling of the mind, force the conviction upon us more or less precisely, that we are dependent, and that there must consequently be some being to whom this conviction of dependence directs us *as its co-relative*. The primary feelings of approbation and disapprobation are thus in a measure sustained, and a kind of real moral sentiment, though rarely of a very practical character, is thus preserved to leaven as it were the community. Were this not the case, our world, as has been said, would become a species of hell, for we should have natures assimilated to those which we ascribe to devils. Every kind expression would be regarded, consequently, more or less as deceit, and every kind act more or less as treachery. Nor would this be without cause, since under such an assumption there could be no good ground for belief in anything whatever. If God and nature were regarded as false, it would be difficult to conceive how phenomena derived from them could be trusted. It is absolutely horrible to think of such a condition of things, and yet such must be the condition of human beings apart from religion.

The moment, however, that this element is introduced, everything changes. Our very sense of self-approbation and disapprobation assumes a new character, when they are known to be no more a mere feeling of happiness or depression, but an immediate reward conferred on us by Him who is the King of kings and the Lord of lords, the Creator, the Preserver, and the Disposer of all that exists. It is in seeking this reward, with all its concomitant blessings, after we have satisfied ourselves that it is to be found, that moral sentiment becomes moral principle, and that a power is generated within us which conquers our passions and absorbs our selfishness. We know ourselves to be under a real government now, of which the laws are enacted by an all-wise and perfectly just Being, and which must therefore, from their very essential perfection, bless those who obey, and curse those who violate them. Under such circumstances, we not only become bound to observe those laws in respect of God himself, but we feel that there is an intimate relationship of which we were previously practically unconscious, constituted betwixt us and our fellow-creatures, as children of the same Almighty Father, and consequently as brethren in the highest sense, towards whom all the duties implied in such a relationship are to be fulfilled. On the fulfilment of such duties indeed, personal as well as social, under trust in the realisation of our primary and grand relationship to Him with whom they all originated, it becomes in the very nature of the case evident to us that true happiness must entirely depend. *Duty and happiness are thus identified.* Our duty is our happiness, and our happiness our duty. The attainment of higher degrees of this mental state thus becomes more and more our great desire, because this mental state, implying a love of duty, can alone spiritually unite us with Him, in whose union with us the assurance of present peace and eternal blessedness is involved. As our trust in God, accordingly, gradually grows, our happiness proportionally increases, because our moral principles are thereby proportionally purified and intensified. The divine authority of moral and religious law becomes in this way additionally evidenced in its results. We know that it is of God, because we now feel God working it out in our consciousness, through a closer and closer union with Himself.

It is under this process that morality assumes, in the strictest sense, the character of a science, for thus its principles develop into a precise and definite form, and its motives exercise the most irresistible influence, inasmuch as it enforces and rewards itself, to every one that endeavours practically to realise it. We feel, in fact, that we are placed in this world as in a state of discipline, for the purpose of preparing ourselves *to occupy a higher position in the scale of creation.* We discover that it is the object of the Supreme Being to train us here to self-control by perpetual trial, and thereby to establish in us, through our own persevering efforts, the principles of self-respect and social love, under subordination to, and in consequence of, our love for and trust in Himself. We thus *acquire a character* identifying us with the moral and intelligent universe, as part of a great whole; and it is a character which we cannot lose, because, acquired under discipline, its essential excellence as blessing those who possess it in itself has been confirmed by personal experience.

This, we have no hesitation in saying, is the only possible theory of morality, except that of selfishness, under which we can neither be bound by any sense of duty, nor determined by any obligation of right or wrong. We have, indeed, apart from trust in God, a certain degree of mutual good feeling and a certain amount of prudence, sufficient, perhaps, to save our race from destroying each other. But beyond these narrow limits, personal gratification would be the only rule of our conduct in reference either to ourselves or others. Whereas the moment that we begin to realise the happiness involved in trust on the Almighty, *as contradistinguished from our condition without it*, there is a principle of delight in the enjoyment of the spirit of love generated, which no sensual passion can ever wholly eradicate, nor any amount of selfishness ever wholly destroy. Apart from the system now developed, we repeat that selfishness is the only theory of morals that can admit even the appearance of being logically defended. All others, be they what they may, either merely give names to unknown causes, or confuse incidents and consequences with principles. Indeed, this is so far true also of the selfish theory; but it has the advantage of appealing to a principle which, though *really the reverse of moral,* yet does serve nearly to account for the *ordinary moral conduct* that is exhibited in human life. A desire for our own personal welfare is undoubtedly an operative principle; and we are all so conscious of this, that it gives a plausibility to the selfish theory to which it is in no measure entitled on its merits; and has left it, indeed, almost the only system in modern times which can be said to possess disciples, or to which any precise value is attached.

It is well that men should understand this, and understand the grounds on which the religious theory and this selfish theory respectively rest. The religious theory is founded on the assumption that God having enacted laws by which human beings are bound in a spirit of love towards their fellow-creatures and Himself, requires those laws to be worked out under a system of discipline which ennobles our natures in preparing them for a higher state of existence. Its proof, as will now be seen, is found in its full and thorough explanation of all the phenomena, putting its evidence on a level with the most perfect philosophical evidence of physical science. This theory thus makes morality a portion of the grand scheme of the universe, harmonising and perfecting that scheme in the spiritual, as all men admit that it is harmonised and perfected in the physical world. The selfish theory, on the other hand, implies a system of absolute confusion and disorganisation. It makes the spiritual universe not only something anomalous, but, in contrast with the physical universe, something ridiculous and monstrous. Indeed, if we were to imagine systems the most entirely antipodes, so as to exhibit the parts of nature mocking each other, it would be the perfect adaptations and organisation of the physical, as compared with the incongruities, inconsistencies, and contradictions of the spiritual world, *assuming the truth of the selfish theory of morality.* But the fact is, that the selfish theory of morality is untenable, not only on the ground now mentioned, but, as we trust has been proved, under whatever aspect it is possible to regard it. It can only, indeed, admit of the appearance of a defence under the supposition that there is no God in whom we can put confidence, no truth in the teaching of nature, and no future state of existence; that consequently, as there can be no happiness here, except by deadening spiritual thought, so when the brief season of life passes away, we descend to the grave, rot, perish, and are forgotten. IF THIS WERE THE CASE, OF ALL DECEPTIONS OUR WORLD WOULD BE THE WORST, AND OF ALL LIES OUR NATURES WOULD BE THE MOST ATROCIOUS.

CHAPTER III.

DETAILS OF MORALITY.

RECAPITULATION—DETAILS OF MORALITY—MORALITY CONSISTS NOT IN ACTS, BUT IN INTENTION AND A STATE OF MIND — ILLUSTRATED—CATEGORIES UNDER WHICH THE DETAILS OF MORALITY ARE COMPREHENDED—LOVE OF OURSELVES—LOVE OF OUR FELLOW-CREATURES—LOVE OF OUR GOD—THERE CAN BE NO SUFFICIENT MOTIVE OR OBLIGATION TO MORALITY APART FROM RELIGION—NATURE OF MORAL LAW ACCORDING TO THIS THEORY, AND MODE OF ITS REALISATION—EFFECT OF THIS REALISATION ON CHARACTER.

WE have now determined the nature and obligations of morality. Morality, we have seen, consists in realising the spiritual laws of our natures, so that each may preserve its proper place, and each particular exist in its own suitable subordination. The obligations of morality result from the effect of such realisation of spiritual law in blessing each individual and the whole of the human race with the highest possible amount of happiness attainable under the natures with which they are constituted. The proof of the obligation is found in the teaching of nature, that such not only will be, but must be, the result; because as we are compelled by the constitution of our natures to seek the highest happiness attainable, there is in this a declaration of nature that we ought to seek it by the most earnest and assiduous use of the means which are in our power. The supposition that nature may be deceiving us, or that reason may be deluding us, we have already shown to be inadmissible, because the teaching of nature and reason is all that we have to trust to in any case; and therefore to disbelieve them practically, is to deny the validity of our faculties, and this evidently involves what to us must imply a contradiction in terms.

This highest happiness which we are to seek, as we have farther seen, must regard our future as well as our present happiness, since our grand object in life is not only to secure intense, but also permanent happiness. Such happiness, however, can neither be assured by anything that we can do, nor by any assistance that we can receive from our fellow-creatures. It must be the gift of the Supreme Being through that trust in Him which is the highest of our moral states, as implying the most intense and permanent happiness in its own enjoyment. Such trust is to be acquired by a perpetual endeavour at fulfilling His laws. This is made manifest from the self-approbation which our efforts for the purpose generate, as well as from the general happiness of our race, which the success of our efforts at fulfilling the spiritual laws of our natures has an invariable tendency to realise. Such efforts, indeed, constitute true practical prayer, through which the moral character is gradually constituted, and without which mere formal prayer would of itself be absolutely worthless. By thus endeavouring to live continually under a sense of God's presence, we bring God every moment more and more into union with our souls. It could not be otherwise, because we are using the means which God has appointed; and in this, accordingly, the principle which ought to rule all our relationships in life acquires practically by degrees an irresistible influence.

The special modes under which this principle is realised, so far as our reason enables us to discover them, constitute the details of morality. It will now, however, be perceived that the character of these details is something very different from what is usually imagined. It is now clear that the assumption of certain external *acts*, as constituting the details of morality, and thence being universally obligatory, is as absurd in theory as it is inconsistent with all experience. This error, into which almost all writers on moral philosophy have fallen, originates in a misconception of the very nature of morality. Morality is a state of mind, and has nothing to do with external acts, except in so far as they may realise such state of mind. This of itself shows that universal rules cannot be laid down with respect to external acts, nor can such acts at all times be obligatory. The very act which might proceed from a spirit of love in one case, might proceed from a spirit of selfishness in another; and the act which in one case might be for the public good, might in another prove detrimental to it.

There can, for example, be no more universal precept than that which commands us not to kill. Yet even this precept must be received under many exceptions. The act which, under one set of circumstances, would be murder, may under other and different circumstances be admissible, or even meritorious,—as in the case of a soldier fighting for his country, or an executioner fulfilling the law. The case may be made even stronger. To us the slaughter by the clans of a former age of those who had previously put to death their clansmen, seems, and is frequently spoken of as, indefensible. Yet the very same thing is sanctioned under the Old Testament dispensation. The Goel or blood-avenger of the Jewish law was simply the nearest relative of a man who had been slain, armed with divine authority to slay the slayer. Nor can there be any doubt that this was perfectly in conformity with the principles of morality. It was the best arrangement that could be made *under the circumstances*. It prevented greater evils. It was the criminal law of a low stage of civilisation.

In the same way amongst us, the purity of the female character is perhaps, of all other things, the most essential to human happiness. Yet amongst the Jews, polygamy, concubinage, and divorce were, if not formally sanctioned, at all events permitted; and again we say there can be no doubt that it was perfectly in conformity with the principles of morality. To understand this, it must be observed that marriage and concubinage amongst the Jews meant substantially the same thing. Concubines were wives, the families of whom were deprived of some of the privileges of succession. These concubines were persons of inferior rank, frequently slaves. That such persons should be bound by legal ties to a husband, was evidently conducive to the interests of society. Morally, therefore, the arrangement was right; for the object of morality is not, as we have seen, any external act or condition in itself, but the realisation of such acts or conditions as may promote the highest welfare of society physically and spiritually. To have left the inferior class of females, and especially slaves, subjected to the brutality of men in a low state of civilisation, would have degraded both them and their families infinitely more than to give them the character of married women, and their families the character of legitimate children. That the privileges of families were unequal, in so far as the rights of succession were concerned, no more implied an immoral arrangement, than the privileges accorded to eldest sons among many civilised nations. This arrangement of Judaism under such a state of society practically tended much more to the promotion of the general welfare, and to moral purity, than the unrecognised connections that were usual among the heathen, under which, even in Greece and Rome, men's own children became their slaves, and the female character was so degraded as to deteriorate to a great extent the moral habits and principles of whole nations. On exactly similar grounds may the laxity of divorce allowed by the Jewish law be morally defended. It was the remedy for that harshness and those divisions which, under such a state of society, and in connection with polygamy, must have been productive of incalculable evils, had the marriage tie in every case been indissoluble, or even nearly so. For those who were divorced, moreover, a certain provision was made, so as to check and control the worst consequences which loose divorce might have occasioned.

From all this it will still further appear that morality does not consist in any act, as is usually supposed, but in intention and a state of mind. Acts are only of importance in so far as the individual doing them is concerned, as embodying and fostering the state of mind. Wherever they are inconsistent with what ought to be the state of mind, they increase the evil and augment the sin. Even where they are of all others most calculated to promote the public welfare, they are not moral acts, as the selfish theory implies, unless they proceed from that love which is the essence of moral principle. Hence it is manifest that the ordinary systems of moral philosophy, as they are called, are not really systems of moral philosophy, but either systems more or less perfect of jurisprudence, or more frequently mere systems of casuistry. The true details of morality consist in the determination of those *states of mind* which constitute morality. When these are determined, no doubt rules for the guidance of our conduct in particular cases may be deduced from them. This, however, is not moral philosophy. As has been said, the moment that we depart from the determination of mental states, in connection with the general character of conduct which they imply, and enter on a determination of the nature of acts, *as suitable for various conditions and circumstances of society*, we instantly begin to appeal to a new science. This appears manifest from the consideration that morality is immutable, but the special acts that embody it vary, as we have seen, with every change in human intelligence, and every modification of human circumstances. We do not mean, however, to maintain that rules for the regulation of human conduct may not be applied to special or growing degrees of intelligence. Quite the reverse. They may be so, and ought to be so, if it were only for the sake of illustrating principles. But we maintain that if they be suitable for a high degree of intelligence and civilisation, they can only gradually be brought into practical operation. In such cases, therefore, they ought to be only very generally stated in connection with the principles which they are intended to embody, so that their details may practically evolve themselves, as society, in the progress of civilisation, becomes capable of receiving them. The details of morality, therefore, instead of being complicated by multitudes of exceptions, and of exceptions to those exceptions, as in systems of jurisprudence or casuistry, are most singularly simple, precise, and intelligible. They may be comprehended under the three categories of love of ourselves, love of our fellow-creatures, and love of our God.

1. Love of ourselves. It may at first sight seem surprising that we should consider love of ourselves as a portion of morality. This arises, however, from the general misconception as to what morality means. For it means the realisation of the spiritual laws of our whole natures; and it will not, we presume, be denied that love of ourselves constitutes a portion of those laws. Indeed, love of ourselves—or, in other words, an incessant desire for the most intense and permanent happiness—constitutes the motive, as we have

already seen, which impels us to obey any spiritual law. This love of ourselves is not selfishness, but, on the contrary, is frequently the very reverse of selfishness. Hence the absurdity of those who have called the purest morality a species of selfishness. This is a mere abuse of terms. Selfishness is a love of ourselves which *excludes* the love of others, and therefore implies the violation of spiritual law. True love of ourselves seeks its enjoyment in the maintenance of our natures, both physical and spiritual, under such conditions as will give the fullest scope for the gratification of *all* the spiritual laws of our natures, and must therefore ultimately secure our most perfect happiness.

On this account it commands the preservation of our bodily health, the increase of our physical strength, and the maintenance in their fullest vigour of all our intellectual powers and moral tendencies, as essential for the practical development and perfection of our being. Any conduct, therefore, which may, without sufficient cause, impair our bodily health, or physical strength, or, still more, weaken our mental faculties or our moral tendencies, is morally wrong. We say in the former case, *without sufficient cause*, because our essential characteristic being the spirituality of our natures, it follows that, in the performance of spiritual duty, mere physical results can be considered as comparatively of little consequence, and this the more especially as our physical frames can only last for a short time, whilst our spiritual being is to last for ever. Hence the maintenance of our intellectual powers and moral tendencies in their full vigour must be our primary object. Gluttony, therefore, drunkenness, profligacy of every kind, together with all studies, ideas, and feelings calculated to weaken the intellectual powers or the moral tendencies, are, by the laws of our natures, strictly forbidden. On the other hand, temperance, courage, self-control, together with all studies, ideas, and feelings calculated to strengthen our intellectual powers or moral tendencies, are by the same laws commanded.

In this view it will be easily perceived that we must specially guard against self-deception, because it opens an entrance for every kind of practical evil. All our moral habits, and consequently all our moral feelings, would necessarily in a longer or shorter time become perverted by the permanent indulgence of false principles or opinions. A knowledge of ourselves, therefore, with the least possible admixture of prejudice or error, must necessarily be the steady aim of those who desire to regulate their conduct by the laws of nature. This consideration implies the duty of truth. No doubt we are morally bound to truthfulness from the very nature of our beings. Our power of speech, and generally our capability of communicating our ideas and feelings to others, could not have been bestowed upon us *for the purpose of deceiving*, or, in other words, *for the purpose of concealing such ideas and feelings*. It would be as reasonable to suppose that our eyes were given for the purpose of being closed, or our ears for the purpose of being stopped. But, besides, falsehood necessarily leads to self-deception. By a law of our natures we cannot habitually deceive others without partially deceiving ourselves; and thus a habitual liar, we know, as matter of experience, comes absolutely to lose the power of discriminating betwixt truth and falsehood. In like manner, he who accustoms himself to reason under the influence of prejudice, as having adopted particular theories *without knowing himself*, comes to lose more or less the power of discriminating strict logical truth. He looks at every process of reasoning which affects his prejudice through a distorting medium. The same result follows in the case of those who, from whatever cause, acquire a *habit* of disputation, and who are, therefore, prepared to pervert the ordinary sense of words, or to use them in a sense under which they are manifestly not employed by their opponents, in order to secure an argumentative triumph. Such persons, again, absolutely lose the power of discriminating strict logical truth, and become necessarily a species of sceptics under a hallucination that they are searching for fundamental principles! We have in such results the constitution of a moral obligation of the strongest kind. The proof is farther confirmed, if it needed confirmation, by the destruction of social relations, which habitual falsehood *of every kind* involves, and this will still more fully appear from a consideration of the second category of moral detail to which our attention is next to be directed.

2. Love of our fellow-creatures. That there is such a feeling as love of our fellow-creatures, our own consciousness assures us. We know, farther, in our consciousness, that we love our fellow-creatures in a greater or less degree, according to the intimacy of relationship which subsists between us and them, or substantively in proportion to the degree in which we believe them really to love us. But, more or less, we sympathise with them all. On the other hand, we desire that they should love us, and as this desire is realised, a closer connection is constituted between us. This love of human beings towards each other is beyond all doubt a primary emotion. It is of the very essence of our natures. A desire for the advantages which our fellow-creatures have it in their power to bestow might generate external courtesy, but could not possibly originate a spiritual emotion of love. It could not therefore originate a disposition or character with which mere considerations of personal interest have nothing whatever to do. It is love alone which generates love. A man

might load us with benefits, and might be prepared to augment them indefinitely, and we might meet his liberality with profuse professions of love; and yet if we did not believe that he loved us, we could not possibly love him in the proper and spiritual sense of the term. Even supposing our sympathies with the joys and sorrows of others were explicable under a sort of identification with what we might imagine would be our own joys and sorrows in identical circumstances, this would in no measure account for the variety of degrees in the intensity of our sympathies. Love and the feeling of sympathy, under any aspect in which the subject can be regarded, imply original tendencies, or rather an original tendency, for they are substantively the same feeling. Its constitution under a secondary form cannot be explained by any imaginable process. Hence it follows that this tendency must be universal; and this accordingly is found to be the case. All human beings have a certain pleasure in doing good to their fellow-creatures; and as we sympathise with the joys, so do we, in a still greater extent perhaps, sympathise with the sufferings, of all that come under our cognisance.

The conclusion thus derived from our admitted feelings is amply confirmed by the mutual dependence upon each other under which human beings are constituted. Indeed, our happiness so depends upon our fellow-creatures that we should not only be miserable were we without society, but apart from the love and care of their fellow-creatures, our race could not continue to exist. No doubt, our sense of dependence is felt in its highest extent with respect to those who are the most intimately connected with us. There is, however, no human being of whom we can be said to be absolutely independent. Every one near us may have an opportunity of doing us good, and certainly might, if so inclined, do us a serious amount of harm. Even those who inhabit the most distant lands, and know nothing of us personally whatever, may by their wars and discords, by their energies and science, by their instructions and discoveries, by their principles and conduct, tell most materially on our welfare.

If, therefore, we are thoroughly to realise, so far as lies in our power, that spiritual law of nature which is thus manifestly intended to bind us to our fellow-creatures, we must seek the welfare of our race, looking not merely to the indulgence of individuals for the moment, but to the most intense and permanent happiness that can be secured for all mankind. Specially, we are forbidden to indulge one of our fellow-creatures at the expense of another, not merely because the universal adoption of such a principle would disorganise society, but because it is a manifest violation of the law of love, *as disturbing the Almighty's arrangements.* From the nature of the relationship which unites us with Him as creatures to a Creator, our love for Him ought to be infinitely the most intense of all; and proportionately great, of course, ought to be our reverence for all that He has appointed and done. In like manner, we are forbidden to concede lesser gratifications at the moment, although people may eagerly desire it, at the expense of higher and more permanent happiness ultimately.*

From these premises results our obligation to all the moral duties of truth, equity, and purity. They all spring from the primary feeling of love, realised in its fullest and most perfect form. Of course, however, this does not imply that we should love all human beings precisely in the same degree. Nature has bound us to some by more intimate relationships, and there are multitudes of acts of kindness and affection which we ought to realise towards those more intimately connected with us, proportionately to the intimacy of connection, but to which others have no claim. Our love to our fellow-creatures, farther, under these principles, ought to be modified according to the measure of their moral excellence. From the very nature of love, indeed, we must hate immorality, and crush it by every means in our power, since, being opposed directly to the spirit of love, it must necessarily

* Looking to this world alone, the same act might be useful to one and injurious to another. Connecting this world with eternity, however, *that which is right must be beneficial to all, and that which is wrong injurious to all.* It is evidently a false morality which divides society into majorities and minorities.

prove destructive of that happiness which love stimulates us to secure for every human being. Immorality, indeed, or excess of selfishness, it will now appear manifest, is a moral disease generated partly by the abuse of free-will and partly by the power of habit, and, as tending, consequently, both to individual and social misery, is to be eradicated by every legitimate instrumentality. It is the abnormal growth of one portion of our spiritual natures at the expense of the rest, and, unless timeously checked, must end in hopeless wretchedness.

Now, for the purpose of checking it in ourselves, we must, in the first instance, watch over our *actions* in connection with the motives influencing us. We have already described the effect of our actings on the character of our minds, and every one must be sensible of it from personal experience. A continued course of selfish acts will harden our hearts, so as almost to destroy the power of love; a continued struggle, on the other hand, against selfishness, and a continued perseverance in kind acts, will steadily strengthen the power of love, and change that conduct, which we realised at first as a matter of duty and wisdom, into the highest and most heartfelt happiness. Nor will the effect be limited to ourselves; our example will tell upon others. So soon as the conviction is forced upon them that we are sincere, our example will influence not merely the generality of our fellow-creatures, but the most debased and degraded of them. Our morality will thus be doubly blessed. No doubt, our advice, our exhortations, and our precepts may also be most useful; but we must never forget that, apart from our example, they will not only be in vain, but, as believed to be manifestations of hypocrisy, may prove absolutely pernicious. The infliction of punishment, moreover, for the purpose of compelling men to be moral, it will now be obvious, is altogether inadmissible, except in so far as the punishment can be identified in the mind of the sufferer with the *criminality of the intention.* For morality consists in a state of mind, and arbitrary punishment, consequently, neither directly nor indirectly connected therewith, may make men hypocrites, but could never create moral dispositions in them. Hence the caution which should be exercised in the chastisement of children, which, if inflicted arbitrarily, or, as they believe, undeservedly, will do a vast deal more harm than good. We are indeed entitled to inflict arbitrary punishment for breaches of the moral law *which disorganise society;* but this, though consistent with morality, is not for the purpose of generating moral dispositions, but for the purpose of regulating human conduct; and is, therefore, not justifiable strictly under moral law, but under another form of spiritual law, which God has sanctioned in the constitution of political government.

According to this view, the fundamental principles of morality assume, in so far at all events, a new character. That which is called the science of casuistry, by which the relative suitableness of acts is determined, and the rules of which must therefore change with the changing phases of society, ceases to be regarded as a branch of moral philosophy, because moral philosophy has nothing to do with acts, apart from the motives which generate them. Whatever we do with a sincere desire to preserve our own faculties in vigour, and at the same time to bless and benefit individuals where individuals only are directly concerned, or society at large where the interests of society at large are involved, is done in conformity with the principles of morality. It is the intention, and not the act, which is morally right or wrong. We may be utterly mistaken as to the effect of the act, and yet our moral rectitude may be unimpeachable. No doubt we must endeavour carefully to ascertain what is best calculated to preserve the vigour of our faculties, and to bless and benefit mankind; but this is for the very purpose of giving the fullest effect to our intentions. Some knowledge of medicine, therefore, as well as some knowledge of casuistry, seems to be necessary for the full practical realisation of our moral principles. Neither, however, constitutes part of moral philosophy; nor is a knowledge of the *details* of these sciences of any material importance. The more minute details of either medicine or casuistry, indeed, rarely admit of being absolutely ascertained, because their determination depends upon circumstances, which are liable to an almost infinite series of modifications. In endeavouring, therefore, to ascertain that which will be for the most intense and permanent happiness both of ourselves and others, we can hardly require any knowledge either of the one or the other, which is not common, through their own experience, to every individual of the human race. Right intention is consequently almost all that we practically need for the purpose of realising our moral principles in our practice.*

In thus far, then, we have a very plain, and at the same time a strictly logical argument, proving that there are spiritual laws directing us how we ought to feel, and generally how to act, both with reference to ourselves and our fellow-creatures. Here, however, in the details of morality, as we found previously in determining its general prin-

---

* The intention must originate in a love for others *identical in the effects which it produces* with love of ourselves. Hence it must be the same in principle. We would thus no more injure a fellow-creature than we would injure ourselves; and we have a similar pleasure in doing them good, according to the intimacy of relationship that they bear to us. This state of mind, in so far as it can be attained, is a gradual approach to the restoration of the balance of our moral natures. Thus it will be seen how entirely a realisation of the principle of moral law will supersede even in practice the necessity of the precepts of casuistry.

ciples, we are met by counteracting tendencies. These tendencies cannot indeed be called laws of nature, because they are simply excesses of law— or, in other words, spiritual diseases, which incidental causes have produced. They are abnormal expansions of portions of our spiritual natures. Hence they destroy the balance of those natures, so that some portions of them being indulged at the expense of others, ultimate misery is the result prognosticated by that immediate sense of remorse or self-disapprobation which was formerly described. It looks, at first sight, as if nature, designing a certain purpose, had either left it imperfect, or that some incidental change had been introduced under the working of spiritual law, which had counteracted the proposed result. A more careful examination of the phenomena of the spiritual world enables us thoroughly to resolve the difficulty. Without attempting to discover what may have been the primary moral condition of mankind, we are assured, on irresistible evidence, that they are now existing in a state of discipline as essential to the perfection of their moral natures. Such being the case, we are assured farther, in the very nature of the fact itself, that sufficient means must exist under this state of discipline, through which, if we choose to make them available, the balance which ought to subsist among the parts of our spiritual being may be restored, and the grand object of our creation thus rendered attainable. Accordingly, we can discover, on still farther inquiry, not only that such means actually exist, but that the whole phenomena of the universe attest them. There is a power everywhere displaying itself that meets the very want under which we labour, and which is sufficient not only to restore the balance among the parts of our spiritual being, but of itself to elevate us to a higher and nobler position in the scale of existence, blessing us with peace here, and everlasting glory hereafter. This brings us to a consideration of the third form of love, which completes the details of morality.

3. Love of God. That there is a feeling of love for our fellow-creatures, or rather, perhaps we should say, a tendency to love our fellow-creatures, implanted in the human mind, seems ascertained beyond contradiction, and also that such feeling or tendency implies trust in the love of those whom we love. True love, therefore, or love in principle, must be limited to moral qualities, and must be proportioned to the degree in which we believe those whom we love to possess such qualities. For the possession of moral qualities, implying, in so far as they are possessed, the subjugation of selfishness, necessarily implies also the only character which can be loved. Selfishness cannot be loved. Even the most unprincipled, consequently, ascribe some moral quality to those whom they really love. They may be greatly

mistaken with respect to the measure of the quality or qualities which they ascribe to them, but they must ascribe to them some love for themselves, or it would be impossible, in any intelligible sense of the word, that they could love them; and hence persevering kindness will ultimately conciliate the love of every one who is not utterly depraved. It is, on the contrary, hardly possible that a mother could love even her own child, did she believe it devoid of every moral feeling.

To realise any approach to perfect love, therefore, we must manifestly realise the existence of a perfectly moral being, whose very essence is love, and who, abhorring every excess of selfishness, would reciprocate pure love with the most intense affection. Now, as we have already seen, such is the essential nature of God. We are connected with Him by the closest of all relationships, as creature to Creator, as preserved to Preserver, as dependent on Him who is absolutely independent, and from whom alone, therefore, every blessing must come. A breach of our relationship with God, consequently, implies a breach of all our other relationships; since, if we fail to love Him who is love, and to whom we owe everything, it is impossible that we can truly love His creatures, whose love can be only a shadowy reflex of that of their Creator, seeing that they are as dependent upon Him as we are. The man who repudiates the obligations of a higher relationship knowingly, cannot be trusted with respect to a lower relationship, when its obligations interfere with what he believes to be his personal interests. He that violates, for example, the love which he owes to parents who have manifested towards him the most unceasing and affectionate tenderness, could not be trusted by any one else where his own interests or passions were liable to be traversed. Still less can he who violates the love which he owes to his God * be trusted by men, since not only is the relationship infinitely closer than any other, but the dependence of creatures on their Creator is infinitely greater than on any other being, and can never for a moment be suspended.

All this becomes the more striking when we consider that moral law, however certainly enacted by nature, can, away from trust in God,

---

* It is quite true that a certain love must be realised towards our fellow-creatures before we can properly realise love for God, because we know their relationship to us before we can know the nature of God, or, consequently, His relationship to us in any distinct form. This, however, has no bearing on our present subject. Our argument merely amounts to this, that lower obligations must be subordinated to higher when we are made acquainted with them, or else it is a proof that that which we mistake for love is a mere form of selfishness. It may also be added, as will be now manifest from the whole tenor of our argument, that to appreciate in its fulness the immensity of the love of God, *we must connect that purpose of discipline on account of which we are placed here, with the glorious results which it is calculated to work out on our position in the universe and our everlasting blessedness.*

imply no sufficient obligation. On the contrary, *trust in God is the only effectual obligation which nature has provided for urging us to morality.* It may be *wise* for us, no doubt, to observe the moral law in the generality of cases, because this may in an exclusively selfish sense tend to promote our welfare. It is right to observe the moral law, because right means simply obedience to law. It might, however, be argued, that if right mean "obedience to law," it would seem right to obey the strongest law, which would be the desires that our inclinations for the time press most vehemently upon us. No doubt these really do not constitute "law," but, as has been said, "the excess of certain laws," as counteracting certain other laws, in which we have the proof and measure of the excess. Yet the tendency which we have to indulge such excess of law in certain cases, weakens our sense of obligation involved in the operation of the law itself. For the measure of obligation can only be ascertained by the struggle of self-control required to outweigh the influence of immediate impulse. It is impossible that the measure of "obligation" could be otherwise determined. If a man feel satisfied, therefore, that on the whole his highest and most permanent happiness would be promoted by what is usually called immorality, or by special acts of such immorality, it seems obvious that, so far as the word "obliged" could be used with propriety at all, he would be *obliged* to act immorally. No doubt he would be mistaken; but it is a mistake into which we are assured from experience that a great proportion of the human race would fall. This is a conclusion against which there seems no possibility of contending. That must be right which is in conformity with the spiritual laws of our natures, and those must be the regulating spiritual laws of our natures, *even when really in excess*, which seem likely, on the whole, to afford us the most intense and permanent happiness. These both reason and common sense would necessarily urge us, therefore, proportionally to obey. Nor does it make the slightest difference to the conclusion that we introduce such words as conscience, remorse, approbation, or disapprobation, since except in so far as they imply the approbation or disapprobation of the Supreme Being, they can mean nothing save forms of happiness or unhappiness. It is true that these words are frequently used in a sort of mysterious or magical sense; but to do this is merely to deceive ourselves by attempting to cut the knot which we find ourselves unable to untie.

It is a matter of demonstration, therefore, that we must appeal to a higher form of love and of law, or the difficulty is insuperable. Nothing save such happiness begun here as would involve in itself the assurance of intense and permanent happiness growing here, and perfected in a future

DETAILS OF MORALITY. 259

world, could constitute such a moral obligation as that the spiritual laws of nature would be sufficiently strengthened for the purpose of sanctioning and vindicating themselves. For this purpose, therefore, we must endeavour to realise a fuller and fuller trust in the Supreme Being. We must try to see Him in every event of life, and feel a consciousness of His presence in every thought, motive, and feeling. We must learn not merely theoretically and in profession, but practically, to realise our entire dependence upon Him, and to look to His love alone for the attainment of every blessing in life.* This effort will vindicate, *as obedience to every natural law must do*, its own propriety and its own power. We shall be made to feel in our consciousness that it is effecting its object. When this state of mind is attained, or

---

* The theory that all things comprehending our spiritual states are ruled by general laws, which the Supreme Being has indeed primarily called into operation, but over which, *notwithstanding the disorganisation which may be caused by the acts of free-will creatures,* He subsequently exercised no control, which was the doctrine of certain of the ancient philosophers, is really atheism in disguise. It implies that the Supreme Being has, *for a time at all events,* ceased to realise the practical relationship which binds the Creator to His creatures. But *this is just what we mean by immorality,* and consequently the theory—if that can be called a theory which is self-contradictory—implies a direct charge of immorality against God. That we are not sensible directly, through our perceptions, of God being present with us every moment, is true, but we can be made sensible of it in our conscious experience if we use the means, and through them seek to realise the assurance.

is attaining, our sense of its conformity to our higher nature gradually expands. It is more and more becoming its own reward, because it is becoming felt and known as that trust in God which excludes all fear and supersedes all suffering. It is what we speak of as the joy of heaven beginning on earth, by realising to us that union with God which enables us to regard Him as a father. Our duties, as has been said, are now therefore no longer duties but pleasures, and thus the harmony of all the spiritual laws of our nature is perfecting, which, as is evident, constitutes, and must from the very nature of things constitute, the consummation of spiritual blessedness.

Whether all this can be fully attained under the teaching and influence of natural religion, is again quite another question. With that question at present we have nothing to do. It is certain that such happiness can be attained by some means, unless nature be purposely deceiving us, since nature is perpetually urging us to seek it. It is, moreover, certain that it cannot be attained apart from religion, since apart from religion we can neither have thorough peace for the present, nor *any security whatever* for the future, either in this world or beyond the grave. It is still further certain, that without it there can be no approach to any solid foundation for a theory of morality, inasmuch as there is no other conceivable way under which the laws of nature could be made to balance, and thus to vindicate themselves. We do not, of course, mean by this, as will be obvious from our previous observations, that apart from religion there is no argument against vice, and in favour of virtue. On the contrary, we maintain that *generally* it would be wise to resist vicious propensities, and to cultivate virtuous dispositions, as a mere matter of worldly prudence. But we equally maintain, what no one with any knowledge of the world will venture to dispute, that apart from religion *it would be a matter of no great consequence* if a man could only play the part of a hypocrite pretty well. Apart from religion, indeed, morality would in many cases be exceeding folly, as depriving us of such gratifications as the world can afford, and exposing us to serious worldly loss and suffering without any prospect of equivalent compensation either here or hereafter. We maintain, further, in conclusion, that as matter of fact, apart *altogether* from religion, men would become practically indifferent to morality, and, when not acting under impulse, would at the best be guided by the most exclusive views of selfish prudence in whatever conduct they might choose to pursue. Really disinterested kindness must of necessity vanish from the earth, and any domestic or social happiness which human beings could enjoy would be of the lowest and most debasing kind, without one hope that it could be either elevated or augmented.*

It is pure trifling, as we have partially indicated, to speak of approbation or disapprobation in such a case, as felt either by ourselves or our fellow-creatures, since it is clear that, if they

---

* It has been suggested that instinctive affection, such as mothers bear to their children, would constitute a motive in addition to selfishness or mere self-gratification. The fact is, however, that love *in all cases* is an instinctive emotion in the sense of its being a primary and essential emotion of our natures. That a mother's love is generally more intense, may be perfectly true, though it also may be superseded by selfishness; but the love which we have to any of our fellow-creatures is just as thoroughly an instinctive feeling as a mother's love. It is the want of intensity that causes the ordinary love which we bear to our fellow-creatures to be less effective, and consequently more easily superseded; and it is religion alone that can give it the necessary intensity, by *identifying* it with our highest and most permanent because essential happiness. Bringing us into communion with God, it gives love a character which otherwise cannot be realised, as both blessing us in itself, and assuring us of every other blessing through which our natural desires can be gratified. Without any trust in God, therefore, to sustain it, love must quickly be superseded by the irresistible power of selfishness strengthened by habit; and there would consequently be no domestic or social love even, except in so far as the members of families or societies might flatter each other's vanity under a sort of tacit compromise, or might feel some interest in those who were necessary to the promotion of their own enjoyments and comfort. The love felt under such circumstances is just a mere remnant of the instinctive feeling preserved and cherished as a species of selfishness, and essential to selfish enjoyment; and instead of being of the pure and disinterested character which the word is understood to express, must necessarily be of the low and debasing kind described in the text.

possessed any adequate power, they would vindicate themselves. It is, if possible, still more absurd to speak of the obligation to morality involved in the laws of nature, inasmuch as, apart from religion, the obligation involved in the laws of nature would not only be an insufficient motive, but would in many instances actually *incline against morality*. Apart from religion, indeed, our conduct would of necessity be regulated solely by a consideration of that which on the whole would be most conducive to the gratification of our own desires and the promotion of our own interests. Were this the actual condition of society, so that even the *unconsciously operating* influences of religion were wanting, human life would be a curse, and intelligent existence a diabolical mockery.

Religion, therefore, as expounding and realising the nature of the Supreme Being, and the relation in which we stand to Him, can be the only sound foundation of morality. Apart from religion, morality is little more than a mere delusion, having no solid basis on which to rest, and no sufficient, nor nearly sufficient, motives to enforce it. Whereas, on the contrary, if religion be assumed as its basis, it constitutes a perfect science, realising the grand object of human life in ascertaining and securing the most intense and permanent happiness of which our natures are susceptible. This is the crowning evidence for the truth of the theory. It fulfils all the conditions, and explains all the phenomena. The force of this evidence, which is all that we require, and generally all that is possible in the case *even of a physical theory*,* is still further enforced by the consideration, that there is no other possible assumption under which the spiritual laws of the universe can be reconciled, or the object of nature in the creation of the universe appreciated.

The theory is therefore philosophically true beyond question. It is indeed impossible to deny, that if morality *in itself* imply the existence of intense and permanent happiness here and hereafter, then we have in the system now propounded a perfect theory of morality, fulfilling all the conditions and explaining all the phenomena of the spiritual world. We believe, further, that it has millions on millions of times been actually realised in practice. Socrates † is an example of one among the heathen who partially understood it, and at all events attempted to give

---

* We know nothing, for example, of the nature of "gravitation," and of course have no evidence for such a power, except that the assumption of it "fulfils all the conditions and explains all the phenomena" of the perceptible motions of inanimate existence throughout the universe. This is the *only* ground of our belief in such a power, but it is irresistible. The same thing holds true in all similar cases.

† In the 'Memorabilia' of Xenophon, we find Socrates repeatedly appealing to the relationship betwixt God and man as a fundamental principle of morality.

effect to it in his own life. In the Christian world there have been countless instances of the same thing, although the very humility which their faith enjoins, induces real Christians frequently to withdraw from public observation, and struggle in quietly performing the duties of life for the purpose of attaining a more entire union with their God. Any human being, however, may try the experiment for himself; and as surely as God and nature are true, so surely shall he prove successful, if he tries in a right spirit, under the use of God's appointed means. The sorrows of the world will disappear. A peace, such as he never felt before, will be diffused over his mind. Duty and happiness will become the same thing, viewed under different aspects. A growing power over himself in repressing selfishness and cherishing love will give him a sense of a closer and closer union with the divine nature, and this will be in his own consciousness an assurance and a foretaste of eternal blessedness beyond the grave. If we only believe thoroughly in a Supreme Being, and in our moral relations to Him, the result is certain. The victory is indeed won, and the gates of heaven are thrown open to receive us.

The moral law, therefore, according to the theory which we have now generally developed, is merely another name for the spiritual laws of our being, as expressions of the divine attributes. These attributes—of course, we speak only of the moral attributes — are all really comprehended under the word *love;* for God *is* love, and accordingly as He must approve of love wherever it exists, so must He abhor malignity under every form, and by connecting suffering with its manifestation, thereby do all consistent with leaving us free-will, for the purpose of promoting or eradicating it. Thus in conformity with the perfection of His laws, He exacts, in so far, the penalty of malignity, or that excess of selfishness from which it flows, not only under incidental evils, but *in the very nature of the feeling itself;* for malignity being the result of a disorganisation or disease of our spiritual natures, it is no more possible to be malignant without spiritual suffering, than to labour under physical disorganisation or disease without bodily suffering and decay. It implies, indeed, a greater penalty ultimately, in respect of its being a result of free-will. We are accursed in thus far because we have chosen to be so.

Yet from experience it would appear, as we have seen, that this sanction, however *absolutely* tremendous, is insufficient under our present circumstances to vindicate spiritual law, from the fact of its being to a great extent practically ineffective. This is because for the present we have power to deaden our spiritual sufferings by spiritual opiates; just as we can *for a time* deaden physical sufferings by material opiates. In the distractions which we can realise through the business of life and the pleasures of the world, we also find *for the time* those spiritual opiates, and we take them. Would we only allow ourselves to think, would we still more allow ourselves steadily to meditate on our present condition till we had thoroughly appreciated our own weakness, as unable for one moment to preserve ourselves from misfortune, sickness, death, and, it may be, eternal misery, it would be impossible that we could continue to live in contempt of God and of His laws. For a man without religion to meditate on futurity as a matter of habit, would be to subject himself to inevitable wretchedness. It would drive him to insanity or to suicide, or else it would necessarily force him to seek peace where alone it is to be found. So long as we delight in the mere gratifications of selfishness, therefore, whenever thoughts of futurity, with the possibility or probability of misfortune, sickness, death, and eternal misery, occur to us, we turn away from them, and by plunging, as has been said, into business and pleasure, we deaden our feelings and our fears for the time. Yet though we may deaden, we can never thoroughly eradicate these feelings and fears. Though the criminal condemned to death may by intoxication or similar excess deaden for a time the horrors inspired by his prospective doom, yet it would seem, as has been said, that even under such circumstances the object cannot be thoroughly effected. In like manner, though we, who are just as surely as he is condemned to death in the body, may by spiritual excess deaden to a certain extent our fears of futurity, yet we cannot altogether eradicate them. The sting lies latent in our hearts, and pains us more or less incessantly even in the midst of our engagements and enjoyments. In our attempts, however, at deadening our feelings and fears, there are other instrumentalities at work. We are specially aided by doubts as to the reality of divine superintendence, *which we encourage*, and reckless hopes of mercy, which to him that cherishes malignity *is impossible in the nature of things.*

That there should be such means of deadening our feelings, is the result of our being placed in a state of discipline. Were we not permitted to deceive ourselves, or were we forced by assurance of immediate punishment to act in a particular way, as the Jews were under their *temporal* system, there could be no moral discipline, and consequently, in creatures such as we are, *no possibility of forming stable and constituted characters.* Those who are never tried may at any time fall. It is the man who has known both good and evil, and who under such knowledge, experimentally acquired, has by an earnest struggle against himself won the victory in rejecting the evil and realising the good, whose permanent character is alone to be depended on. He alone, having through trust in God subdued selfishness under the self-discipine which he has had the means of exercising on earth, can be assured of enjoying the blessedness of love for ever, both in earth and in heaven.

Practical morality—or, in other words, the application of our moral principles to acts—therefore, is to endeavour, with respect to every particular, to do that which will promote the most intense and permanent happiness of ourselves and of all mankind. We say of ourselves and of all mankind, because *it must be the same,* if we include the love of God amongst the motives to morality, not only as belonging to them, but as that, according to the argument which we have now proposed, on which the others must rest, and on the validity of which, consequently, they must be entirely dependent for their own validity.

PART III.

SCIENCE OF POLITICS

SCIENCE OF POLITICS.

INTRODUCTION.

DEFINITION OF POLITICAL SCIENCE—ITS ORIGIN—ITS RELATION TO MORAL SCIENCE—IT CONCERNS CONDUCT RATHER THAN STATES OF MIND—NECESSITY OF GOVERNORS FOR ADMINISTERING POLITICAL LAW—NO DIRECT NATURAL LAW ENTITLING ONE MAN TO RULE OVER ANOTHER, EXCEPT THE LAW OF THE STRONGER—NO POLITICAL RIGHTS, THEREFORE, UNDER DIRECT NATURAL LAW—MISCONCEPTIONS ON THE SUBJECT.

POLITICAL science treats of the manner, circumstances, and extent in which and to which human beings are entitled to combine for determining rights undetermined by nature, and for the mutual defence of person and property under a system of more or less arbitrary laws. That men are so entitled to combine is self-evident, where they are all agreed as to the terms. Nor can it be doubted, from the very nature of our mental tendencies and worldly relations, that they are entitled to compel others to submit to the laws which they may frame. When the welfare of all depends upon such an arrangement, as must be the case with communities inhabiting the same district, their interests are so interwoven as to render it impossible that they could exist under any measure of peace and safety, unless all were subjected to the same laws. Hence the necessity of forms of government.*

It is the common impression that forms of government originated on the model of the natural government of families, where the father gives the law to his children, and grew out of it. There may be some truth in this, though it seems quite clear that human beings must have combined for protection of person and property apart from all such considerations. That there is a tendency thus to combine for political purposes, is manifest from the conduct of all nations and tribes. It is, however, no *direct* tendency, but an indirect result necessarily flowing from its obvious necessity. It cannot, therefore, be ascribed to a primary law of nature, except perhaps in so far as a natural tendency may impel us to assist those who are oppressed, but merely to a rational conclusion

---

* We have seen that morality has strictly nothing to do with acts, except in so far as they flow from a state of mind and realise it. Acts beyond this are left to be regulated by human laws *under subordination to, and in conformity with,* the principles of morality. Hence, as explained in the text, the science of politics.

with respect to circumstances which no primary law seems to have provided for. Had men, indeed, lived purely moral lives, a large amount of political law might have been dispensed with. But even in that case there would still be a number of civil rights to be determined and regulated, for which no natural law has made any provision. These, however, are not to be determined capriciously, but *according to the principles of moral law*, so as to show that some sort of political government must have been implied in the constitution of our race.

It thus appears that the sciences of morality and politics are not only intimately connected, but are absolutely interwoven with one another. Political science, indeed, in its principles, is to a great extent merely a subordinate branch of the general science of morality, and is under another aspect supplementary thereof. It determines certain rights left undetermined by nature; and enforces moral duties in the *practical conduct* of human life by arbitrary punishments and rewards in those cases where, under the exercise of free-will, moral motives are found insufficient for the purpose. It is not, therefore, feelings, but conduct, with which political science has mainly to do. Hence human laws forbid crime, not merely because it is wrong in itself, but mainly because it disturbs and disorganises society.

Thus it will be seen that political science has,

or at least ought to have, little to do directly with intentions and feelings. Its great object is to guard person and property. No doubt, so far as it is in the power of a government to direct intentions and feelings into a right channel, they are bound to exercise it, not only because they thus take the most effectual means of regulating conduct, but because no man can throw off his responsibilities with respect to any duty, especially his duty to God, in any position of life, whether as legislator, magistrate, or individual. It is as absurd to argue that a government is not bound to provide the means of moral, as it would be to argue that it is not bound to provide the means of intellectual, knowledge for its subjects. It is, indeed, more so, since on their moral knowledge must depend their obligation to political obedience. But all appeals to the intentions or feelings of their subjects should be by persuasion only. Acts alone can be regulated by human laws, save to a very limited extent, and under very special circumstances.

When an ecclesiastical government, indeed, takes cognisance of immoralities, the tendency must be as far as possible to determine the character of motives, because, in an ecclesiastical point of view, it is the motive which constitutes the crime. A religious man is bound to avoid even the appearance or suspicion of evil; and therefore an ecclesiastical court is not only entitled but bound to take into consideration the extent to which an accused person may have placed himself in circumstances justifying suspicion. If he has done so voluntarily or recklessly, he in thus far has manifested indifference to character, and, consequently, must be held guilty of all that the act implies, unless he can by positive evidence relieve himself from the charge. Even in that case his indifference to character is ecclesiastically censurable. But, in ordinary criminal jurisdiction, the question of motive only constitutes indirectly the subject of consideration, because it is not only very difficult in many instances to determine the motive, but because it is the act, and not the motive, which *directly* affects the public interests. Hence in criminal cases under political law, though the accused can defend himself by showing that he had no intention of committing wrong, the intention is *assumed* by the accusing government.*

* This is not conformable to the common idea upon the subject. In this country—in the case of murder, for example—malice is libelled, and therefore it is assumed that malice—meaning, in judicial language, purpose or intention—*must be proved*. But on accurate consideration, it will be perceived that the act is held as implying the intention, unless the evidence *prove the contrary*. Evidence proving that there was no intention on the part of the slayer to commit murder is truly exculpatory, *whichever party may offer it*. If one man kills another, and there is nothing in the evidence to prove that it was unintentional or impulsive, the criminal must be held either insane or a murderer. The usual maxim that a doubt should be given in favour of the criminal, applies to a doubt of the fact, and not of the motive. In every instance the act, *as proved in evidence*, implies the motive. Were it otherwise, no man could ever be

Still it is almost impossible to shut the eyes of either judges or juries to the character of motives in criminal cases. In civil causes, however, the assumption of motives, or of the feelings and intentions of parties, ought to be altogether excluded from consideration, except in so far as they may be distinctly expressed or clearly implied in their own deeds and utterances. The legal character of an act *when it was done,* and the legal sense attachable to words *when they were spoken or written,* ought, without exception, to be taken as expressive of the motive or intention of the parties in every judicial case. It may, indeed, be said that there is great difficulty in determining what might have been the legal sense attachable to deeds or words of an old date; nor is there, perhaps, any point which has led to a larger amount of litigation than in attempts at determining such matters. Yet the principle is clear and precise. Whatever has been undisputed during years of prescription, ought in every instance to determine the legal sense intended either by acts or writings.* No doubt, if there were proof

condemned, since even in the worst of cases there must ever be a doubt as to the motive; and in cases of murder there is generally very serious doubt either as to the motive or the sanity of the criminal.

* This is equally true of legislative acts as of private deeds. It is utterly iniquitous for a court of law to assign a new sense to any act of which the sense has been determined either positively or negatively by prescription. The mere words of an act may seem often to imply a very different sense from that

noviter veniens ad notitiam, and which had previously been *necessarily* unknown, it might invalidate even prescription under ordinary circumstances. But it is otherwise clear as matter of principle that in every instance undisputed prescriptory belief ought to determine legal construction with regard to *every* subject. In such cases, transactions *have been bonâ fide;* and, considering the necessary uncertainty of mere legal deductions, ought, as matter of justice, to be unchallengeable: to this principle, save in the case formerly stated, there are really no exceptions. Prescriptive belief constitutes a legal construction, sanctioned not only by common sense, but by the laws of nature, and, were it duly recognised, would prevent a large proportion of the litigation which disgraces civilised countries, and give a stability to property which it has never hitherto realised.

Such being the character and object of political government, it is obvious that in making provision for its due exercise many arrangements must be made, and great expense consequently incurred.

originally attached to it, because the views of the legal bearing of words may be wholly different at different times; but if a sense has been attached to the words of a legislative act by long prescription, not merely by positive decisions, but negatively *by no attempt having been made at attaching a different sense*, this ought to be considered the true meaning. It is easy to perceive the immense effect which this would have in checking litigation, by assuring every one of the possession of property of every kind which had been held during the years of prescription unchallenged.

To provide for this, there must be governors with the power of making and executing suitable laws. These governors must, of course, have a certain authority over those whom they govern; and hence arises the primary and fundamental question in political philosophy—Under what right can one man be entitled to exercise authority over another?

This question is in so far settled by the actual constitution of nature. As matter of fact, some men are created superior to others, both with respect to physical strength and mental ability. It is, therefore, impossible that an equality of authority, or, consequently, of temporal advantages, could be preserved among them. These personal differences can only be compensated by a union of men among themselves. The compensation, however, cannot in any case be complete. No arbitrary arrangement can altogether neutralise the primary distinctions of nature. The strongest, physically and mentally, will of necessity exercise the greatest influence in such a union, and thus the foundations of political government are, in the first instance, laid as resting on personal qualifications. To the political government thus constituted all within its sphere in each case must accede, inasmuch as a compact and united body would necessarily crush the opposition of isolated and outstanding individuals.

This, therefore, introduces us to a new principle. As time progresses, and the influence of circumstances, and especially of civilisation, begins to be felt, the mode of selecting governors changes by the introduction of the strength of united masses, in place of the direct action of individuals. Still, however, the selection must depend upon the will of the stronger party. In such cases the governor or governors may be very weak in themselves, but the party selecting them sustains their authority. While, therefore, nature evidently forces on men some form of political government suitable to the respective circumstances of successive stages of human progress, it must still be the government in each case of the stronger individual or party, and in thus far has no other right except the right of the strongest.

Under such circumstances it is absurd to speak of political rights apart from mere power. There can be no such rights, because *in thus far* power is the origin of them all. Moral rights have a natural sanction in feelings of love and sympathy common to our race. But political rights have no such sanction, nor, indeed, have they *directly* any natural sanction at all, except in the law, if it can be called a law, which enables the stronger to rule over the weaker. It is positively ludicrous to read the misconceptions into which men fall upon this subject. They speak of political rights as if their nature and limits were obvious to the most superficial observer. Whereas it is manifest, from what has been already said, that the foundation of political rights implies considerations which are by no means generally recognised, and that the practical determination of their nature and limits has never been ascertained with even an approach to accuracy.

These are the points, therefore, to which our attention must be directed before it is possible to come to any definite conclusion with respect to the details of the science, or the relative advantages of particular systems.

CHAPTER I.

NATURE AND FOUNDATION OF POLITICAL RIGHTS.

IMMEDIATE SOURCES OF POLITICAL POWER—IN SO FAR THE WORDS "RIGHT," "OUGHT," AND "DUTY" CAN HAVE NO PLACE IN POLITICAL SCIENCE—THEORY OF COMPACT, AS THE FOUNDATION OF POLITICAL RIGHTS, UNTENABLE—THEORY OF A TACIT ADMISSION OF SUCH COMPACT UNTENABLE—SUBMISSION TO A GOVERNMENT DOES NOT NECESSARILY IMPLY A RECOGNITION OF ITS AUTHORITY—UTILITY OF GOVERNMENT DOES NOT NECESSARILY IMPLY A RECOGNITION OF THE RIGHTS OF THOSE THAT ADMINISTER IT IN ANY PARTICULAR CASE—PALEY CORRECT IN RESTING POLITICAL RIGHTS ON "THE WILL OF GOD," BUT WRONG IN ASSUMING "THE WILL OF GOD" TO BE COLLECTED FROM "EXPEDIENCY"—"THE WILL OF GOD" DECLARED IN THE ACTUALLY EXISTING CONSTITUTION OF THINGS—THIS THEORY EXPLAINED AND VINDICATED.

IN so far, then, we have now seen that political power, in the first instance, results from superiority of strength. It matters nothing, in the present stage of our argument, whether this strength consist in physical force or mental ability, or a combination of both modified by circumstances. What the circumstances are which may thus modify physical force and mental ability in the constitution of political government, it is, moreover, impossible with any minuteness to describe, because they are innumerable. They comprehend climate, geographical position, intellectual cultivation, the external action of events, and an infinity of other particulars. It is, however, self-evident that, taken together in connection with the physical faculties and mental qualifications of men, they explain in every instance the causes of the constitutions of all governments, and of the influence which individuals acquire in the special administration of each. In this very fact, however, it is still farther proved that the comparative strength, whether of individuals or parties, however acquired and however preserved, is the foundation both of forms of government, and of individual influence in such governments. Yet it does not follow that those who wield this strength can employ it for any purpose that they please. In saying this, we do not allude to the limits which the obligations of the moral law impose upon them, which we shall consider subsequently, but of those limits which, under the very causes out of which they themselves derive their power, will control the exercise of it. For where it is carried beyond certain limits, they will, under the constitution of human nature, more or less speedily lose the support of those on whom they had previously depended. A portion of their own friends will desert them, so as to compel them to regulate their proceedings with a greater respect for the opinions and feelings of society, under the penalty of being deprived of their authority altogether.

Within those limits, however, there can be no doubt that those who govern solely by the greater strength, may employ it for any purpose that they please. There is indeed a tendency equivalent to what may be called an indirect law, under which certain portions of each society combine their strength for the purpose of supporting each government, and there are tendencies in the same manner equivalent to indirect law, which give to certain persons controlling influence in such governments. This, however, manifestly constitutes as much the law of the strongest, as if a man with his knee on the breast and his hand on the throat of a weaker fellow-creature, were to threaten him with mutilation or death unless he should agree to obey his commands. It is true that the influence of strength does not appear so manifest, when shrouded under the numerous complications of civil government; but its operation is just as evident to any one capable of estimating the character of the authority by which a claim to the obedience of subjects is tacitly implied, under the greater proportion of systems which treat of political science.

In thus far, therefore, again, it is clear that such words as "right," "ought," or "duty" can have no place in political science. Neither the government nor the governors, indeed, can have any right, except the right of force, nor can the subject be bound to any obedience, save under the law of fear. In other words, there is no real obligation upon any one to obey human laws, except in so far as the rulers can compel obedience by physical strength. There would consequently be no willing obedience under a sense of duty, and every one would be entitled to evade obedience by all the indirect means in his power. Were such the true state of the case, human laws would have comparatively little effect in attaining the object for which they are usually understood to be designed, *because sedition and treason would not be crimes.* Attempts to undermine and overturn existing governments would simply imply a fair and legitimate struggle against an arbitrary and unauthorised exercise of physical force.

The only shadow of political government, as resting on the constitution of the human mind, is to be found in the relationship connecting parents and children. Whether there be even in the minds of children, however, a natural sense of the duty of obedience to their parents, or whether the obedience of children to parents may not be the result of circumstances, a habitual sense of practical authority, and therefore merely an indirect law of nature, is a question which it is very difficult positively to decide. Even assuming, however, that children have a natural sense of parental authority, or generally of that of their

OF POLITICAL RIGHTS.

guardians, *as those on whom they depend under the arrangement of nature,* this could not imply any claim on the part of others to exercise authority over persons who owe them no particular obligation by nature, and with whom they are entirely unconnected, save as creatures of the same race.*

In such a case it is evident that the claims of both parties are precisely the same. We have just as good a claim, so far as natural right is concerned, to exercise authority over others, as they have to exercise authority over us. If there is to be authority, therefore, exercised by the one over the other, we must just fall back again on the law of superior strength. The stronger individual or party has the *right,* just because he or it has the *power,* of ruling over the weaker.

* It is said, and would of course be said in this country by those unaccustomed to reasoning, that in free countries men are governed by their representatives. But if this mean anything, it must mean that all persons are treated unjustly who have no representatives. All the nations of the world, therefore, have been and are unjustly governed, except perhaps America and Britain with her dependencies. But even in America and Britain many are unrepresented. There is therefore no real right in the government of *any* nation. This, however, is not all, for it must be observed that men may object even to a representative system, and *desire to govern themselves.* They may be *forced* to submit to a representative government, but there is no natural obligation on men to submit to a parliament, or a house of assembly, or a congress, more *than to a despot.* We come back to the law of the stronger again. There can be no answer to this under the assumption of political power being a natural right.

In order to escape from this difficulty, it has been assumed by some that there is a sort of compact among men, according to which they have agreed to concede obedience to the respective governments under which they dwell. The assumption has originated in despair. Where no other approach to a legitimate claim could be discovered on the part of governments to the obedience of their subjects, this theory of a mutual compact was proposed. But assuredly there could not be an assumption more utterly unfounded. There are multitudes, indeed, who are so far from agreeing to any such compact, that they detest the forms of government under which they respectively live. It is in vain to say in reply to this, that the majority favour such an arrangement; for under what law can it be pretended that a majority acquires the right of ruling over an unwilling minority, or even an unwilling individual, except the law of the strongest?

We are occasionally told, indeed, that in yielding to a government, and taking advantage of the protection which it affords, we *tacitly* confirm a compact, or at all events indirectly sanction a claim to obedience. We deny, however, *that there ever was a compact at all ;* and it is impossible to confirm that which never existed. Trace the history of every government, and we shall find that in each case governments have grown out of circumstances, and never in any one instance rested on a compact universally agreed to. Such has been the case, even with respect to the most popular forms of government. There never has been anything like a universal consent given to them; and even if there had, such a consent could not have bound all future generations. The fact is, that we come into the world generally to find a form of government established for us, with the primary constitution of which we have no more connection than if we had been born at the opposite side of the earth. It is evidently absurd, therefore, to say that we have given our consent to such a form of government, or that under any direct law of our mental constitution we are bound to yield obedience to those who administer it.

Nor is it more to the purpose to say, that by taking advantage of its provisions we thereby give our sanction to the government which we find in existence. We do *not* take advantage of its provisions, except under the pressure of physical necessity; or again, in other words, under the law of the stronger. We should be crushed if we attempted to resist.

Nor does it further in principle involve any other law to argue that if we dislike the government of the country in which our lot has been cast, we may leave it, and seek some other form of government elsewhere more agreeable to us. It is not, indeed, always the case that we can leave our country and seek another. But if it were, where is to be found the law of nature that entitles one man or body of men to say to any of their fellow-creatures that he must leave the country where he was born, unless he choose to obey him or them, except the law of the stronger? There is no such natural law existing in any direct form, nor any approximation to it. The more powerful may, indeed, compel the weaker to obedience, but there is no shadow of direct natural law to justify it. Did the matter, therefore, depend on direct natural law, it is certain that every one would be entitled to resist, by whatever means were in his power, all arbitrary laws, and arbitrary administration of such laws, and consequently all political government.

It is true that political government is useful, and, indeed, from the universality of its existence in some form, we may conclude that it is felt to be essential to the welfare of mankind. It is assumed, therefore, by some philosophers, to be an institution claiming authority from natural law, not indeed directly, but indirectly, as discoverable by inference. A law, however, which does not flow from a principle sanctioning itself, but is enacted from a consideration of probable results, *is not a natural, but an artificial law;* and the theory can only mean, therefore, that there must be some cause or causes in the nature of things to account for the admitted phenomenon. This, of course, is true, but it is a barren conclusion, as it explains nothing. It leaves us just as we were. No doubt, as matter of expediency, reason would recommend the institution of political government, but there would be no obligation binding those to obey it who might deem it inexpedient for themselves. A political government resting exclusively on expediency, moreover, could of course have no claim of right whatever. It becomes once more simply a government of physical force exercised by a tyrant majority for securing that which they believe *most expedient for themselves.*

But granting, what evidently is not the case, that there were something like a direct natural law in favour of political government, where, we again ask, is to be found any foundation for the rights of those who administer it? Whence are they specially entitled to assume a superiority over their fellow-creatures, under which they make laws for their direction, and enforce those laws by arbitrary penalties? The thing will not admit of an argument. There is no direct natural law, thus giving one man authority over another, except the law of superior strength, which of course excludes every idea of right, *except the right of every one to exercise the power which from circumstances he actually possesses.*

According to Paley, "the only ground of a subject's obligation is the will of God." We shall subsequently show that in so far he is perfectly right. But in adding "the will of God, *as collected from expediency*," without any further limitation, he not only leaves it to be implied that political obligation may be predicated of *everything* which involves expediency, but he proposes a mode for discovering "the will of God," which, apart from other considerations, is liable to the most serious objections.*

There cannot, indeed, be a greater error than to suppose, as Paley evidently does, that a government is entitled to interfere with everything which it may imagine calculated to promote the public welfare. It is a common error, and therefore the more dangerous. The power of political government is, strictly speaking, only repressive. So soon as a government is established, its duty is to guard person and property; and except *for the sake of this*, it has nothing to do with anything else. In laying on taxes, in raising armies, in providing means for the intellectual and moral education of the people, the grand aim of a government should ever be their bearing on the main point of protecting person and property. Nothing

---

* The theory of Paley in this aspect is not *absolutely false*, but only very imperfect. It is, indeed, so imperfect, that taken by itself it would lead to the most pernicious practical results. As will be subsequently seen from the text, it is not expediency, but the actual existing condition of things, which teaches us the "will of God" with respect to the constitution of governments. There must be something more than expediency to guide even our political conduct.

can be more mischievous than the meddling spirit which induces governments to attempt forcing masses of arbitrary laws on their subjects, having merely what may be called the general welfare of society in view. Let men be sure of the safety of person and property, and they will find the means of assuring their own interests and happiness in a way greatly more effectual than any government can provide it for them. But the fact is, that no government can arbitrarily interfere to any considerable extent with the opinions, habits, and pursuits of its subjects, without interfering with personal rights, which, as we shall subsequently see, belong to a higher class, and are sanctioned by stronger obligations.

But further, as we have said, the assumption that "the will of God" is to be "collected solely from expediency," is a theory liable to the most serious objections. On the face of it we are struck by the language of a theory which proposes to resist powers and subvert governments, *because they are inexpedient.* The notions which men entertain as to expediency are so various, that were every one entitled to conspire and excite sedition whenever he believed that a change of government might be expedient, there would be no settled peace in any country. This apparent absurdity seems, however, to be modified by a subsequent limitation when it is said, "So long as the established government cannot be resisted or changed without public inconveniency, it is the will of God that the established government be obeyed, and no longer." This, however, would lead to the opposite conclusion; for were we never to "resist or change" a government when it caused "public inconveniency," it is manifest that we should never resist nor change a government at all.

There is, indeed, a want of precision in the theory which renders it practically useless. It nowhere clearly appears what Paley means by the "interests of society," which he considers the alone proper object of political government. Specially, he nowhere determines whether society means all human beings, or the majority of each state. Under the former of these assumptions, political government would become practically unworkable, since its complications would be so enormous as to render it impossible for any human intelligence to resolve them, while the possible collisions of interests betwixt different states would subject each government to a perpetual succession of insuperable difficulties. Under the latter assumption, which there can be little doubt is that which he means, not only might the interests of the majority of one state interfere with the rights of other states, but it would follow that individuals, and not only individuals, but colonies and provinces—as, for example, in this country, Ireland or Scotland—might be outraged, and yet would not be justified in seeking redress, because the interests and convenience of a larger number in other provinces might be injuriously affected. The case actually occurred on a recent occasion in America, where the interests of the South being compromised by a tariff convenient for the North, a civil war was the consequence. Under such circumstances it has always appeared clear to us, that where a tariff is fixed, not for the purpose of providing necessary supplies for the use of the state, but for the purpose of promoting the private interests of parties, the *right* of separation is indisputable.

In fact, this theory of Palcy's, whatever sense we attach to the word expediency, really assumes the whole question. How do we know that the "public interests" of an arbitrary district called a State indicates "the will of God"? May it not rather be, if experience is the only guiding principle, that the "interests," or supposed interests, of each body of men connected with one another by mutual pursuits, as in the case of trades-unions, indicates "the will of God," in so far as they themselves are concerned? To us it appears that, under one aspect, the argument is stronger in the latter case than in the former, since in the latter case there is a natural and voluntary, while in the former there is only an arbitrary and compulsory, bond of combination. Under this assumption, the public interests of states would be subservient and subordinate in the nature of things to the public interests of trades and professions, or other natural combinations. No doubt trades and professions may fall into mistakes as to their own interests; but so may governments; and if it be left, as Paley leaves it, to every man to judge for himself, there can evidently be no more blame attachable to the one than to the other.

There is, however, a still more important element substantively omitted by this theory; we mean, that of men's own individual interests. Is it clear that we ought to yield them for the sake of promoting the public interests? Paley says that we ought, because it is expedient even for ourselves. This, however, is by no means, in all instances, the opinion of mankind. They are of opinion that our direct "interests" indicate the "will of God" more than the "public interests," which can only indirectly benefit us; and in so far they are undoubtedly right. The position, however, which this principle occupies in Paley's theory nowhere distinctly appears; and yet, practically, it is of the most material consequence. Unless we precisely ascertain its authority, the theory, apart from all other objections, must be entirely indefinite.*

---

* Paley has fallen into this error by assuming that each individual is to judge for himself. This would not only supersede political right altogether, but leaves the great question undetermined as to the parties whose advantage is to be ascertained. Why should that which is expedient for a majority in a particular district indicate the will of God? Where, more-

We have dwelt on this theory at some length, because it is beyond doubt the best form under which the utilitarian theory has been applied to politics, and because Paley has defended it with masterly ability. Yet, though there is much more to be said in favour of such utilitarianism as a political than as a moral theory, we trust that it has now been proved, even as a political theory, to be untenable, though regarded under the most favourable aspect. It assumes that which is to be proved, and evades the difficulties which such assumption implies. We need not now dwell, therefore, on the ordinary form of the utilitarian theory. The assumption that the object of political government is "the greater happiness of the greater number," not as probative of the "will of God," but *absolutely*, will not admit of a defence.*

over, is the expediency of one set of men ruling rather than another? The theory is evidently without any definite basis on which to rest, while the different propositions by which he supports or explains it are mere assertions, which he does not sustain by an appeal to principles of any kind.

* To promote the "greatest happiness of the greatest number" is in itself no motive at all, and can imply in itself no obligation. To take it even as a test of political obligation, might imply the subjection of the minority to intolerable tyranny. It is in vain to argue that this would not promote the "greatest happiness" even of the majority. In a mere worldly point of view, and for a certain length of time, we are convinced that it frequently would promote the "greatest worldly happiness" of the majority. Such has, moreover, been the conviction of *every nation of the world, and almost at every stage of their history.* Where the theory of the "greatest happiness of the greatest number," therefore, is avowed, it is under the assumption that

It is not only liable to all the objections with which Paley's theory is chargeable, but to a multitude of others, and is a theory, indeed, which no government would dare avowedly to realise. It depends for any plausibility which may be claimed for it on being mixed up with a cognate theory of morals, which again has been made to rest on the inconsistent theory of selfishness; and thus the whole has been so complicated as to prevent its incongruities from being immediately manifest. In this way it has in so far served the purpose of a certain school, and been patronised by it.

But while Paley's theory, in so far as it rests our knowledge of the "will of God" on expediency, is wrong, or at least imperfect, he is unquestionably right in regarding "the will of God" as the sole possible ground of political obligation. Under any assumption of a compact, or indeed under any direct form of natural law, as we have seen, political government can have no claim of right whatever, since natural law gives no authority to one man, or body of men, to rule over others, except the law of the strongest. Supposing that it could be proved that the people of each kingdom are bound to enact laws among themselves, there is no natural law under which the parties entitled to make or to administer such

all the rights of the minority are reserved, which makes the theory itself little better than a play upon words.

law can be determined. It is only when we go under and behind natural law that we discover the true key to the mystery. It is only when we consider all things as constituted and regulated by the Supreme Being that we discover the source of political obligation. Moral obligation is indeed founded on direct natural law, but this cannot be the case with respect to political administrations. Under any form of theory referring the rights of political government to the obligations of direct natural law, we are invariably involved in contradiction and confusion.*

If, however, we look upon the system of the universe as the design of one overruling Intelligence, who has constituted every event as it actually exists, and has given to every individual the position which he actually occupies, then the mass of contradiction and confusion which involves all the theories to which we have previously referred immediately vanishes. The arrangements of the universe assume the character of a magnificent scheme. God is the grand Legislator and Governor of the whole, and rulers are merely His vicegerents. From that moment the law of the strongest, which had only rested on physical force, becomes the law of intelligence and right, *because it is subjected to the principles of morality and order.* All things are seen to have been wrought out for a particular purpose, and the union of men

* Appendix C.

for the general welfare is sanctioned by the very fact of its rational necessity, as carrying forth the decree of an almighty Lawgiver. Everything that exists, and *as it exists*, according to this theory, is His doing, in so far as it is consistent with the moral law; and, consequently, every individual is in the position which he occupies by His appointment, in so far as it has been legitimately attained. Whatever influence, therefore, or power it involves, has been conferred by Him, is exercised under His authority, and *is to be limited and controlled by the terms of His moral commandments.**

This is farther illustrated when we observe, what is manifest even on the most superficial consideration, that the law of the strongest necessarily accommodates itself to the intellectual and moral condition of each people. In the lowest intellectual and moral condition of mankind, personal strength and courage invariably exercise the chief influence, more or less modified by the intellectual character of the individuals. Laws in all such cases are necessarily lax, and irregularly administered, so as to be suitable to the comparatively

---

* It by no means follows from this that men are not entitled to advance their worldly interests, or to seek for a higher position. On the contrary, they are impelled to do this by the laws of their natures, which are the laws of God. But they are bound to do it in subordination to the social circumstances and political government of the country in which they live, because these are determined by the decree of God, just as much as their natures are constituted by His appointment.

OF POLITICAL RIGHTS. 301

low moral tone of society. But as intelligence increases, and the importance of union for the common welfare of society begins to be appreciated, a nascent desire for freedom from the tyranny of pure physical force appears. Mental ability commands greater respect. Kindness of heart and zeal for the general happiness acquire a predominating influence. It is no longer, in a word, the physical strength of individuals which constitutes, even in a measure, the ruling power, but the intellectual and moral strength of the masses, subjecting themselves by a more or less unconscious process to the government of the wisest and best, with a view to the higher interests of each and of all. Thus, a desire for and a realisation of liberty progresses according to the forms most suitable for each people; and thus, accordingly, by taking the circumstances of each people into consideration, we can discover more or less accurately the causes of the form which each government has gradually assumed.

It is, therefore, still truly the law of the strongest—using the word in the most general sense—which regulates the constitution and administration of governments; but in so far as the principles of government are understood and applied, it is that law as enacted and overruled *by the strongest of all; and while the strongest, also the best and the wisest.* It originates, in other words, with the Supreme Being, who, in determining the position which each of His creatures is to occupy, determines in that very fact the influence, direct and indirect, which each is entitled to exercise. Whoever goes beyond this assumes a power which he has not received, violates a divine law, and therefore in thus far may with justice be resisted. It is in this assurance, which is felt by all men, and known to all men more or less precisely, that we have the only source of political right, and the only measure of political obedience.*

The theory, therefore, which affirmed kings to hold their sovereignties *jure divino*, though now almost universally repudiated, was, *in a certain sense*, not only correct, but is the only theory on the subject capable of logical defence. The error lay in not pushing the theory to its legitimate results. For not only kings, but all other magistrates, and indeed every human being, occupies the position which each respectively holds on the direct authority of God, and is not only entitled, consequently, but bound to exercise all the duties and privileges that legitimately appertain to it. Nor, under the same argument, is any one entitled to deprive another of the position which he legally holds, nor to interfere with him in the performance of its legitimate duties.

* This argument, it is hardly necessary to say, implies that neither any power, nor the exercise of any power, can be of God, when either *attained* or exercised in opposition to the moral law of God. This subject, however, will be more particularly adverted to afterwards.

It does not, however, follow from this, that every one is perfectly suited for his particular position, not merely because the Supreme Being has purposes in the administration of His providence, which we cannot know, but because the selection of office-bearers is usually left by Him to be determined under the influence of free-will. The blame, therefore, of improper appointments rests with human beings themselves, since God could not interfere with His creatures in the exercise of free-will, without subverting the system of discipline on account of which they have been placed in this world. But for evils of this character there is a remedy provided.* When men fail to perform the duties of their stations, they may justly be deprived of them under the authority of God; and they will be deprived of them, should their failure reach such a point as to offend thoroughly the judgment of that ruling power on earth, which must ultimately rest *in the decided majority of the strength of every people.* In this we speak not of culpability, but of incapacity; of culpability we shall speak afterwards, merely remarking at present that there are limits beyond which the magistrate in any country, however despotic, dare not go, and that

* It is in this case almost exclusively that Paley's theory of expediency determining "the will of God" is admissible, and it is an expediency which must be ascertained either by the decision of a superior, or by the overwhelming voice of society.

those limits become narrower just as despotic interference might more injuriously tell on the higher principles of the people, *and consequently on their moral discipline.*

From all this it is clear, that while strictly moral rights may be rested on natural law, as discoverable in the primary feelings of the human mind, political rights must refer their origin solely to that anterior cause on which moral rights are also, no doubt, dependent, and consequently are to be ascertained inferentially. Their authority rests exclusively on the will of God, as discoverable from *the actually existing constitution of things*, which so exist under His decree, and according to His good pleasure, *in so far as it is realised in subordination to His moral law.* In thus far, therefore, no one is entitled to resist them.*

---

* Hence it is arranged by nature, that sudden changes on forms of government for a long time render all government in the countries where they occur mutable and precarious. A long-established government is felt by habit to be *jure divino*. Men come to regard it, therefore, as a sort of immutable. They never perceive gradual changes, but sudden and violent changes unsettle their belief. Every man, under such circumstances, evolves for himself a new theory, imagining that some sort of perfect system should be established, now that change has begun. We have thus governments framed by men, instead of being worked out under the spiritual laws of nature and of God. Hence innumerable factions. There is nothing fixed in men's minds. The result is necessarily a falling back on first principles, without any regard to existing circumstances. Hence again anarchy, and ultimately a military domination.

Such is the nature of political rights, and such the authority on which they exclusively rest. We hardly think, indeed, that any one will venture expressly to maintain that there is any other foundation on which we can *logically* rest them. We are convinced, indeed, that the thing is impossible. Away from religion, apart from the providence of a God by whom all primary laws are enacted, all events arranged, and the validity of all natural feelings and desires guaranteed, there can be neither moral nor political right in any proper sense, nor, consequently, any moral or political obligation. Moral and political rights and duties must rest on the sanction of an almighty and omniscient Lawgiver, or else moral rights and duties can only have a very imperfect foundation, and political rights and duties *can have no sort of foundation at all.* Political right, if we are to use such a term, can only, in such a case, rest on the law of physical strength, and political duty on the law of physical compulsion.

We press this argument, because it is full time that men should know what they are doing, and on what principles they can alone put their trust. There can be no question that loose, materialistic, and selfish theories are spreading widely over the

---

This being inconsistent with the aspirations of civilised society, there arise further commotions. What form such a state of things might ultimately assume, our experience hardly enables us to determine.

world, sustained in most cases, we firmly believe, by an utter ignorance of what are the practical consequences which must follow from them. For as such theories strengthen themselves by habit, moral duty must gradually become of no force, except in so far as enforced by human law, and human law of no obligation, except in so far as enforced by physical power. Were such a state of things realised, the world would become one mass of anarchy and misery; and the nearer we approach to such a state of things, the more will anarchy be strengthened and misery intensified.

The special danger lies in people having their eyes opened, during such practical times as those in which we live, to the absurdity of "the beauty of virtue," and "the greatest happiness of the majority," and suchlike principles. Multitudes have no doubt hitherto been influenced by some reverence for the mysterious meanings which they have been taught to attach to these phrases. But it cannot last. Even the humblest and poorest orders are beginning to think much more than they did, and they will inevitably discover that to the man who has no belief in an overruling Providence, "virtue" has no beauty, or, at all events, is frequently not half so agreeable as vice; while "the greatest happiness of the greatest number" principle is a mere grandiloquent phraseology, intended for inducing the poor to rest satisfied on the whole with the existing state of things. Indeed, much as the recommendation of the "greatest happiness of the majority" principle is *really* for the advantage of the rich, too many of them only adhere to it in practice so far as it suits themselves.

Such hyphotheses, indeed, have never been very available. It is because they have been supplemented by a more or less unconscious sense of *the perpetual presence and overruling providence of God*, that they have aided in preserving the peace of society. Eradicate this supplementary belief, and all such hypotheses in themselves would be laughed to scorn. There are few in the present day so ignorant as not in some measure to appreciate their utter inadequacy as foundations of political rights. We do not indeed think that such a belief in an overruling Providence can be *altogether* eradicated, because the conviction of an overruling Providence, we have seen, necessarily results from the constitution of the human mind. It may, however, be greatly weakened, and in the process of restoring its legitimate power through suffering, which appears almost the only means of restoring it, there can be little doubt that the most disastrous consequences must be incurred. Apart from personal and domestic and social considerations, such a process, widely extended, must necessarily involve fearful convulsions of nations.

This danger is enhanced, of course, by every

advancing step in the progress of civilisation, for every such step accustoms men more and more accurately to think, and consequently shows more and more clearly the utter futility of all the grounds, apart from religion, on which political rights and obligations have been rested. It is on this account that we deem it of such incalculable importance to lay the true foundation of their authority under a train of reasoning which is demonstratively logical, and at the same time so plain that it can neither be met by argument nor evaded by sophistry.

CHAPTER II.

LIMITS OF POLITICAL RIGHTS.

LIMITS OF POLITICAL RIGHTS—THEY ARE LIMITED BY THE MORAL RIGHTS OF OTHERS, AS OF SUPERIOR AUTHORITY—CLASSIFICATION OF MORAL RIGHTS AS RELATING TO GOVERNED AND GOVERNORS: 1. RIGHT OF PERSONAL LIBERTY—2. RIGHTS OF LABOUR AND PROPERTY—3. RIGHT OF POLITICAL POWER.

WE have now determined the nature of political rights, and the foundation on which they rest. The very same argument enables us to determine their limitations. For it is evident, that as political rights, having been bestowed by God, must be valid as against any inferior or merely human right, so must they in turn be subordinated to those moral rights which, as flowing from the direct spiritual laws of God, necessarily imply a superior obligation. In order, therefore, thoroughly to understand the limits of political rights, we must appreciate the moral rights which relate governed and governors to one another. These are comprehended under three classes: 1. The right of personal liberty; 2. The rights of labour and property; 3. The right of political power.

1. The right of personal liberty. It is evident from what has been said that every one is entitled to resist such an interference with his personal liberty as would put it in the power of another to control his moral conduct, or that of those whom the Supreme Being has placed in immediate dependence upon Him. This consideration at once condemns slavery, and indeed every form of government giving to one such an arbitrary control over the conduct of another as to imply slavery.

This, however, of course, involves the assumption that the parties enslaved are more or less cognisant of the moral evils resulting from slavery. Unless this were the case, though the enslaving another might be an immoral act on the part of him who was guilty of it, yet the argument would not in so far imply a right of resistance on the part of him who had been enslaved. A man cannot be entitled to act under a principle *which he does not know.*

When, however, a man feels that slavery interferes or may interfere with the duties which he owes to his God—and more or less we are inclined to think that all must feel this—he is not only entitled, but bound to resist. For if the law of morality be of paramount obligation, as we have proved to be the case, it demonstratively follows that no one can be entitled to exercise such a dominant control over the conduct of another as to interfere with its obligations. We do not say that morality and slavery cannot possibly coexist in certain cases, because the master may only require what is consistent with morality, and the slave may refuse under any penalty to do that which is inconsistent with his moral convictions. But it is obvious that morality, considered as the realisation of religion, is theoretically inconsistent with slavery, as rendering—so far as human means can effect it—the moral and religious conduct of one man dependent on the caprice, or at all events the will, of another. Every one, therefore, has a right to personal liberty by a law of God anterior to any political obligation, so long as he does not interfere with the property or privileges of others, and is consequently entitled to resist even by force any individual or government which may attempt to deprive him of it.

No doubt a man can be compelled to submit to slavery. This, however, has nothing to do with the question of right. It is simply a matter of prudence, or rather of necessity. For no man is justified in continuing a slave one moment after he has reasonable ground for hoping that he can relieve himself from a thraldom under which not only he himself but his children may be compelled to violate the moral law of God, either by direct force, or through being trained to mental and moral degradation.

Hence it follows that every privilege which is *essential* to the acquisition and maintenance of moral principle, and the performance of moral duty, is an inalienable right, superior to all other rights. We are entitled, therefore, and even bound to defend such privileges by force when we clearly see that they are endangered, and to resist every form of political government that may attempt to take them away.

2. Rights of labour and property. Besides personal liberty, which is of the strictest form of right, every man is entitled to the undisturbed possession of his own property and the fruits of his own labour. In other words, the fruits of every man's labour are his own, and every man is entitled to exercise without molestation all the rights implied in the possession of property. This is essential to his full performance of moral duty, for to deprive a man of the use of his property is in so far to reduce him to slavery, by controlling the means which the natural laws of God have given him for the purpose of attaining to a higher moral position, and of realising those moral relationships in which, by the laws of God, he stands to his fellow-creatures. No doubt a man's property is subject to such claims for taxation as may be essential for the public good, because the very necessity of the

case proves that by the decree of God this is a burden with which all property is chargeable. At the same time, taxes ought to be fairly levied in proportion to the respective capabilities of individuals, so far as these can be discovered, and always for the main object of guarding person and property, or, in other words, the essential rights of the subject. Hence, of course, all taxes for the private advantage of individuals or classes are unwarrantable, unless it can be demonstratively proved that this is only an incidental consequence, and that they are actually in their direct effects benefiting the community at large.

Yet it by no means follows in this, as in the former case, that we are entitled to resist by force every act, or even every series of acts, which may seem to imply a deviation from principle. Not only is it sometimes very difficult to apportion taxes with perfect fairness, but it is never to be forgotten that a determination of the rights of labour and of property has been left by the laws of the Supreme Being very much to human arrangement. Hence, although human law cannot be entitled to compel one man to work for the benefit of another, nor to take away property which it has once *absolutely* given, yet the extent to which labour may be taxed, and the mode in which property is to be distributed, as well as the terms under which it is to be held, must from the nature of the case be very much left to arbitrary decision. It is no sufficient ground of resistance, consequently, that the laws of any country may be unwise, except in so far as such resistance may be legitimately provided for by the laws themselves, because the expediency of the laws is, under the authority of God, to be determined by the governors, and not by the governed. Nor are we entitled forcibly to resist human laws because we happen to be placed in an unfavourable social position under the operation of circumstances. Such circumstances have been worked forth under the action of Providence, and we are consequently placed in the position which we occupy under the direct sanction of the Supreme Being. It is the very purpose of God that men should perform their duties in the respective positions which they occupy, and submit to the inconveniences involved in them. If suffering and privation be requisite, therefore, it is a proof in itself that such are the means by which it is the will of the Supreme Being that those subjected to them should be disciplined, and thus prepared for that happiness which it was intended that the events of life should enable us to realise.

There can be no doubt, however, on the very same grounds, that resistance even by force is allowable where the rights of labour and property are purposely trampled upon in such a manner as to render one class of men entirely dependent upon another. In such a case the moral law is violated, and men are necessarily reduced to a condition of substantive slavery. The time for this, however, will almost invariably be indicated by the condition of society. A case, indeed, can hardly be conceived in which public opinion will not be made to tell on the proceedings of any government, ere recourse to violence become an absolute necessity. Strange as it may appear, however, there actually have been instances of governments persisting in such oppression of classes as almost to compel resistance; and experience proves, that when the torrent bursts its bounds there is hardly any possibility for a time of regulating or checking its impetuosity. The passions become so inflamed as to urge sufferers to extravagance. This is specially the case where a nation, having at some particular time made rapid advances in civilisation, suddenly discovers not merely that the rights of labour and property have been violated, but that a real slavery had been introduced among them, through the crushing of their intellectual powers and the degradation of their moral natures. Matters become infinitely worse if the people believe religion to have been made an instrument for working out such results. We have the phenomenon exemplified in the condition of the French at the time of their great Revolution; and we can neither blame them for having had recourse to force, nor even wonder, perhaps, at the degree of their extravagance.

3. Right of political power. Every human being, under every form of government, enjoys a certain measure of political power, in so far as his strength of body and faculties of mind give him a certain indirect influence. This influence, of course, increases proportionally with the progress of civilisation. Hence there is a class of political rights, apart altogether from official position, that flows from the relative qualifications of individuals. In this way a man without any official position may have indirectly a great weight in political government. From this it follows, and we know it to be true as matter of fact, that be the governors what they may, every system of political government must be suitable to the wants, the opinions, and generally the circumstances of the governed. This is the enactment of the Supreme Being, and will work itself out, therefore, in the very nature of things, under a process which we have described already. If it is not effected gradually under regulated changes, the result must ultimately be sought through convulsion and violence. From this we have a manifest instruction of Providence, that governors are bound to see to it themselves.* They are bound

---

* It is sometimes argued in recent times, that men ought to receive political power in order to dignify them in their own eyes, and thereby raise them in the scale of society. It is an

to watch the progress of society, and to introduce changes on the system of government, so as to accommodate it to the progressive changes in the condition of those whom they govern. No doubt it is impossible to make any system perfect, but the state of society, again, will in every instance indicate clearly enough how far changes are practically necessary, so as to prevent violent national convulsions. In some instances, indeed, there may be too great a tendency to make changes under the influence of mere democratic impulse, mistaken for the general convictions of society, but this is only a ground for teaching us to exercise caution and discrimination, and by no means an argument against all change. On the contrary, the real opinions and feelings of intelligent men, uninfluenced by personal ambition, indicate the will of God, because it is the voice of reason; and those governors who neglect the clear manifestations of these, subject their country and themselves to those penalties which necessarily follow contempt of nature's laws. It is in this way that, as men

---

argument so very silly, that perhaps it hardly requires a reply. We may just remark, that if it apply to those who have the suitable qualifications, there is little difference of opinion as to the desirableness of giving such parties political power, if it can be accomplished. But if the claim be meant to apply to those who are unqualified, apart from its manifest other absurdities, it would imply that for the sake of an *incidental object*, *the end and aim of political government itself should be sacrificed.*

generally become more intelligent, the foundations of government require to be enlarged, not because every intelligent individual has a right to enjoy official power, but because its widest safe expansion gives the best assurance of impartiality in its exercise.*

From these considerations it will appear that the use of force, for the mere purpose of acquiring political power under a direct or official form, is inadmissible under almost any circumstances. No man, we have seen, has a natural right to it, and consequently we can only be justified in using force to procure it where a government persists in maintaining *and exercising* privileges which are equivalent to the reduction of a portion of its subjects to such slavery *as may interfere with the performance of moral duty*. Under any other circumstances, the strength which could alone gain the object by violence will ultimately and probably more quickly accomplish it by moral influence. Even when a government persists in

---

* Governments, under ordinary circumstances, change gradually so as to meet progressive changes in the state of society. Sudden and violent convulsions usually result either from knowledge outgrowing political progress, or from wealth accumulating in the hands of a small number, so that the masses are oppressed. The immediate causes of such changes, however, are innumerable, and their forms very various. Such changes in monarchical and aristocratic governments are, strangely enough, for the most part led by aristocrats under the influence of vanity or ambition. In democratic governments they are for the most part directed by a dominant military chief.

maintaining privileges which may be abused, and indicates, as it may seem, an inclination so to abuse them, the utmost caution should still be exercised in having recourse to force, considering the strong tendency which men have to seek for power merely for the sake of power, and the risk thence arising of self-deception. We must ever bear in mind that no ground of mere expediency can warrant forcible resistance of an established government, because every established government has its authority from God. Nothing, in fact, can warrant it, but a conviction of its interfering with privileges of its subjects *essential to the performance of their moral duties*. Violent resistance to an established government, on the ground of supposed *political* rights being withheld, is inconsistent with the law of nature, and consequently with the will of God.

CHAPTER III.

SUMMARY OF THE PRINCIPLES ESTABLISHED IN THE PRECEDING CHAPTERS, AND DEVELOPMENT OF POLITICAL SCIENCE AS FLOWING THEREFROM.

SUMMARY OF THE PRINCIPLES ESTABLISHED IN THE PRECEDING CHAPTERS—GOVERNMENTS ARISE FROM CIRCUMSTANCES, SO AS TO BE MORE OR LESS SUITABLE TO THE PROGRESS OF SOCIETY—THIS IS A DECLARATION OF THE WILL OF GOD—EVILS ARISING FROM A SUDDEN CHANGE ON THE ESSENTIAL CHARACTER OF ANY GOVERNMENT—COMMON RESULT OF SUCH CHANGES, AND THE CAUSES THEREOF—FURTHER CHANGES FOLLOWING ON SUCH RESULT—PROBABLE MODE OF RESTORING A GOVERNMENT UNDER SUCH CIRCUMSTANCES TO WORKING ORDER—ILLUSTRATED IN THE CASE OF CROMWELL, AND IN THE PRESENT PROCEEDINGS OF THE FRENCH EMPIRE—LIBERTY OF THE PRESS—CLASS OF PERSONS IN WHOM POLITICAL POWER MAY BE SAFELY VESTED—DANGEROUS CLASSES—POINT OF VIEW IN WHICH POLITICAL POWER OUGHT TO BE REGARDED—CAUSE OF MISCONCEPTIONS ON THIS SUBJECT.

POLITICAL power, as we have now seen, humanly speaking, rests on superiority of strength. It may be physical strength, or mental power, or a union of both modified by circumstances. Regarding the subject under this aspect, it will be obvious that those who wield this strength may, within certain limits, employ it for any purpose that they please. There is a tendency, equivalent to an indirect law, under which certain portions of each society combine their strength for the purpose of sustaining each respective government; and there are various causes perpetually in operation which give certain persons greater or less influence in such governments. This influence is, of course, realised, therefore, through the possession of superior strength; and, humanly speaking, it rests upon no other foundation whatever.

To civil government thus viewed, the words "right," "ought," and "duty" are, as we have seen, perfectly inapplicable. Neither the governors nor the government can have any right, except the right of force; nor is the subject bound to any obedience except by the law of fear. Yet this is not the general impression with respect to the authority of civil government; on the contrary, there seems a universal conviction, even among those whose theory logically nullifies the conclusion, that magistrates, on some ground or other, are *entitled* to obedience. This universality of conviction is in itself a proof that there is either a law, or some tendency equivalent to a law, assuring us of its authority, since a universal effect can only be accounted for under the assumption of a law direct or indirect; that is to say, a law either realised directly in our feelings, or indirectly indicated by the character of our circumstances. Hence, as we have attained an indisputable conclusion to the effect that the authority of political rights rests on no direct law, there is no other possible assumption, save that it rests on the character of circumstances, and thus must derive its authority from the will of God, *as expressed in the arrangements of His providence.* In this we have a full explanation of the universal conviction that prevails upon the subject, and which can be explained in no other way. To say that this conclusion may not be true, is simply to say that the arrangements of Providence, which necessarily involve natural law in themselves, constitute a system of deception, and hence that the laws of nature implied in them are delusions and falsehoods. If we can bring ourselves to absolute scepticism *with respect to all things physical and spiritual,* such a supposition may perhaps be a suitable mode of expressing it in this case. But if we believe anything whatever with respect either to physical or spiritual existence, it is a supposition evidently absurd and untenable, and is indeed substantively a contradiction in terms.

From all this it follows that every form of government is really a species of theocracy. The Supreme Being does not, indeed, *directly* prescribe any form of government, nor does He name the persons by whom any form of government is to be administered; but indirectly, through the arrangements of Providence, He sanctions the form of government in each case, as well as the authority of those who administer it. That neither governments nor those who administer them are in all respects perfect, nor even in many instances such as they might and ought to be, is true, because both must depend in so far on human judgment. To select their respective forms of government, and the persons who are to administer them, is in so far not only left to men themselves, but is a part of the system under which they are tried and disciplined. Yet the general result will be found suitable to the circumstances of each people, because it will flow necessarily from the arrangements of Providence. Both governments and governors, consequently, as they actually exist, have in so far divine recognition, and are thus entitled to obedience, in as far as they do not violate the anterior laws under which God has limited their powers.

Whether, therefore, a government be despotic, constitutional, aristocratic, or democratic, we are certain that it is in so far suited to the then condition of the governed while it is exposed to no serious threatenings of violent opposition.* We

---

* It will be evident that the same argument applies to all kinds of government, civil and ecclesiastical. That the Supreme Being may by direct revelation prescribe a special form of government is true, but in that case it must be administered more or less *by superhuman instrumentality*. This is manifest; because the same form of government applied to nations in different circumstances, and different stages of civilisation, *would not work under the ordinary laws of Providence*.

are certain of this, because no government can be in a state of security, or free from threatenings of violent opposition, which is inconsistent with the widespread and profound convictions of its subjects. Threatenings of violent opposition, however, do not necessarily prove that a government is bad. They may in some instances merely prove a widespread immorality among certain classes of the people, urging them to ambitious aspirations, in the hope of promoting their selfish interests by change. In this case the subjects are manifestly violating divine law, and if successful will probably soon pay the penalty of such violation. Governments are, therefore, entitled *jure divino* to the obedience of their subjects in all cases where they do not violate, nor show a purpose of violating, privileges essential to the observation of the moral law. When, on the contrary, they do this, they may *jure divino* be resisted, because they thereby substantively repudiate the only right under which political government can be exercised. Under this very limitation, however, governors are clearly bound to introduce changes on their system of administration, when God through a change of circumstances has indicated His will to transfer power in so far from one class to another. No doubt such changes often take place silently both in circumstances and governments. When, however, they take place in circumstances, and legislators refuse to make corresponding changes on governments, it must ultimately lead to distractions and violence.*

This is specially the case where the ruling influence in nations is, from whatever causes, rapidly passing from those who actually exercise official authority into other hands. In such cases there must be a serious risk of political convulsion from the one party being eager to grasp, and the other unwilling to relinquish. There is, indeed, a manifest danger when such a change is in progress, that the former system of government being practically subverted, a new government may supersede it, under the operation of incidental and arbitrary causes, which will, therefore, be anomalous in its character, and, of course, unworkable in its administration. Should this be the case, generations may pass away ere a smoothly-working machinery can be reconstituted. There generally, indeed, results under such circumstances a widespread restlessness, originating in the discontent of those whom the change has not satisfied, and consequently spasmodic struggles

* As people advance in civilisation, a higher amount of political privilege is necessary for enabling them to fulfil the exactions of the moral law as applicable to the change on their intellectual condition. Thence, again, the obligation of governments to extend such privilege as civilisation progresses. Of course, where this is neglected, and subjects feel conscious that the performance of the moral duties which their circumstances demand is thereby prevented, they are not only entitled, but bound, where it can be done without generating greater moral evils, to take possession of it for themselves.

between the various factions approaching more or less nearly to anarchy. These almost invariably end in some species of despotism. All ultimately begin to feel the necessity of peace and of a firm government for the preservation of life and property. Thus some able adventurer, usually the favourite of the military, is, with the tacit concurrence of the more powerful section of the people, endowed with supreme authority.

Yet this will not last in countries advanced in civilisation. No doubt perfect personal liberty, and entire respect for the rights of labour and property, may exist under the rule of a despot. A despotic government, indeed, under a firm and wise governor, has often, and perhaps truly, been called the best of all governments. Unfortunately, however, few are to be found capable of wisely and firmly regulating unlimited power. No one would feel this more than a wise and firm governor himself; and looking to the possible characters of those who might follow him, such a ruler would probably prepare for contingencies by training his people to the exercise of self-government. Giving them more or less popular institutions under his own control, he would endeavour to leave to posterity a system realising constitutional principles begun, and capable of working itself into such a shape as would prove suitable to the condition and growing political intelligence of the people.

It must be confessed, however, that this is a process of which we have no experience. We think the germs of such an attempt can be traced in the government of Oliver Cromwell, certainly one of the ablest and greatest men that ever occupied the position of chief magistrate of a nation. We are also inclined to believe that such germs of intended development are discoverable in the present government of the Emperor of the French. It is indeed almost certain that Louis Napoleon is influenced by some form of this theory, and it would assuredly be the most glorious triumph of statesmanship did he succeed in giving it practical effect. The present government of France cannot last. The realisation of the theory which we have now suggested, seems the only possible means of preserving the throne to his family, or a permanent government to his people.

It is indeed true that, as a proof of his despotic tendencies, the Emperor of the French has been accused of overbearing the liberty of the press. But the extent to which entire freedom of the press is compatible with the existence of almost any government, is probably of all problems the most difficult to be solved, and is indeed one of the grand political problems of the present age.*

* In Britain we have no *sufficient* experience. *Entire* political freedom of the press is a novelty. America teaches us more upon the subject, but little or nothing bearing on our present purpose. For, passing over the moral and social effects with which the freedom of the press is usually attended, it must be

Our imperfect experience upon the subject hitherto seems only to show that freedom of the press has a decided tendency to foster democracy. It could not, indeed, we may venture to say, be otherwise. The primary object of all writers who are not devoted to the interests of truth only, must be the sale of their writings. This holds specially of the periodical press, of which the journals are for the most part mere objects of mercantile speculation. Now, the sale of writings can be most thoroughly effected by encouraging the prejudices and stimulating the passions of the largest numbers. No doubt other motives will have a greater or less effect, according to the strength of moral principle in different individuals. But there are multitudes over whom higher motives have little or no influence; and as surely as human nature is human nature, these writings—especially in

observed, that while an immense majority of the people possess property, as is the case in America, the press will, under the argument which we have stated, necessarily defend property; and, indeed, any writing that attacked property would be crushed. But where a majority have no property, but depend on manual labour for subsistence, the press, under the very same argument, would be led to attack the rights of property; and, as we have said, the result is unknown. We cannot, however, conceive anything that could prevent anarchy in such a case, except high moral principle prevailing among the great body of the people. There may be other motives which would operate, but we cannot form the slightest notion of what they are. Apart from moral principle resting on religious grounds, the "greatest happiness of the greatest number" would, amongst the masses, be a motive rather to anarchy than to order.

the case of cheap publications—will have the widest circulation. It is indeed but justice to the cheap press of our own country to say, that it is as yet, on the whole, conducted with wonderful moderation. Yet its ultra-democratic tendency is manifest to every human being. Now, we do not say that this is wrong, nor do we desire to enter at all on the question of its probable results. We only state an indisputable fact, in order to show that neither the Emperor of the French, nor any other man contemplating the object which we have ascribed to him, can be blamed for regulating the liberty of the political press. Its full development would be absolutely destructive of the possibility of rearing up a permanent government in any country which had recently been subjected to a series of revolutionary changes.

Governments, then, it is clear, are not the result of any formal selection, except to a very limited extent, but flow out of the constitution of things as arranged by the providence of God. That they may be modified for good or evil by the exercise of human will is true, but this applies to the details rather than the essential character of the systems. These last must in all cases be in some measure conformable to the intellectual and moral progress of each people. Hence it is that any sudden change on the essential elements of a government must be attended with the greatest political danger. It is hardly in any case to be attempted, indeed, unless where such government is manifestly exercising a prejudicial effect on the moral habits of the people. We say *hardly*, because it is conceivable that circumstances might occur which, in a purely political point of view, would render sudden political changes absolutely necessary. Generally, however, even legitimate and constitutional changes *of a very decided kind* should never be made, unless to obviate practical evils.

Absolute theoretical symmetry in government under the present condition of things is unattainable. Changes for this purpose will invariably lead to other evils, unforeseen and unexpected. Indeed, changes for the mere purpose of giving political power to discontented parties who *plead no practical evil*, must, under the principles which we have now endeavoured to establish, be exceedingly dangerous in the nature of things. The foundations of government are no doubt more broadly laid, but they are partially laid on quicksands. Those who are thus introduced to political power are more likely to subvert than to strengthen the structure, while no limit can be constituted against the perpetual recurrence of additional claims. As we have seen, there are no political rights, strictly speaking, except in so far as political power is actually realised; and even then it is a trust rather than a right, as is proved from its originating in an indirect, and not a direct law,* which we are required by God to perform, not for our own advantage, but for the general welfare of the community. If, consequently, it seem desirable that political power should be extended to a larger number, not from any practical evil to be remedied, but for the sake of resting the government on a broader foundation, it should be done with the most extreme caution. From the very nature of the case it is evident that there are dangerous elements at work. There is a spirit of pure love of power in operation, which, if gratified beyond certain bounds, will, as matter of necessity, acquire irresistible strength, and must therefore soon subvert the order of society. It

* Judicial is a species of subsidiary political power, and the determination of the parties in whom it is vested involves consideration of the most immense importance to the welfare of society. Singularly enough, in modern times this subsidiary political power has become more and more limited to a class or profession. The result has come to be, that men believe actions at law to be almost pure gambling. The Romans allowed no professional judges. The ablest men were selected annually to preside and direct certain parties to whose decision generally each case was referred, and who somewhat resembled modern juries. Neither the presidents, nor generally the jurors, were paid. That such a system, carefully constituted, would meet some of the evils of modern times, especially in the diminution of the advantage which rich suitors possess over those that are poor, seems clear, and probably the decisions on the whole might, if less technical, be quite as equitable. As democracy advances, it seems at all events highly improbable that judicial proceedings can continue as they are. The subject is deeply interesting, but the nature of our purpose prevents us from entering on it at length.

rests on selfish desire, inconsistent with that principle of obedience to the laws of Providence, under which political government can alone permanently exist.

In truth, there are only two classes of persons with whom it is safe to intrust political power, supposing intellectual qualifications to be equal. The one consists of those who, from a high sense of principle, seek the true interests of the community as a moral duty. The other consists of those who are possessed of property sufficient to make them afraid of political convulsions, and who, therefore, from motives of self-interest, will watch the circumstances of the times, and so regulate their political conduct as to preserve life and property unassailed and unassailable. Where those who seek political influence on mere selfish grounds constitute the ruling power, and the majority are without property, life and property can only be preserved through the use of bribery, or similar means addressed to their passions or self-interest. Mere ability and knowledge, apart from high moral principle or self-interest, are rather dangerous than otherwise in persons possessed of political power.* Yet perhaps even

---

* The theory that education will fit men for the possession of political power, in the sense of making them safe custodiers of life and property, apart from moral principle and self-interest, is too absurd to deserve a reply. It is little more tenable to maintain that education will teach those who have nothing, to oppose the equalisation of property as injurious to their inte-

OF POLITICAL SCIENCE. 333

more dangerous still are the persons who, with a smattering of superficial knowledge, believe themselves to have an inherent right to political power, and are prepared to exercise it, if it can be procured, for the realisation of some scheme of what they profess to consider political perfection, but which seems invariably to end, as matter of fact, in flattering their own prejudices, and gratifying their own selfishness or vanity. When a government falls into the hands of such parties, its doom is sealed.

In a word, as we have already indicated, political power is not a right, but a social trust, to which the nomination partly flows from the arrangements of Providence, and partly results from the exercise of free-will in the people among

rests. The assumption is not true. It is not, at all events, injurious to their interests *for the time*, which is the motive by which the mass of men is influenced; and in the case of multitudes it is not injurious to their permanent worldly interests. It is vain to tell men that a week's time would make differences again, as the idle and profligate would quickly spend what they had got. Every one would answer, "That would not happen in my case;" or if there were any honest enough to admit the possibility of such a thing in regard to themselves, they would at all events be prepared to take their chance, and indulge their desires while their money lasted. But even supposing, under a philosophical deduction, it could be found for their worldly advantage that the rights of property should be maintained, *which it could not be*, yet it must be remembered that desire, jealousy, envy, malignity, are to be thrown into the scale; and he who believes that respect for property would outweigh all these in the present state of the world, must be imbued with a spirit of hopefulness which sets all experience at defiance.

whom it is enjoyed. So far as the latter element is concerned, it should only be open to those who exhibit industry, energy, and high character. When, therefore, a man has proved himself to be possessed of these qualifications by that success in life which is the best practical test of them, he should be admissible to a share in political power. He has proved himself to be worthy of it, and capable of exercising it for the public good, by a test which, though extremely imperfect, yet seems to be the only one practically possible, while the property which he has acquired gives security for him that he will endeavour to preserve the peace of society. Yet it ought to be distinctly understood that he has no right to it, except in so far as his being in a position to receive it gives him a right from God, under the conditions and limitations which every divine right must imply. He is bound to regard it, in other words, as a trust rather than a right; and to understand that he receives it as a mark of the approbation with which his countrymen regard his past, and the confidence which they repose in his future conduct. Let this theory be adopted by any people as the basis of their political government, and the very nature of the case demonstrates that the best and noblest administration of it that is possible will be secured.

These details are not only deducible from the principles which have been established, but are evidently conformable to common experience and common sense. Into more minute details it is not our intention to enter. The character of more minute details, it will be manifest from the whole of our argument, can only be predicated with respect to *special* forms of government. These, however, are to be determined, as we have seen, according to circumstances. Hence the common discussion as to whether monarchy, aristocracy, democracy, or any given combination of them, is to be preferred as a form of government, implies in its very expression a misconception of the condition of human beings, and consequently of the foundation and purpose of government. One form will be best for one state of society, and another for another. In some states of society a despotism would be impossible; in others a democracy would be impossible; in many a constitutional or mixed form of government would be impossible.*

* From this it is manifest, that to apply the form of government suitable for a particular kingdom to the provinces dependent thereupon, but of which the people are in an entirely different intellectual and social condition, must prove ruinous to their peace. It matters nothing though the form so applied should be of the highest excellence. Hence appears the wisdom of the ancient Romans, who left the governments of their conquered provinces as nearly as possible just as they found them. To have forced on them the government of Rome, however superior it may have been in abstract excellence, would, they saw, have been to disorganise them. But they left them as they were, and thus retained them in comparative tranquillity, sometimes under very unfavourable circumstances. The most un-

The peculiar modifications most suitable in each case are perfectly undiscoverable *a priori*, and can only be determined by actual circumstances, as they emerge under the operation of an infinity of different causes. With a knowledge of those principles, however, and those more general particulars which we have now endeavoured to establish, there can be no serious difficulty in arranging details, as experience develops the character and interests of each people.

It would indeed be very interesting, and might serve to illustrate our conclusions, did circumstances permit us to analyse a variety of political constitutions, so as to exhibit the advantages and defects of each respectively. This, however, would involve an extension of the present work far beyond the bounds which we had contemplated, and would imply an appeal to considerations of a purely incidental character, either altogether away from *fundamental* spiritual truth, or, at all events, only indirectly connected with it.

It is enough for our purpose if it has been proved, as we trust has been thoroughly done, that the foundation of political government must be rested exclusively either on mere force, or else on the decree and ordination of the Supreme

---

tenable theory, that a constitutional government, because fitted for the circumstances of one country, is therefore most suitable for the circumstances of all countries, is, however, not only entertained by many, but is openly avowed !

Being. Of His will, consequently, in respect to the administrators of government, the influence appertaining to the position which each *actually* occupies must constitute the proof and the test. We may take our choice of these as the foundation of political government, but there is no other supposition possible.

Yet even this choice only implies a *conceivable* result, for our feelings assure us that force is *not* the only foundation of political authority. Every man is conscious of an undercurrent of conviction pressing on him, that there is a higher authority sanctioning political arrangements, and obliging him to obedience. In this way we hear appeals continually made to political right even by the most unthinking and illiterate, while no one seems exactly to know in what such political right consists, nor, consequently, does any one, of course, pretend to determine its precise limits. Hence the extreme vagueness under which men have been content to receive theories of political government. They have rested satisfied with a political philosophy which, on any other subject, they would have rejected with merited contempt. But *feeling* that there is something, be it what it may, beyond the theory sanctioning such government, they supplement the one by a *tacit* belief in the other.

Now, this tacit or partially unconscious belief we trust that we have succeeded in putting into such a form, in connection with our previous argument as to religion and morals, as will secure for it a recognised and conscious conviction. In this way political government, ceasing to depend on mere empirical belief, is made to rest on the conclusions of a strictly philosophical science; its principles being understood, and its purposes in the highest sense being rendered practically available.

APPENDIX.

A, page 84.

VIEWS OF M. COMTE, AND THE POSITIVE PHILOSOPHY.

In thus reducing the argument for the being of a God as arising from the adjustment and organisation of the universe *to its principle*, we specially claim the sanction of those who belong to what has been called the "positive" school of philosophy. The argument, in fact, is conducted on the strictest principles of positivism. "Nous renonçons à chercher l'origine et la destination de l'univers," says M. Comte, "et à connaître les causes intimes des phénomènes, pour nous attacher uniquement à découvrir, par l'usage bien combiné du raisonnement et de l'observation, leur lois effectives, c'est-à-dire leurs relations invariables de succession et de similitude." In this view it simply constitutes natural theology an essential branch of the "positive" philosophy.

To understand this clearly it must be kept in view, although few even of M. Comte's avowed disciples seem to be aware of it, that the "positive" philosophy and the "Comtian" philosophy are two entirely different things. It is utterly a mistake to suppose that the "positive" philosophy implies atheism. The "positive" philosophy is simply another name which M. Comte has been pleased to give to the old "inductive" philosophy commonly ascribed to Bacon. It is not opposed, therefore, to the inductive philosophy, as many seem to suppose, with which it is, on the contrary, perfectly identical, but to what M. Comte calls the "theological and metaphysical stages of philosophy."

It is indeed true that M. Comte, while repudiating anti-theism, yet professed himself to be an athiest in the ordinary sense of the word, but it was on grounds which had nothing whatever to do with what he called the "positive" philosophy. This was a part of the "*Comtian*" philosophy, which assumes that the being of a God could not be proved *inductively*. It is this assumption which, we trust, our argument demonstrates to be erroneous. We have shown in the text that the adjustment and organisation of the universe is a phenomenon, as much as the adjustment and organisation of a steam-engine is a phenomenon; and that we must refer the former to an intelligent agent, under *exactly the same process* as we refer the latter to an intelligent agent. We prove thus that belief in an intelligent God is *an essential part of the "positive" philosophy*, unless, indeed, Comte had been prepared to deny that belief in the intelligence of our fellow-creatures is a part of the "positive" philosophy, in which case his whole system must have fallen to pieces.

To illustrate this matter more fully, it may not be without advantage to give a sketch of the leading principles of the Comtian philosophy, not as being a matter of any importance in itself, but because we hear a mysterious profundity not unfrequently ascribed to it, and which renders it eminently the philosophy of multitudes who do not know what it is, and who would assuredly laugh at it, and at themselves, did they know the true nature of the deity which they worship.

It is founded on the notion that there are three modes of philosophising which do and must follow each other in successive order *with respect to every subject*—viz., the theological, the metaphysical, and the "positive" or inductive modes. The first, or theological mode, Comte thinks, refers all effects to supernatural agency. The second, or metaphysical mode, refers effects to occult qualities. The last, or positive mode, explains effects by the action of phenomena on phenomena, and its philosophy consists thus in generalising the relations of phenomena; or, in other words, in ascertaining their laws. The theory is an utter delusion.

It is an entire error to suppose that in the early ages of the world, or in any state of society, men attributed or attribute *all* effects directly to superhuman causes; or, in other words, philosophise by a theological mode. When a stone sank through the water, in early ages they attributed it to the relative character of the two bodies, *and they generalised this knowledge so as to believe that under the same circumstances* the same effect would invariably follow, so that in thus far they were as much metaphysical and positive philosophers as the men of any other age. When the people of those times chewed their meat, they did not in like manner attribute it to any superhuman agency, but to the action of their teeth upon the food; and they also generalised this knowledge so as to believe that under the same circumstances the same effect would invariably follow. The same thing held true with regard to an infinity of other particulars. It held true of every particular of which the *direct cause was known*. It was only *unknown causes* that they attributed to superhuman agency, and unknown causes all men did, and *do still*, attribute more or less to superhuman agency, thus showing that a belief in superhuman agency somehow necessarily results from the condition of the human mind.

That which M. Comte calls the "metaphysical" mode of philosophising is, again, common to all ages. Every direct cause is an "occult" cause. Unless it be with respect to our own minds, we do not know the absolute or essential nature of any cause whatever. The ancients, indeed, imagined that we had some *absolute* knowledge of qualities, which we know to be a mistake, our knowledge being purely relative, but this made no difference to their mode of philosophising. They attributed no more to entities than we do to qualities. They philosophised by induction, as men have ever done and ever *must* do. The alchemist, for example, philosophised as much by experiment as the chemists do in the present day. The real error of the ancients, which M. Comte seems to misapprehend, lay in their assumption of *a priori* hypotheses, to the realisation of which they directed their experiments *exclusively*. They thus had their attention turned away in a great measure from the really useful conclusions, to which their experiments, conducted under a correct knowledge of the use of hypotheses, would have probably led them. We say under a correct knowledge of the use of hypotheses, because all men philosophise under some form of hypothesis, and must do so; but in modern times they modify their hypotheses according to the progressive results of their experiments, and thus are enabled much more readily to ascertain true causes. In this we have the source, and the only source, of the superiority of modern science.

As knowledge extended, of course the number of effects attributed to direct superhuman agency diminished, not from any change in the *mode* of philosophising, but because the direct causes of effects became known to a greater and greater extent. Men still attributed the more remote causes of effects or phenomena, and those of which no probable theory could be imagined, to superhuman agency. *Indirectly*, therefore, they did, and do, and ever will, attribute all effects to superhuman agency—*i.e.*, they recognise the action of qualities directly, but they consider the *causes of those qualities themselves* to be superhuman. Our modes of philosophising, therefore, instead of being divisible into theological, metaphysical, and positive stages, are identically the same *in principle* now as they ever were. The only difference is, that our knowledge of direct causes is increased and extended. We just as much as ever regard qualities as the direct means of producing effects, and superhuman agency as the indirect or final means. The modes of philosophising are, therefore, precisely what they ever were, and what it seems certain they must ever be. As our knowledge extends, we are able to refer a larger number of effects to direct causes; but the causes of these causes, and generally all phenomena, of the causes of which we can conceive no probable theory, we are compelled to attribute to the action of intelligent superhuman power.

What M. Comte means by assuming philosophy to be the investigation of laws, it is very difficult under his theory to understand. A knowledge of laws must imply a knowledge of causes; or, in other words, *a tacit recognition of occult powers operating.** But if we recognise occult powers operating, his philosophy, so far as it involves anything which can be called his own, must immediately vanish. Why should we not in that case recognise the operation of entities? Why not of superhuman agency? We have seen none of Comte's disciples who have attempted to meet this apparently insuperable difficulty, nor does Comte himself appear to have felt it. Yet the assumption that we can somehow appreciate the nature of causation, and the action of causes, lies at the foundation of his system, and must indeed lie at the foundation of every philosophical system.

---

* It seems quite inconsistent with his general theory, which appears to limit all knowledge to *the phenomena of perception*. Causes are not phenomena of perception. How, then, do we come to know them? Comtists say that we know them from *experience*. It is substantively the theory of Hume, with whom, singularly enough, almost every form of scepticism having the appearance of plausibility has originated. But experience can only tell us of that which *is past;* it cannot assure us of that which *is to come*. It cannot assure us that *all* effects must have causes, or that certain causes will be followed by certain effects. There is a something behind which induces us *to believe in experience*, and which *does not arise from perception at all, but is purely mental*. We have already explained that it is our personal sense of the nature both of physical and efficient power. But *it matters nothing what it is*, if it be admitted, as it must be admitted, that it is a *mental tendency*.

Without it all philosophy, and indeed every pretence at philosophising, must be annihilated. If we do not admit the existence of occult powers which *must* act permanently in the same way, science of every kind is at an end. Mr J. S. Mill * is of opinion that Comte intended to admit the existence of physical, but not of efficient causes. We should like to hear a reasonable ground for believing in physical, and not in efficient, causation. At all events, we trust it has been proved in the text that all men do believe in efficient causation, if they believe in the existence of their fellow-creatures. On this whole subject of causation M. Comte seems to have been specially at sea. His most devoted disciples hardly know what is to be made of his theory in regard to it.

As to the classification which Comte derives from his imaginary series of modes of philosophising, it just comes to this, that sciences which depend upon other sciences *are posterior in date to those on which they depend.* Of course they are. It is unnecessary to dwell on the specialities of his classification, however liable to objection, for it has no bearing upon our subject; but his principle is undoubtedly true, and we believe has been accepted as true in all ages. We are not aware that in stating the proposition formally, or in applying it, he has made it available for *any useful or practical purpose whatever.*

Comte repudiates psychology, or the observation of our mental states, and consecutive induction therefrom. It is a result of his materialistic philosophy. Hence the only intellectual philosophy that he conceives to be possible is phrenology. He singularly forgets, as Mill has demonstra-

---

* I have adopted Mr Mill's view of Comte's philosophy in these remarks, because, though professing to differ from him in many particulars, Mr Mill is generally an admirer, and almost a disciple, of his philosophy. It has been my wish to regard every man's opinions under the most favourable and defensible aspect. Had I given my own view of the nature of Comte's philosophy, it would have been very different.

tively shown, that there can be no such science as phrenology, granting it to be a science, except by comparing the structure of the brains of different men with their moral characters, *as discovered by psychology*. We could not even conceive the idea of feelings and faculties, &c., by merely looking at the brain. A certain amount of anterior psychological investigation is manifestly essential to our knowledge of feelings and faculties, and even of the existence of mind at all. This theory, which is thus *manifestly impossible*, is Comte's theory of the "positive" philosophy of mind. A mistake so manifest and so enormous could hardly fail, one would think, to stagger the faith even of those who are most inclined to be his disciples.

This theory of the truth of phrenology, however, being assumed, it might have been expected to constitute the groundwork of Comte's sociology. We should suppose that every one, under this view, would be educated according to the structure of his brain. In that case there could be no doubt as to what his character must be. We should have a sort of realisation of the theory of Plato's republic. Every man, up to the extent of his education, would feel exactly what he ought to feel, and do exactly what he ought to do; with this immense advantage, that every science would soon be perfected by our having an opportunity of selecting the individuals most suited for the study of each, and of providing them with the most suitable instructors. Something like this, indeed, Comte seems actually to have had in his mind, but finding the attempt to form any system under such a theory hopeless, he, whether consciously or unconsciously, falls back on psychology, that very psychology which he had repudiated, and endeavours to explain the philosophy of the social world by psychological considerations, intermixed with a vast deal of mere arbitrary assertion, which he strives to verify by an appeal to history. In all this we cannot discover anything in M. Comte's social philosophy which can be of any practical use. The tendency of his historical narrative seems much to resemble that of the writings of the late Mr Buckle, in showing that men in all ages are influenced by the same general causes. This, in so far, is undoubtedly true, but it appears difficult to conceive why so much time and trouble should have been spent in proving it. The fact has been admitted and acted upon by men in all ages, although it never can be proved in the extreme form in which these writers have adopted it. They both have fallen into the system of the earlier ages, and adopted an *a priori* theory which they afterwards set themselves to prove, *in defiance of all counteracting considerations.*

The social philosophy of Comte, consequently, affords no practical results, except such as are so manifestly extravagant as of themselves to shake all faith in his system. Thus, for example, in the words of Mr Mill, according to Comte, "The undisputed authority which astronomers possess in astronomy will be possessed on the great social questions by positive philosophers, to whom will belong the spiritual government of society, subject to two conditions: that they be entirely independent within their own sphere of the temporal government, and that they be peremptorily excluded from all share in it, receiving instead the entire conduct of education." * The general proposition would extend the authority of positive philosophers over the universe. The conditions are evidently contradictory and impossible.

Yet there can be no doubt that the principle which Comte intended to form the basis of his theory of sociology is perfectly correct. I give it again in Mr Mill's words: "Personal interests and feelings in the social state can only attain the maximum of satisfaction by means of cooperation, and the necessary condition of co-operation is a common belief. All human society, consequently, is grounded on a system of fundamental opinions, which

* 'Auguste Comte and Positivism,' by John Stuart Mill.

only the speculative faculty can provide, and which, when provided, directs our other impulses in their mode of seeking their gratification." This theory, pushed to its legitimate extent, gives the precise system of morality which we have advocated. But it cannot be pushed to its legitimate extent, apart from the assumption of an intelligent and morally perfect God. Apart from this, the very idea of men "obtaining the maximum of satisfaction by means of co-operation," is manifestly absurd. We want the co-operation of the very being that can alone, *by possibility*, afford us the "maximum of satisfaction." The co-operation of all our fellow-creatures, taken together, can never assure us of one moment's satisfaction, and still less of "the maximum of satisfaction," which must not only be intense, but permanent.

As to M. Comte's religious system, it appears so extraordinary as almost to exceed belief. It simply shows that every man who attempts to frame a system of spiritual philosophy will be absolutely forced to recognise some sort of religion. We all hanker after it. His God, or the *grand être*, as he calls it, is the whole human race, past, present, and to come. This God is to be worshipped in our mothers as representatives of the past, our wives as representatives of the present, and our daughters as representatives of the future. What obligation lies on us to worship the *grand être*, or why it should be worshipped in our mothers, wives, and daughters, nowhere clearly appears. Religion, if it be anything, is the science which teaches us our relation to superhuman beings. If it does not mean this, it means nothing at all. The theory of M. Comte, therefore, is not a theory of religion in any sense, but a wild theory of morality; nor can it, consequently, in any measure meet that belief in superhuman agency, which, under some form or other, is spread over the whole world. So strongly does M. Comte feel this, that, in entire opposition to his materialism, he ultimately introduces into his system a sort of Fetishism, according to which each particular existence is regulated by its particular God. Mr Mill insinuates that this part of his writings was probably not composed until his mind had begun to weaken. We cannot think this supposition warranted. There are many passages in M. Comte's later writings which prove his mind to have been as vigorous as ever. His religion seems merely the result of an attempt at working out his system *to some measure of consistency and completeness.* But he necessarily failed, because no system of sociology or morality of any kind can be made consistent and complete, so as to explain the phenomena, except under the assumption of the existence of an intelligent God, infinite in all His attributes. Apart from this assumption, the condition of human beings is an inextricable anomaly. If other theories of materialism seem less extravagant than that of Comte, it is because *their authors stop short, and never attempt to complete them as wholes.* They are thus mere fragments, which rest upon an arbitrary assumption, that all things physical and moral are regulated solely by the ordinary laws of nature, *the origin of which is left entirely unexplained.*

Under such an assumption, however, the existence of human beings and the constitution of human society become, as we have indicated, unaccountable and monstrous anomalies; to attempt the determination, consequently, of anything like principles of sociology or morality must end in contradiction and extravagance. We do not dwell on M. Comte's system of worship, nor on the strange and *superstitious* dogmas in which he professes to believe, because we have no wish to say anything disrespectful of him, and still less to ridicule his system. Every man is entitled to hold his own opinions, and if we believe any man's opinions ruinous to his happiness, we are rather bound to grieve for his errors, and to seek their remedy in a right spirit, than to mock and to vilify them.

We have thus sketched M. Comte's system of spiritual philosophy *under the most favourable aspect* in which it can be regarded, because it is said to be exercising a great influence on mankind, while we are convinced that few in this country, at all events, have anything like an accurate notion of its real character. "Positivism," which is merely another name that M. Comte has chosen to give to the inductive philosophy, has been confused with materialism. That M. Comte was himself a materialist is true, but *not as a positivist*. He has, however, in substance refuted his own materialism by his system, and under a process more thoroughly effective than probably any one else could have employed. We are all, therefore, "Positivists;" but if people really knew what "Comtism" is, there would, it is certain, be very few Comtists in the world.

B, page 90.

There are two forms which this theory assumes. Under the one all living organisms are supposed to spring from a single existence by a continued series of developments. According to the other, all kinds of embryo creatures being produced by nature, those which are strongest are supposed to survive, and thereafter to propagate, and by development to perfect themselves, while the weaker and more imperfect perish. Neither of the theories proves the universe to be eternal, but rather the reverse, since the question manifestly recurs, Whence did the primary existences derive their origin, whether one or many? and whence specially the organisation which involved in itself such prodigious powers of progression and adjusted development?

Setting this aside, however, it may be remarked in regard to these forms of theory, that under the former it is impossible to explain the *generic* differences of living organisms; while under the second it is equally impossible to explain the universality of that archetypal identity in all such organisms which the transcendental anatomy appears to have demonstrated.

It is useless, however to dwell on mere difficulties with respect to a theory which, under either of its forms, implies an assumption which the text proves to be false and impossible apart from intelligent agency. Were it worth while to suggest the absurdities involved in it, we might ask how natural products of the earth could, under any natural process, develop animals out of vegetables? and where are to be found the gradual and continuous manifestations of such a process? How under any mere *natural* process these animals, again, could develop lungs *relating them to the air?* how teeth, stomach, and bowels, *by a circuitous process relating them to the vegetables on which they are sustained*, and to other animals of a different kind—how under any natural process they could have developed eyes *relating them to the sun?* There is no end to the extravagances and impossibilities which such a theory involves. Granting that development of some kind were possible which implied self-subsistence, a farther *natural* development, *involving the dependence of the subject on external objects* WITH WHICH IT NATURALLY HAD NO CONNECTION, is not only inconceivable apart from intelligent agency, but the very expression of it seems a contradiction in terms. Though these forms of theory seem not only improbable but impossible, they would not, therefore, in the slightest degree interfere with our argument for the being of a God. On the contrary, there is no theory that can even be imagined which can evade or weaken it.

C, page 299.

It may be worth while to illustrate this by examples. I take them from the Duke of Buckingham's 'Courts and Cabinets of William IV. and Victoria.' The Duke has extracted the following passages as samples of the style of writing circulated among the humbler orders about the time that the Reform Bill of 1832 was passed:—

"And are the people of England such sorry slaves that they can only talk and sing of freedom? Will not they, too, resist the laws of these tyrants? Will not they, too (as well as the French), have a glorious revolution? We must resist it, for be the laws binding on you, they are not on us. *We have not consented to them. We have never authorised, but have ever denied the power of any man, or any set of men, or any William Guelph, or any other Guelph, to control our actions, and make laws for us. We deny such power now, and we will not be bound by their laws.*"—*Poor Man's Guardian*, 1831.

"But citizen Hetherington does not acknowledge the validity of an Act of Parliament under which he has been convicted. It is not binding on him. He has nothing to do with it, except to defy it. And why does he defy it? *Because he had no representation in the Parliament in which this villanous ordinance was passed.* He considers the damnable, knowledge-taxing mandate of the borough-mongering parliamentarians as much binding on the *unrepresented* people of England, as the contemptible, impotent ordinances of Charles Capet were binding on the people of France."—*The Republican; or, The Sovereignty of the People,* 1831.

"I make no exception. The royal family of England is as great an evil in England as the royal family of Spain is in Spain, of Portugal in Portugal, of France in France, of Prussia in Prussia, of Turkey in Turkey. . . . With the voice of a man, with the spirit of a good man and a citizen struggling to be free, I cry out to all Europe, and more particularly to my own countrymen, Down with Kings, Priests, and Lords! . . . Either in war or in peace, Kingcraft, Priestcraft, and Lordcraft, is a system of murder, plunder, and spoliation; then *down with Kings, Priests, and Lords!*"—*The Prompter*, 18th June 1831.

It is unnecessary to dwell on the vanity and violence exhibited in these passages. But his Grace does not even attempt to answer the argument involved in them, and which, had the writers known its principle, might have been pushed a great deal farther. He only hints, by a reference to "the three tailors of Tooley Street," that they had not the power to carry their theory into effect. It is strange that his Grace did not perceive this to be precisely the argument of the writers whom he quoted, somewhat more decently expressed. It is as much an appeal to force as if he had replied in so many terms that the existing government had the military and police on their side. The argument can only be logically answered on the principles laid down in our text, and it well behoves all who desire the maintenance of existing government on a *claim of right* to ponder this consideration. If they imagine that any other principle can enable them to reply to such reasoning, let them tell us what it is? None of the ordinary theories of politics enable us to answer it, and we cannot doubt, *from the very nature of the case*, that no other form of theory can possibly do so, except the assumption that all governments enjoy their power under the direct authority of God, so long as it is exercised in subordination to His moral law. Apart from this assumption there can be no political right, and consequently the true principle of political government apart from it would be a principle of ANARCHY.

PUBLISHED BY

WILLIAM BLACKWOOD & SONS,
EDINBURGH AND LONDON.

Professor Crawford.

THE FATHERHOOD OF GOD,
Considered in its General and Special Aspects, and particularly in relation to the Atonement; with a Review of Recent Speculations on the Subject. By THOMAS J. CRAWFORD, D.D., Professor of Divinity in the University of Edinburgh. Second Edition, revised and enlarged, with a Reply to the Strictures of Dr Candlish. In post octavo, price 7s. 6d.

"It is with sincere pleasure that I declare my concurrence in the whole substance of these two lectures (on the Atonement). Dr Crawford has rendered a signal and seasonable service to the cause of truth, by the clear, cautious, and able exposition which he has given of the great catholic doctrine of the Atonement, and by his thorough vindication of it against Socinian and Neo-Socinian objections, founded on its alleged inconsistency with right notions of the character and government of God. If he were to give the Church the benefit of this exposition and vindication—which is not only very complete in itself, but sufficiently independent of the rest of his book to admit of separate publication—I, for one, would hail such a use of it with all my heart."—*Dr Candlish's Reply to Professor Crawford, p. 19.*

Rev. Dr Nicholson.

REST IN JESUS.
By the Rev. MAXWELL NICHOLSON, D.D., Minister of St Stephen's. Third Edition, price 4s. 6d.

"We heartily commend this book to our readers. They will find in it vigorous thinking and true feeling and manly piety without a trace of mawkishness, combined in honest, earnest directions for Christian living, by one who is clearly giving them the results of the experience of his own life."—*Glasgow Herald.*

Professor Macpherson.

THE RESURRECTION OF JESUS CHRIST:
With an Examination of the Speculations of Strauss in his 'New Life of Jesus,' and an Introductory View of the present position of Theological Inquiry in reference to the Existence of God, and the Miraculous Evidence of Christianity. By ROBERT MACPHERSON, D.D., Professor of Theology in the University of Aberdeen. Price 9s.

The Moderator of the General Assembly.

I.
ADDRESS DELIVERED AT THE CLOSE OF THE GENERAL ASSEMBLY OF THE CHURCH OF SCOTLAND, 3d June 1867. By the MODERATOR, T. J. CRAWFORD, D.D., Professor of Divinity in the University of Edinburgh. 2d.

II.
PRESBYTERIANISM DEFENDED AGAINST THE EXCLUSIVE CLAIMS OF PRELACY, As urged by Romanists and Tractarians. 2d edition. Also, PRESBYTERY or PRELACY, which is the more conformable to the pattern of the Apostolic Churches. By the Rev. T. J. CRAWFORD, D.D. 2d edition, 2s.

Principal Campbell.

THE THEORY OF THE RULING ELDERSHIP: Or the position of the Lay Ruler in the Reformed Churches Examined. By P. C. CAMPBELL, D.D., Principal of the University of Aberdeen. Price 3s.

"Principal Campbell deserves the best thanks of the whole community for setting forth this subject so opportunely, and in a work so lucid in arrangement, so accurate in statement, so irresistible in reasoning, and so perspicuous and pleasing in style. We most heartily recommend his production to the most anxious attention of the churches and the public generally."—*Glasgow Herald*.

"This is a careful and exhaustive argument on the subject of the eldership." —*Aberdeen Free Press*.

Mr Charteris.

LIFE OF THE LATE REV. JAMES ROBERTSON, D.D., F.R.S.E.
Professor of Divinity and Ecclesiastical History in the University of Edinburgh. By the Rev. A. H. CHARTERIS, M.A. With a Portrait. Octavo, price 10s. 6d.

"The memoir of Professor Robertson now published shows a depth in his spiritual life, a simplicity and energy in his faith, a genuine warmth of heart, love of evangelical truth, and high-toned self-consecration, that was but imperfectly indicated in his public life, and could scarcely have been guessed at by those who only knew him as the Assembly debater. . . . Who can read his letters to his 'inexpressibly dear Robert,' dying at Jersey, without being deeply moved? They are such as have been seldom written amidst the distractions of life—so deep and true, so intensely fervent, so genuine as utterances of the loving smitten heart of the friend, father, and spiritual guide of the afflicted youth."—*Witness*.

The Church Service Society.
EUCHOLOGION; OR, BOOK OF PRAYERS:
Being Forms of Worship issued by the Church Service Society. Price 6s. 6d.

"We anticipate great good from the publication of such a work as this. It can hardly fail to encourage and carry forward that effort to improve the worship of our Churches which not a few feel to be the most urgent demand of the day. In conclusion, we commend this work to the laity as well as the clergy. If the latter ought to be the pioneers and guides in all Church reform, the former may be assured that what they are their ministers will in great measure be."—*Aberdeen Journal.*

"Their volume is, therefore, a magazine of prayers rather than a manual of devotion, consisting of specimens or examples of prayers—original but mainly selected, as full, as suggestive of solemn, earnest devotion as words can be, and these very skilfully arranged, so as to fit in with the simple order of the existing service. Wellnigh every similar work of any value seems to have been consulted, and as every selected sentence is referred to its source, the result is a work of very considerable interest."—*Dublin Evening Mail.*

Mr Innes.
THE LAW OF CREEDS IN SCOTLAND:
A Treatise on the Legal Relation of Churches in Scotland, Established and not Established, to their Doctrinal Confessions. By ALEXANDER TAYLOR INNES, M.A. In octavo, price 15s.

"The regal results of these many Scottish conflicts of Church *v.* State—and several of the English also—are recorded in this volume in a neat, graceful style, fully, accurately, and impartially, by a man of industry, and of an order of literary taste, scholarship, and ability far from common among lawyers. He has studied the subject historically, and he has treated it in that aspect, giving, in a series of appendices, admirably compressed accounts of judicial decisions, and other authoritative utterance."—*Scotsman.*

"A most admirable contribution to our ecclesiastical literature."—*Edinburgh Evening Courant.*

Professor Milligan.
THE DECALOGUE AND THE LORD'S DAY,
In the Light of the General Relation of the Old and New Testaments; with a Chapter on Confessions of Faith. By the Rev. WILLIAM MILLIGAN, D.D., Professor of Divinity and Biblical Criticism in the University of Aberdeen. 4s. 6d.

Dr Woodford.
THE ANSWERS IN THE SHORTER CATECHISM.
Adapted for reading in continuous Text, with the Questions and Proofs subjoined, Grammatical Notes, and a Historical Preface, containing Extracts from the Original Draft-minutes of the Westminster Assembly of Divines. By EDWARD WOODFORD, LL.D. Price 8a

Rev. Dr M'Crie.

A New and Uniform Edition of his works. Edited by Professor M'CRIE. Four Volumes, crown octavo, 24s. Sold separately,—viz. :

I.
LIFE OF JOHN KNOX.
Containing Illustrations of the History of the Reformation in Scotland. Crown octavo, 6s.

II.
LIFE OF ANDREW MELVILLE.
Containing Illustrations of the Ecclesiastical and Literary History of Scotland in the Sixteenth and Seventeenth Centuries. Crown octavo, 6s.

III.
HISTORY OF THE PROGRESS AND SUPPRESSION OF THE REFORMATION IN ITALY IN THE SIXTEENTH CENTURY.
Crown octavo, 4s.

IV.
HISTORY OF THE PROGRESS AND SUPPRESSION OF THE REFORMATION IN SPAIN IN THE SIXTEENTH CENTURY.
Crown octavo, 3s. 6d.

V.
SERMONS, AND REVIEW OF THE "TALES OF MY LANDLORD."
In One Volume, crown octavo, 6s.

Count Montalembert.
THE MONKS OF THE WEST.
From St Benedict to St Bernard. By the COUNT DE MONTALEMBERT. Authorised Translation. Volumes I. to III. Vols. IV. and V. are in the press. Octavo, 31s. 6d.

"It is, indeed, a volume (the third) of peculiar interest to Englishmen, as dealing with the religious history of the British Isles; while it is not inferior to its predecessors in vividness and eloquence of picturesque delineation, or in their occasional touches of pathos. . . . On the whole, the intellectual interest of the Count's 'Monks of the West' rests mainly on this, that it is the work of a brilliant and accomplished layman and man of the world, dealing with a class of characters who have generally been left to the arid professional handling of ecclesiastical writers. Montalembert sees their life as a whole, and a human whole; and, with all his zeal as an amateur hagiographer, he cannot but view them with some of the independence of a mind trained to letters and politics."—*Pall Mall Gazette.*

Professor Caird.

I.
SERMONS.
By the Rev. JOHN CAIRD, D.D., Professor of Divinity in the University of Glasgow. Twelfth Thousand. Foolscap octavo, 5s.

"They are noble sermons; and we are not sure but that, with the cultivated reader, they will gain rather than lose by being read, not heard. There is a thoughtfulness and depth about them which can hardly be appreciated unless when they are studied at leisure; and there are so many sentences so felicitously expressed that we should grudge being hurried away from them by a rapid speaker, without being allowed to enjoy them a second time."—*Fraser's Magazine.*

II.
RELIGION IN COMMON LIFE:
A Sermon Preached in Crathie Church, October 14, 1855, before Her Majesty the Queen and Prince Albert. Published by Her Majesty's Command. Bound in cloth, 8d. Cheap Edition, 3d.

Professor Flint.
CHRIST'S KINGDOM UPON EARTH.
A SERIES OF DISCOURSES. By the Rev. ROBERT FLINT, Professor of Moral Philosophy in the University of St Andrews. Crown octavo, 7s. 6d.

Dr Park.
LECTURES AND SERMONS.
By the late Rev. JOHN PARK, D.D., Minister of the First Charge, St Andrews. Crown octavo, 9s.

"Specimens of Scotch preaching at its very best."—*A. K. H. B. in Fraser's Magazine.*

Dean Ramsay.
THE CHRISTIAN LIFE, IN ITS ORIGIN, PROGRESS, AND PERFECTION.
By the Very Rev. E. B. RAMSAY, LL.D., F.R.S.E., Dean of the Diocese of Edinburgh. Crown octavo, 9s.

SERMONS AND ADDRESSES,
Preached at the Induction of the Rev. MAXWELL NICHOLSON, D.D., as Minister of the Parish of St Stephen's, Edinburgh, 11th June 1867. By the Rev. G. T. JAMIESON, Rev. Dr VEITCH, Professor STEVENSON, Rev. Dr NICHOLSON.

Principal Lee.

I.
LECTURES ON THE HISTORY OF THE CHURCH OF SCOTLAND,
From the Reformation to the Revolution Settlement. By the Very Rev. JOHN LEE, D.D., LL.D., Principal of the University of Edinburgh. Edited by the Rev. WILLIAM LEE. Two vols. octavo, 21s.

II.
INAUGURAL ADDRESSES IN THE UNIVERSITY OF EDINBURGH.
To which is prefixed a Memoir of the Author, by Lord NEAVES. Foolscap octavo, 2s. 6d.

III.
PASTORAL ADDRESSES OF THE GENERAL ASSEMBLY.
Foolscap octavo, 2s. 6d.

Principal Tulloch.

I.
LEADERS OF THE REFORMATION:
LUTHER, CALVIN, LATIMER, and KNOX. By the Rev. JOHN TULLOCH, D.D., Principal, and Primarius Professor of Theology, St Mary's College, St Andrews. Second Edition, crown octavo, 6s. 6d.

II.
ENGLISH PURITANISM AND ITS LEADERS:
CROMWELL, MILTON, BAXTER, and BUNYAN. Uniform with the 'Leaders of the Reformation.' 7s. 6d.

"It is a book which, from its style—firm and interesting, dispassionate and impartial, but yet warm with admiration—will be hailed for fireside reading in the families of the descendants of those Puritan men and their times."—*Eclectic Review.*

III.
THEISM:
The Witness of Reason and Nature to an All-Wise and Beneficent Creator. Octavo, 10s. 6d.

"Dr Tulloch's Essay, in its masterly statement of the real nature and difficulties of the subject, its logical exactness in distinguishing the illustrative from the suggestive, its lucid arrangement of the argument, its simplicity of expression, is quite unequalled by any work we have seen on the subject."—*Christian Remembrancer,* January 1857.

A LETTER ON LAY PATRONAGE IN THE CHURCH OF SCOTLAND,
Addressed to the Lord Advocate. By WILLIAM FORSYTH. Price 8d.

LECTURES ON SCRIPTURE CHARACTERS:
Addressed to the Students of King's College at the Lecture on "Practical Religion," founded by the late John Gordon, Esq. of Murtle. By the late Rev. DUNCAN MEARNS, D.D., Professor of Divinity in the University and King's College of Aberdeen. Two volumes, crown octavo, 12s.

A WILLING PEOPLE.
Or the Best Mode of Provoking to Christian liberality.
A Tract for parochial distribution, for the purpose of aiding Clergymen in establishing the method of Collecting from House to House. Price 1d.

ANALYSIS AND CRITICAL INTERPRETATION OF THE HEBREW TEXT OF THE BOOK OF GENESIS.
Preceded by a Hebrew Grammar, and Dissertations on the Genuineness of the Pentateuch, and on the Structure of the Hebrew language. By the Rev. WILLIAM PAUL, A.M. Octavo, 18s.

INDEX TO THE ACTS AND PROCEEDINGS OF THE GENERAL ASSEMBLY OF THE CHURCH OF SCOTLAND,
From the Revolution to the present time. By the Rev. JOHN WILSON, Dunning. 5s.

THE COURSE OF TIME:
A Poem. In Ten Books. By ROBERT POLLOK, A.M. Twenty-fifth Edition, foolscap octavo, 3s. 6d.
"Of deep and hallowed impress, full of noble thoughts and graphic conceptions—the production of a mind alive to the great relations of being, and the sublime simplicity of our religion."—*Blackwood's Magazine.*

AN ILLUSTRATED EDITION OF THE COURSE OF TIME.
In large octavo, bound in cloth, richly gilt, 21s.
"There has been no modern poem in the English language, of the class to which the 'Course of Time' belongs, since Milton wrote, that can be compared to it. In the present instance the artistic talents of Messrs Foster, Clayton, Tenniel, Evans, Dalziel, Green, and Woods, have been employed in giving expression to the sublimity of the language, by equally exquisite illustrations, all of which are of the highest class."—*Bell's Messenger.*

Publications of the General Assembly's Committees.

PRAYERS FOR SOCIAL AND FAMILY WORSHIP.
For the use of Soldiers, Sailors, Colonists, Sojourners in India, and other Persons, at home and abroad, who are deprived of the ordinary services of a Christian Ministry; also, Prayers and Thanksgivings on particular occasions. Third Edition, crown octavo, 4s. Cheap Edition, 1s. 6d. Another Edition, on toned paper, 2s. 6d.

FAMILY PRAYERS:
As authorised by the General Assembly of the Church of Scotland; to which is prefixed a Pastoral Letter from the General Assembly on Family Worship. Price 4s. 6d.

HYMNS FOR PUBLIC WORSHIP.
Selected by the Committee of the General Assembly of the Church of Scotland on Psalmody. In various sizes of type—price, respectively, 4d., 6d., and 1s., bound in cloth; also, an Edition for Schools, at 1½d.

In the Press.

KNOX'S LITURGY: AND THE WESTMINSTER DIRECTORY.
With Introduction and Historical Notes.

THE SACRED POETS OF THE SCOTTISH REFORMATION,
And their relation to those of Germany. By Professor MITCHELL, St Andrews.

NATURAL RELIGION:
An Inquiry into the Fundamental Principles of Religious, Moral, and Political Science. By W. R. PIRIE, D.D., Professor of Divinity and Church History in the University of Aberdeen.

THE RELATIONS OF THE SCIENCES TO ONE ANOTHER,
And to Philosophy, Religion, and Morality. By the Rev. ROBERT FLINT, Professor of Moral Philosophy in the University of St Andrews.

www.ingramcontent.com/pod-product-compliance
Lightning Source LLC
Chambersburg PA
CBHW020302240426
43673CB00039B/683